George Mallory

George Leigh Mallory

George Mallory

DAVID ROBERTSON

FABER AND FABER
24 Russell Square
London

First published in 1969
by Faber and Faber Limited
24 Russell Square London W.C.1
Printed in Great Britain by
Robert MacLehose & Co Ltd Glasgow
All rights reserved

SBN 571 08759 0

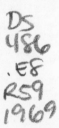
137941

For the grandchildren
of George and Ruth

Preface

This book, though it recounts George Mallory's experiences on Everest, largely in his own words, was not conceived as an 'expedition book'. It has to do with all of Mallory's life, including his climbs. My hope has been to set him among those who knew him best and thus to see his traits discovered.

Consequently, I have drawn much from letters and from conversations.[1] Beridge Robertson began the sorting of papers left by her parents, and since her death in 1953 I have had most generous help from other members of the family: John Leigh Mallory and Clare Millikan, the son and elder daughter of George and Ruth; George's sisters, Mrs. Ralph Brooke and Mrs. Harry Longridge; and Ruth's sisters, Miss Marjorie Turner and Mrs. Robert Morgan.

I am particularly indebted also to Mr. T. S. Blakeney, Sir James Butler, Mrs. John Carleton (Janet Adam Smith), Sir Claude Elliott, Mr. Alan Goodfellow, Sir Rupert Hart-Davis, Mr. R. L. G. Irving, Sir Geoffrey Keynes, the Right Reverend E. R. Morgan, Professor Noel Odell, Lady O'Malley ('Ann Bridge'), Mr. H. E. L. Porter, the late Sir David Pye, Lady Pye, the late Geoffrey Winthrop Young, and Mr. Jocelin Winthrop Young.

My father read the first three chapters not long before his death in Baltimore. For assistance in the United States, I am grateful also to Dr. and Mrs. Robert Bates, Mr. Henry S. Hall Jr., Professor and Mrs. Craig Hugh Smyth, and Dr. J. Monroe Thorington. To my wife, Victoria Bryer Robertson, I give particular thanks.

16 September 1968   DAVID ROBERTSON

[1] A note on Sources and Acknowledgments will be found on pp. 255–263.

Contents

Illustrations

PLATES

Illustrations

MAPS

CHAPTER 1

Mobberley and Winchester, 1886–1905

George Mallory was born on 18 June 1886 at Mobberley, Cheshire, the second child and first son of the Rev. Herbert Leigh Mallory, rector of the parish. At baptism the boy was given the Christian names George Herbert Leigh. It was not until 1914 that his father adopted by Royal Licence the surname of Leigh-Mallory.

There is no reason to search for a connection with the author of the *Morte d'Arthur*. George's forebears in the paternal line were in fact the Leighs of Oughtrington, a junior branch of the ancient Cheshire family of Leigh, of the West Hall, High Leigh. His grandfather George Leigh, clerk in holy orders, married on 28 February 1832 Julia, only child of the Rev. John Holdsworth Mallory, youngest of a line which for more than two hundred years had given Mobberley its rectors and lords of the manor. Mallory died at the end of May 1832. George Leigh succeeded his father-in-law as rector and obtained before the year was out a Royal Licence authorising him and his issue by his wife Julia to bear and use the surname of Mallory in lieu of that of Leigh. Julia died in 1835, leaving a son and a daughter. Fourteen months later, the widower remarried, taking as second wife his cousin Henrietta Trafford. To George and Henrietta ten children were born, five sons and five daughters.

The youngest of the ten, born in 1856 at the Manor House, Mobberley, was Herbert Leigh Mallory. He went as a boy to King William's College in the Isle of Man – the Roslyn School of Dean Farrar's *Eric; or, Little by Little* – and at nineteen was admitted as a pensioner to Trinity College, Cambridge. In 1879, after he took his B.A., he was ordained a deacon and appointed curate of St. Andrew the Less, in the Newmarket Road. On 20 June 1882, at St. Mary Abbots, Kensington, he married Annie Beridge Jebb, posthumous daughter of the Rev. John Beridge Jebb, of Walton Lodge, Chesterfield, and of his second wife, Mary Frances,

daughter of the Rev. John Simon Jenkinson, vicar of Battersea.
The Jebbs had been established for many years in Derbyshire.
John Beridge (1808–1863), son of Joshua Jebb (1769–1845), was
named for one of his great-grandfathers, the eighteenth-century
evangelist; he had gone up to Peterhouse, Cambridge, and then
taken orders. By his first marriage he had a son, John Beridge
Gladwyn Jebb, who spent his life in improbable and often
hazardous adventures, as manager of a coffee plantation in Brazil,
buffalo-hunter in the old West, and gold-miner in Mexico. Rider
Haggard, with whom he planned a search for the lost treasure of
Montezuma, said that Jack was too sanguine and too romantic
for the nineteenth century, but doubtless would have made a
brilliant crusader or knight errant.[1]

Annie Beridge Jebb, twenty-two years younger than her half-
brother, saw something of him when he returned to England
from his wanderings; she regarded him with a mixture of admiration and concern. But she grew up at Walton as an only child, with
no man living in the house. The relations she came to know well
were on her mother's side – Jenkinsons and Greys. Her grandmother Jenkinson, third daughter of Captain Sir George Grey,
who fought at Trafalgar, was a niece of the second Earl Grey,
Prime Minister at the time of the first Reform Bill, and a sister of
Sir George Grey, Home Secretary under Russell and Palmerston.
Sir Edward Grey, later Viscount Grey of Fallodon, was Annie
Beridge Jebb's second cousin. The spirit of adventure which made
her ride a pony alone on the moors, and which reappeared in her
children, may well have been stirred by Jack Jebb and the Greys.

In 1885 Herbert Leigh Mallory succeeded his father as rector of
Mobberley; he remained in that position until 1904, when he
became vicar of St. John the Evangelist in Birkenhead. At
Mobberley the four children were born: Mary, George, Annie
Victoria (Avie), and Trafford. Adjoining Knutsford, only fifteen
miles south of Manchester, Mobberley is a pleasantly sprawling
village parish, with plenty of trees to climb and Mobberley brook
to explore – good terrain for a boy whose instinct always was to
look for things that would be difficult to do and then to do them.
George loved to make adventure; he was eager, as a good brother,
to share it with Mary and Avie and later with Trafford. Avie
recalls:

[1] Introduction to Mrs. J. B. G. Jebb, *A Strange Career: Life and Adventures of John
Gladwyn Jebb* (1895), p. xxiv.

It was always fun doing things with George. He had the knack of making things exciting and often rather dangerous. He climbed every-thing that it was at all possible to climb. I learnt very early that it was fatal to tell him that any tree was impossible for him to get up. 'Impossible' was a word that acted as a challenge to him. When he once told me that it would be quite easy to lie between the railway lines and let a train go over him, I kept very quiet, as if I thought it would be quite an ordinary thing to do; otherwise, I was afraid he would do it. He used to climb up the downspouts of the house, and climb about on the roof with cat-like sure-footedness.

At the age of seven, on being sent to his room for bad behaviour at tea, he vanished; he was not to be found in his room. At last he was seen climbing on the roof of the church. 'But,' said he, 'I *did* go to my room – to fetch my cap.'

'I think we were rather exceptionally unruly children,' Avie has said. The good books chosen for Sunday reading would send them into gales of laughter. Their father, though full of kindliness and good cheer, was a thoroughly conventional parson who expected things to go on pretty much in the usual way. He noticed unortho-doxies of dress or opinion and discussed ticklish theological questions only with reluctance, and he started evening services at the Church of St. Wilfrid and St. Mary only after he had seen that the Methodists were drawing good evening congregations to their chapel. His wife, though deeply religious and strong-minded, was by nature readier with sympathy for the unconven-tional. She thought of herself as rather delicate and sometimes grew irritable, but she would be up and about if there was any-thing going on. Untidy, with no concern for dress, forever doing the unexpected, she was really great fun, and she could always manage a laugh at her own expense. She left the four children very much on their own and kept quite calm over their adventures. Her annual resolution to find a safe place for the summer holidays was no more than a properly maternal but inevitably vain gesture.

Once when the family were staying in Derbyshire, George and Avie quickly discovered the possibilities in a walk with four-foot walls running beside it: each would take one wall and try to keep the other from dashing across and jumping up. Avie decided that she would not be budged; George came after her, and down the two of them tumbled. Trying to protect Avie against a bump on the head, George broke his arm. They retired to the house for a dose of sal volatile and a brief lie-down, but then set out again, planning to explore a stream. This expedition, they told themselves, would be 'safe' – but Avie nearly fell in, and George had to rescue her with his good arm.

The seaside always had great possibilities. When George was eight or nine, the family spent a holiday at St. Bees. One day George went out and perched atop a rough rock, meaning to stay until the incoming tide had surrounded it; he felt quite confident that the tide would turn before the waves touched his feet. On hearing what George was up to, the family hastened to the shore; they could see him very easily, clad in the bright blazer of his first preparatory school. The high spring tide had already cut him off and would soon cover the rock. Grandmother Jebb begged someone to bring the boy in, and with considerable difficulty a young bystander did so. George himself remained quite confident and calm.

Another time, at their mother's suggestion, the children made a sea-level route under the cliffs. They were expected at the other end in time for a picnic tea; but the way was long, the tide was coming in, and the pace was slow. At one point George lowered himself into the water between two rocks; the others used his shoulder as a stepping-stone and then pulled him up. With never a thought of climbing straight up the cliff and racing to the rendez-vous on time, they pushed on to the end and started homeward in the dark. A search-party, with lights, had already gone out after them. The children's only worry was that they had missed tea.

At the age of ten George left his first preparatory school at West Kirby, after the headmaster's death, and went to Glengorse, Eastbourne. His weekly letters to 'My dear Mater' were filled with enthusiasm.

George to his mother   *14 February 1897*

We went to St. Peter's Church this morning. I had my first experience of football on Friday, it was a very nice experience. The first damage I did was to charge two boys over on their faces, the second was to kick the ball into a boys nose, and the third damage was to charge a boy over on his ribs. They play chess and heaps of other games on Sunday.

Only one boy of the fifty-four in school seemed 'atal nasty'. George even accepted the rule that the room he shared with five others had to be kept 'beautifully neat'. Apparently, he never grew discontented at Glengorse.

It is clear, anyhow, that in running away from Glengorse,

after a year or two, George acted simply to oblige a friend who did not feel up to running away alone. The escapade was short. The two boys stopped at a shelter of the Church Lads Brigade; the person in charge notified the school; an assistant master swooped down – and observed with interest that George's luggage, done up in a brown paper parcel, included nothing but his geometry books, a young mathematician's necessities. The boys agreed to return to Glengorse, with the understanding that they would not be punished; but alas, they had a beating. George was disgusted.

In September 1900 George entered Winchester College as a mathematical scholar. The headmaster in 1900 was the Rev. W. A. Fearon, who retired the following year and was succeeded by the Rev. H. M. Burge; the second master was Montague Rendall, who in 1911 succeeded Burge. Rendall quickly became, and always remained, one of George's most valued older friends and counsellors.

George recorded in a story, years later, some of his feelings as a 'new man'. Winchester was the best of schools; arrival there was like having a dream come true. He had heard, and quite half believed, strange tales of things suffered at the great school; but he did not really care. 'Already he believed in himself', the story reads. 'What others had to endure he could endure as well as they.' In fact, far from requiring endurance, life in College pleased him enormously.

George to his mother   *22 September 1900*

I like being here very much – ever so much better than Glengorse; and I like the *men* better, too. (Instead of chaps we always say men.) We have plenty of work to do, and I'm afraid I'm running you up a heavy book bill. We shan't begin playing footer – the Winchester game – for some time yet. We get up at 6:15 and begin work – morning lines, it's called – at 7:00.

George to his mother   *14 October 1900*

It's simply lovely being here; 'life is like a dream.' I enjoy it immensely. . . . I spend most of my afternoon time reading in our library. . . .
P.S. Please tell Trafford from me that he must buck up and become a mathematician, and if he can't read decently by next hols I shall kick him.

As a mathematical scholar, George was encouraged to enter

Army Class and prepare for Woolwich. He progressed steadily, but never attained the highest distinction in mathematics and really had no ambition for a military career. At the time of the Woolwich examinations in 1904, he confided to his sister Mary that he did not want to pass – and he failed, by a narrow margin. 'The truth is', wrote one who knew him well, 'that Mallory was just a very attractive, natural boy, not a hard worker and behind rather than in front of his contemporaries in College in intellectual attainments, a boy thoroughly at home and happy in his milieu.'[1]

At Winchester George enjoyed Rendall's play-readings and developed an interest in ancient monuments, particularly churches. Once he visited Winchester Cathedral with Avie, who writes:

We found a small door unlocked, leading up a narrow winding stone staircase. Of course we went up it, and had views of the building from the various heights, till eventually we found ourselves among the rafters where an old man was just about to wind up the clock – hence the unlocked door – and to our great joy we were allowed to wind it.

On another occasion George made an excursion with a slightly younger friend who had come to Winchester in 1902:

George to his sister Avie   *18 May 1904*

I went to Salisbury on Ascension Day and liked it very much outside, but thought it rather a good thing spoilt inside. Eddy Morgan came with me in a trailer, as he is not allowed to bike far; and, as the road was up and down precipices for about 27 miles, I fairly sweated.

As an athlete, George made his reputation chiefly in gymnastics. He worked hard on the horizontal bar, learning the giant swing:

George to his mother   *1 June 1902*

I do a great deal of gymna and enjoy myself thoroughly. Yesterday I managed to do for the first time a thing which I have been trying since the end of last half without success, and which I am particularly pleased at getting because no one else in the school can do it.

In 1905 these gymnastic efforts culminated in the winning of the Silver Medal. At cricket George was less distinguished, but for two years he 'kicked at last-behind' in College VI; that is to say, he played at fullback for College in the six-a-side variety of Winchester football. 'His eye was single,' Edmund Morgan writes, 'and his whole body full of grace.' He played with great enthusiasm, and he did not like to lose.

[1] *The Wykehamist*, 25 July 1927. It is safe to say that the writer must have been R. L. G. Irving.

In July 1904, as a member of the Shooting VIII, George shared in a triumph that might have been imagined by a writer of school-boy stories. For the first time in years, Winchester won the Ashburton Shield at Bisley. The outcome was in doubt to the very end. With two shots to go, Winchester needed seven marks to win over Clifton; with one shot to go, Winchester still needed a bull's-eye. The last man, with his last shot, made the bull's-eye.

George to his sister Avie   *17 July 1904*

It was simply glorious! We won the Public School Racquets last holidays, we badly beat Eton at cricket, and now we have won the Public Schools Shooting, which is really the best of the lot, because every decent school goes in for it, and it comes into public notice much more than anything else. There was a great crowd at Bisley on Thurs-day, and I think our win was very popular.

When we arrived at the station here about eight o'clock in the evening, we found the whole school waiting to receive us. We were seized and carried to a brake which was waiting to drive us down; and we started a procession, the Militia band in front playing 'See the conquering heroes come' – though I didn't hear a note of it because of the cheering, which continued the whole way down from the station.

As soon as the brake drew up at Commoner Gate by the headmaster's house, we were again seized and carried to Flint Court (the three-sided quadrangle surrounded by class rooms); then Burge came and made a very nice speech, there was more prolonged cheering, and the band made another noise. After that, I was carried into College, where I was rescued by Rendall, who came and congratulated me and asked me to go and have some supper with him – 'Ah, I've got a few scraps'. . . .

It is simply ripping here today, and I am lying in a slack chair out in Meads. . . .

No doubt he was dreaming of August, only a fortnight away; he already knew that he would be going to the Alps.

R. L. G. Irving, the College Tutor, had come down from New College in 1900 – an energetic young man, known to be highly skilled at cricket and fives, delighted by all the activities of youth, and pleased by its simple innocence. Whenever he could, he would go to the mountains. In 1902 he had been elected to the Alpine Club, despite the fact that he was fond of guideless climbing, then deplored by the old guard. The death of the friend with whom he had most enjoyed climbing left him wondering what to do. Of the mountaineers among his elder colleagues at Winchester, C. H. Hawkins was dead, and Frederick Morshead and Trant

Bramston were getting on in years. Taking a guide would be expensive; climbing alone would be unsatisfactory – even if all questions of safety could be set aside – because one wanted to be able to talk. After a last solitary trip to the Sierra Nevada at Easter 1904, Graham Irving resolved that he would find a couple of likely young Wykehamists and train them as recruits. 'It wasn't hard to do so,' he wrote; 'living in rooms almost adjoining mine were the very persons I wanted.'[1]

One of them was H. O. S. Gibson, whom Irving found developing photographs after hours. The boy made a disarming remark about a Swiss photograph, and it came out that he had gone to Zermatt with his father in 1899 and to Grindelwald in 1902. The second recruit was Gibson's friend Mallory, who had climbed nothing higher than the Malvern Hills and read none of the mountaineering books available at Winchester, but possessed extraordinary grace and balance. 'He was tallish,' Irving later wrote, 'with long limbs, supple and not over-muscled as gymnasts are apt to be. He was extremely good-looking, with a gentleness about the features, and a smoothness of skin that might suggest effeminacy to a stranger; it never did to a friend.'[2]

The boys were enthusiastic, and their families willing; and by the end of June Irving had begun to work out plans for an Alpine holiday. Without troubling to inform him, George and Harry ventured across College Street one day to practise climbing on the ruins of Wolvesey Castle, the original bishops' palace. When a piece of wall collapsed, George leapt several yards to avoid injury, and he landed not all of a heap but poised for the next move. Irving felt confident that such a recruit would do well in the mountains.

The party crossed from Southampton to Le Havre on the night of August 2nd and reached Martigny about noon on the 4th. Now George had his first sight of the great snow peaks. By one-horse char the three proceeded toward the Great St. Bernard, as far as the ancient village of Bourg St. Pierre, where they rejoiced on finding no 'respectable' people in the Hôtel du Déjeuner de Napoléon I. Filled with eagerness, they planned an early-morning start on the 5th.

For this first climb Irving had selected the Mont Vélan (12,353 feet), between the Great St. Bernard and the Grand Combin. From the summit one could study the lay of the land for miles

[1] 'Five Years with Recruits', *Alpine Journal* (hereafter *A.J.*), 24:369 (Feb. 1909).
[2] 'A Great Mountaineer', *The Listener*, 35:5 (3 Jan. 1946).

around, and the ascent normally involved no great difficulty; indeed, the Vélan had been one of the first snow peaks in the Alps to be climbed. But the day on the Vélan, George's first in the Alps, ended ingloriously:

George to his mother   *Bourg St. Pierre, 6 August 1904*

Yesterday morning at 2:00 a.m. we got up, had some café et pain, and after an hour's uphill drive arrived at the cantine at the bottom of the Vélan, at about 6000 feet. The first few hundred feet of the climb were in moonlight, and the dawn afterwards was glorious. We breakfasted after ascending steep grass slopes for over 3000 feet – an awful sweat. I didn't feel actually tired, but had no inclination to eat. The sun had risen on Mont Blanc, which was a perfectly delightful pink; and we watched it spread over a range of huge peaks with infinite delight.

After breakfast we had a short descent from our point of vantage, and then crossed over a moraine and ascended a rather small glacier with one or two crevasses, and then came to a perfectly ripping little bergschrund, which we crossed by a narrow snow bridge about twenty yards long. Above it was a steep slope of hard snow, which was easily ascended with the help of an ice-axe. We then took off the ropes and got onto some easy rocks, which we ascended for about 1000 feet to the west arête of the mountain; the latter was a sharp edge which one could just walk along, with a drop of a few hundred feet on both sides.

I was already beginning to feel mountain-sick, but we went on, and after another 300 feet or so I was actually sick. After going up about 1000 feet from the arête, we had a rather prolonged halt and were taken by a storm. I was again sick; and, though we were only 600 feet from the top and could have got there in three-quarters of an hour at most, as we should have had no view and I naturally wasn't much enjoying it, we decided to descend.

Harry Gibson had begun to suffer from the same malady. The party roped up and slithered, frequently halting, down easy shale slopes to the glacier. Lower down, on the moraine, all three went to sleep on rocks described by Gibson as 'extremely uncomfortable'; they awoke refreshed and 'were again able to enjoy life while basking and feeding by a stream.'[1]

Next day they climbed, undaunted, to the Valsorey hut, with designs on the Grand Combin. None of them slept much during this first night in a hut, and Irving had a chill. Consequently, they cut short their expedition on the 7th; but on the 8th they reached

---

[1] Gibson kept the party's journal for the first ten days (Aug. 5th–15th), Mallory for the next three (Aug. 16th–18th), and Irving for the rest of the season (Aug. 19th–28th). The 'Minutes' are now in Mr. Irving's possession.

their summit, and George began to think of himself as a mountaineer.

George to his mother   *Mauvoisin, 9 August 1904*

Yesterday morning we started at six o'clock and went straight up
over snow slopes and shaly rock to about 11,700 feet – a very tiring
proceeding. About 500 feet of rather good rock climbing then brought
us to the west arête of the mountain. From here we had a most interesting and in parts fairly difficult rock climb up the west arête, which we
followed for about 1800 feet. To me this was far the most interesting
part of the climb, as once the rocks were ascended we were pretty sure
of the peak, and I always enjoy rock climbing more than the other part.

After this we traversed to the right, had a little more rock climbing,
and then cut up a steep ice slope, which brought us nearly to the top
of the Valsorey Combin. After this we were on snow the whole time.
We descended 400 feet of snow slope and had a rest and a grub, and then
went up the last 700 feet in fine form in half an hour. The Grand
Combin is 14,100 feet, and of course the view from the top was
perfectly ripping.

The descent to this side was for the first part over steep snow slopes
and then over a huge glacier, the Panossière. The séracs and several
huge bergschrunds by which we wound a complicated way were
perfectly magnificent, and of course there is an infinite delight in looking
down a large crevasse with its bluish ice.

Under a cloudless sky, the party descended by way of the Panossière hut and the Col des Otanes to Mauvoisin in the Val de
Bagnes. Irving long remembered 'the blessed certainty in all of us
that we had spent the best day of our lives.'[1]

On the next day they walked up to Chanrion, at the head of the
Val de Bagnes; and on August 10th they took the High Level
Route to Staffelalp, starting at 2:30 a.m. by lanternlight. They
found their way up the Glacier d'Otemma and turned to the right
over the Col de l'Evêque.

George to his mother   *Champex, 16 August 1904*

The way down from this col was very difficult, and Irving managed
it awfully well. Once, however, he fell down a crevasse which was
completely hidden. I was behind him on the rope, and he only went a
little way in, getting out without much difficulty. The next col, we went
wrong, going over a far more difficult one which delayed us nearly
two hours.

This col, between the Bouquetins and the Mont Brulé, they

---

[1] *The Romance of Mountaineering* (1935), p. 240.

named the Col Gibson. Without further difficulty, they crossed the Col de Valpelline and descended past the Stockje, with the Matterhorn looming on their right, to Staffelalp. This had been a seventeen-hour day.

Recording the walk down to Zermatt, Gibson noted that Irving was 'much disgusted by spectacle of fashionably attired females outside the village.' With a lively sense of mountaineering tradition, Irving took his young companions to the Monte Rosa, where the great Alpine Club men of older generations had stayed; but he saw no need for a protracted visit. There was no time to lose. About sunset on August 12th the trio arrived at the Bétemps hut, at the foot of Monte Rosa itself. The only others in the hut were a taciturn German and his guide. Gibson described the scene outside: 'The whole surface of the Gorner glacier glowed an intense purple colour, while the snows of the Lyskamm glowed a brilliant pink.'

At 3:15 a.m. on the 13th Irving and his recruits, taking a route recommended by Martin Conway, set out for the Dufourspitze (15,217 feet), the highest peak of Monte Rosa; and at 11:20 a.m., after a happy climb up the final ridge, they stood on the summit. 'Italy, as usual,' Gibson knowingly observed, 'was a sea of clouds, but everything else was clear.' Irving led over the Zumsteinspitze, down into Italy by the Lysjoch, and on toward the Colle delle Pisse. From the ridge they looked out over the cloud-filled Val Sesia and saw the spectre of the Brocken. About 9:30 p.m. they reached Gressoney:

Refused admittance as disreputable at the best hotel [Gibson wrote], we got a much needed supper and promise of 'a sofa and two beds' in the parlour of another. The sofa was a fairly normal bed; the two beds were a single straw-stuffed mattress shaped something like the Matterhorn, from which the pillow slid owing to the angle. Nevertheless, we all slept the sleep of the just.

The plan was to ascend from Gressoney to the Quintino Sella hut and to recross the border by the Felikjoch, the high pass (13,347 feet) between Castor and the Lyskamm. On the way to the hut, stopping at a chalet for bowls of milk, the party enjoyed one of those casual Alpine encounters that stay fixed in memory. Gibson's Minute reads:

The old man wandered round us talking incessantly, having broken the ice by putting his hand into a hole in Irving's bags and saying, 'On voit que vous êtes anglais.' He had been a porter to Sella, and gave us directions as to our route, joined with frequent cautions to 'look well when we changed our feet.'

The hut turned out to be a wretched place; bed consisted of 'a broad platform with stones for pillows and a few damp rugs'. When morning came, the three crossed the Felikjoch and had a late breakfast at the Riffel; they reached Zermatt in time for the table d'hôte at the Monte Rosa and then went down to Visp for the afternoon train. Gibson had to go home; the others left the train at Martigny and, after a restful night at the Hôtel du Grand St. Bernard, went on to Champex. There they idled away an afternoon by the side of the lake, with the Combin looming in the distance.

On August 17th Irving and Mallory walked up from Champex to the Cabane d'Orny, intending to cross into France by the Col du Tour or the Col du Chardonnet and so to reach Argentière and Chamonix. About 5:00 a.m. on the 18th they started up the Glacier d'Orny in conditions that seemed anything but encouraging – icy sleet, continuing thunder, and mist almost wholly obscuring the Aiguilles Dorées on their left and the Aiguille du Tour ahead of them, across the Plateau du Trient. George's Minute reads:

We finally reached a fairly low point in the ridge, which we thought might be our col, or possibly the Fenêtre de Saleinaz. The leader ascended on a long rope and looked over the other side, but was not attracted by the prospect of a steep descent which might have led to difficulties on the glacier below. The thought that we were without a map was another deterrent, and it was decided not to try that point. About a quarter of an hour was spent in wandering about in search of a more definite col, but none such was found, and the consideration that our tracks were rapidly being covered up in fresh snow bid us beat a retreat while the way was clear.

But, though turned back, we were not defeated, and decided to descend, if possible, the Glacier du Trient and get to Chamonix by way of Trient and the Col de Balme. With this object, having gone back in our tracks about two-thirds of the distance across the snow field, we had a standing consultation as to which was the proper direction and which end of the compass pointed north. These points having been settled to our satisfaction, we turned to the left, almost at right angles to the line of tracks, and made for the head of the Trient glacier. About twenty minutes' gradual descent brought us out of the cloud, and we were able to see clearly below us. The appearance of the glacier was most forbidding, but the rocks to the right of it looked more practicable, and it was decided to descend by them if possible.

To get to these rocks, it was necessary to cross an ice slope which presented some danger owing to small showers of stones, which were falling fairly frequently. But it was fortunately just not steep enough for steps to be necessary; and, half running across, we reached the rocks without appreciable risk. The conditions were anything but good for the descent of hard rocks: it was still pelting with hail; feet were cold, and fingers numb. The first rocks, however, were fairly easy; and we descended without difficulty until a point was reached where direct descent was impossible and a traverse to the right apparently useless. The only alternative was to traverse to the left underneath the ice slope which we had crossed further up.

This we proceeded to do, and were just about in the middle of the danger zone when a very large rock was seen to be rushing down upon us from above, flying through the air with great bounds and looking most threatening. G.H.L.M. immediately found excellent shelter; but the leader was not so fortunate, and (though his head was well covered) his body was exposed too much for safety. In the ensuing avalanche several big boulders very nearly found the range and went unpleasantly near. The cannonade probably continued, from first to last, for about half a minute, and seemed, both from the noise, which occurred in three main waves, and from the débris, to be fairly extensive. Altogether it was a very interesting and somewhat exciting incident, which inspired us with fresh zeal for the descent.

Irving and Mallory completed their traverse to the left and descended steep rocks, 'in most parts very slabby, though adverse conditions may have made them seem worse than they were'. At 12:30 p.m. they found themselves on dry glacier. Near the end of the glacier, they decided against going all the way down to Trient and then having to reascend to the Col de Balme; rather, they made a short-cut by immediately mounting the slope to the west and following a path to the col, which they reached at 4:30 p.m.

The charming hostess at the inn made us an excellent omelette; and we were delighted by a splendid view of Mont Blanc, which, appearing alone out of a mass of vapoury cloud, in bright sunlight, looked supremely majestic. After completing a very good tea, we walked down to Tour and from there were driven to Chamonix, which we reached at about 6:30, and afterwards did justice to the excellent productions of Couttet's cook.

Couttet's, like the Monte Rosa at Zermatt, was part of a proper introduction to the Alps.

George Mallory

The next week tried Irving and Mallory severely. Intending a climb on Mont Blanc, they crossed the Col du Géant to Courmayeur and made their way on August 21st, despite deteriorating weather, to the Dôme hut. Lacking provisions for a long stay in a weatherbound hut, they had to descend; but on the 24th they returned, determined to have their climb. 'Fine snow dust had found its way somehow through cracks in the walls, and even through the double window fittings,' Irving wrote; 'and the floor was unpleasantly icy.' At 4:00 a.m. on the 25th they started out, not very hopefully, in air 'filled with dry, hard-frozen snowflakes'. They descended to the glacier and then climbed some 1200 feet, but found the struggle through deep snow and against high wind too wearing; they stamped back into the hut soon after 9:00 a.m. 'We had now to face semi-starvation,' Irving wrote, 'but a diligent search discovered a small tin of some sort of tomato paste, some very ancient bread, and a still more ancient piece of cheese. With these treasures we concocted what we both thought a most delicious soup.' Unfortunately, the stove made very little heat; it did not warm the icy floor a foot away. Irving and Mallory managed to wait until 4:00 p.m. for another meal; then they wrapped themselves in rugs. All night long the wind howled and the snow dust blew in eddies.

Dawn on August 26th was clear, with less wind. The two climbers started at 7:00 a.m. and reached in an hour their high point of the previous day. Thence they ascended the west branch of the Dôme glacier and a small ice slope below the ridge connecting the Aiguilles Grises with the Bionnassay arête. At the top of the slope they turned to the right and started up the ridge, which joins the Bionnassay arête between the Col de Bionnassay and the Dôme du Gouter. Irving's Minute reads:

The wind had swept all the snow off, and the leader found his crampons of great assistance. G.H.L.M. managed with great skill to get up with a minimum of steps, and excellent progress was made along the narrow Bionnassay arête till we reached the flank of the Dôme. Here we met the wind, which made us feel as if we had absolutely nothing on. Mallory suffered severely, and his legs seemed likely to freeze altogether. We took shelter for a bit under the wall of a crevasse and, when the gale abated, made our way across to the Vallot hut, which was reached soon after twelve o'clock. Close to the hut we saw a party of six descending from the first Bosse. Two of them had been imprisoned on the summit for four days by the bad weather.

28

After a pause at the Vallot hut for a meal of soup and stale bread, Irving and Mallory started up the Bosses du Dromadaire for the summit. The six descending – the rescued and the rescuers – said that the wind had been terrible. Irving's Minute continues:

> Down at Chamonix, far below, we could fancy the telescope men getting their placards to hang round their instruments: 'Des messieurs sont visibles au Mont Blanc.' What none of those men down below could feel was the thrill in the hearts of those two small specks slowly crawling up the steep ice, and at times pressed close against it to prevent being blown off by the freezing gale that still blew. It is impossible to make any who have never experienced it realise what that thrill means. It proceeds partly from a legitimate joy and pride in life.

Protected by the ridge on their left, Irving and Mallory traversed to the second Bosse in warm sunshine and, in an hour and a quarter from the Vallot hut, gained the summit. They noticed few details of the land spread out below. Sheltering behind the south wall of the Observatory, they felt, as had Leslie Stephen, that here other effects were subordinated to produce the one supreme feeling of height.

Irving elected to descend past the Rochers Rouges and to cut steps down the Mur de la Côte. Near the bottom, believing all danger to be past, he trusted to his crampons and omitted the step-cutting; and Mallory, almost numb with cold, slipped and jerked the leader from his footing. They pulled themselves together after a short slide, with no damage done, and went on to the Grand Plateau and the Petit Plateau, past the Grands Mulets, to the Jonction and so to the valley. Between 8:00 and 9:00 p.m. they reached Couttet's in a famished condition and sat down to an enormous meal, in the course of which they drank to the Sovereign of the Alps. Two days later Mallory left for Martigny; and on August 30th he rejoined his family, who had been understandably worried on reading in the newspaper about 'Two Climbers Imprisoned on Mont Blanc – Feared Tragedy'.

George had not been imprisoned, but he was now enthralled. The days on Mont Blanc finished marvellously the process begun on the Vélan and the Grand Combin. He had set out by lantern-light, under the stars, and seen dawn colour the snows; he had crossed high passes and stood on famous summits. In the company of good friends he had willingly put up with extraordinary discomforts and endured long, fatiguing, wonderful days; and he had learned something of mountain dangers – the crevasse below the

Col de l'Evêque, the mist on the Plateau du Trient and the falling stone on the Trient glacier, the freezing cold on the way up Mont Blanc and the slip on the Mur de la Côte. He had learned also how delightful the pauses and the slack times could be when they seemed really to have been earned – the milk at the chalet and the omelette at the Col de Balme, and the comfortable nights in good beds. Looking upward from the valley, he could say to himself, Yes, I have won my way to these high places, and I am bound to return.

That winter the Ice Club was founded at Winchester, with Graham Irving as President and Leader. The members, all in College, were Mallory, Gibson, H. E. G. Tyndale, and G. H. Bullock. They took to calling each other by the names of the great Alpine guides. Mallory was Almer, after Christian Almer of Grindelwald, whose epitaph described him as 'Der besten Führer einer'.

Lacking mountains, George continued to practise climbing on buildings. On vacation at Birkenhead, where his family now lived, he invited a new friend named Harold Porter to help him climb to the roof of the vicarage:

His idea [Porter writes] was to get out of his bedroom window, whence he could balance up to grasp the overhanging eaves and with an acrobatic kick and swing attain the roof. I was to hold him on a rope from inside the bedroom. All went according to plan, except that his acrobatic kick somehow touched a windowpane, which crashed with a loud noise. His mother, who was a bit of an invalid and was having a siesta next door, quite unaware of our activities, rushed in to find me paying out the rope as George sped over the roof to a known route of descent on the far side, leaving to me the embarrassing task of pacifying his agitated parent till his reappearance.

On an excursion from Winchester, George climbed the tower of the old abbey church at Romsey; and he celebrated Domum Day, the last of the summer term at Winchester, by working his way up between the tower of the gate into Chamber Court and a chimney, with his feet against the tower and his shoulders against the chimney. There was a sheer drop of fifty feet to the paving stones. Edmund Morgan, without experience of climbing, felt almost sick as he watched. Arnold Toynbee, another younger friend who witnessed the exploit, writes that it looked to him like magic.

Proper mountaineering began again with the Ice Club's Summer Meeting of 1905. On August 3rd the President and his sister, accompanied by Mallory, Bullock, and Tyndale, made an early-morning rendezvous at Pontarlier with Tyndale's mother and two sisters and G. S. Leach. The party proceeded to Sion and, having dined at Euseigne as the sunset touched the Dent Blanche and the Ferpècle glacier, reached Evolena in the evening. For the next four weeks, somewhat slowed in their pace by the entirely welcome presence of the ladies and sometimes put off by bad weather, the members of the Ice Club busied themselves on the peaks around the head of the Val d'Arolla.

Many of the ascents were quite modest. To convey a right impression of these enjoyable days, a mere list of peaks does less than a glance at George Mallory's Minutes. George noted, for instance, how the Ice Club came down from the Petite Dent de Veisivi and waited at Satarma for the ladies, who were to bring tea from Evolena and then go on to Arolla, and how they set up a cheer when the ladies arrived in sight, only to learn 'that the grub-bearing mule had actually passed us and was by this time at Arolla'; how the young ladies made their Alpine début on La Roussette, and one of them reiterated in a clear treble, 'Look out for stones'; how Miss Irving, from a little crevasse at the head of the Pièce glacier, declared to the great amusement of the Ice Club, 'You'll never get me out of this!'

Invariably, no matter how trying the circumstances, the morale of the Ice Club was reported as 'excellent'. There was plenty to sustain it. Below the Col du Mont Brulé, the members had 'a hot brew of that delicious beverage Grenadine Punch à l'Irving', a fine stimulant to discussion of possible routes on the Mont Collon; and they spent a good hour over a hearty breakfast on the Col de Pièce, renamed the Col des Gourmandes in honour of the young ladies. One day the party watched from the Pas de Chèvres as sunrise coloured the Pigne d'Arolla, and later from a col below La Louélette saw the Dent Blanche and the Weisshorn gleaming under fresh snow, and then from the summit of the Mont Pleureur looked out to the Oberland peaks and the whole range of Mont Blanc. At the end of that day, bedraggled and penniless, they were recognised, taken in, and fed by the amiable proprietress of the inn at Mauvoisin.

The day of their arrival at Mauvoisin was August 18th. The party returned to Arolla over Mont Blanc de Seilon; and on the

20th Irving, Mallory, and Bullock climbed to the Bertol hut:

George to his mother   *Arolla/Evolena, 22 August 1905*

We went to church on Sunday morning and up to the Bertol hut in the afternoon, getting there in under four hours, shortly before seven o'clock. We had about the most beautiful sunset I have ever seen. . . .

At 3:15 yesterday morning we started by moonlight across the huge snow field, on the most delightful hard crisp snow; and, after the most enjoyable walk and a short scramble over easy rocks, we found ourselves on the arête of the Dent Blanche at 7:15. The sun of course had risen as we neared the Dent Blanche; and, as we had already gone up quite a lot, the view was splendid right over to the Mont Blanc range. It was altogether too inexpressibly glorious to see peak after peak touched with the pink glow of the first sun, which slowly spread until the whole top was a flaming fire – and that against a sky with varied tints of leaden blue.

We had a halt and breakfast for nearly an hour on the arête and then climbed straight to the top in a little over three hours, arriving there at 10:25. There was lots of good climbing to be done, and I can quite understand what an awful mountain it must be in bad condition. Yesterday we had excellent condition; and our time was quite good, I think. We had no difficulty coming down, but a most laborious walk across the snow field. The rest of the party were waiting tea for us at the Bertol hut, as prearranged, and rejoiced with our rejoicing – the Dent Blanche was the one peak we had set our hearts upon doing.

For the next week weather worked against them. On the 24th, however, Irving routed Mallory and Tyndale out of bed at an early hour, proposing to traverse the Dent Perroc and the Grande Dent de Veisivi to the Col de Zarmine. This day was marked by threats of storm and ended in a thorough soaking. On the 28th Irving and Mallory made an exhilarating climb on the ridge of the Dents des Bouquetins and descended to the Arolla glacier, where the other members of the party, waiting and trying to keep warm, had started an impromptu athletic competition, with rope-skipping and a tug-of-war. As snow began to fall, they all retired southward by the Col du Collon and the Combe d'Oren to the inn at Prarayé. The lady of the house helped them to dry their things, meanwhile supplying for the English ladies skirts cut in the latest Valpelline fashion and for one of the gentlemen the curé's best corduroys.

That was almost the end of the summer. 'We found next day,'

1. Arolla: Mont Collon

2. Craig yr Ysfa

Tyndale wrote, 'the truth of the epigram that the Valpelline runs uphill the whole way to Aosta. Wreaths of mist hung low in the wild glens to our left, fleecy washtub clouds enveloped the broad pasturages above the lower valley, and at last, turning north towards the Great St. Bernard, we entered St. Rémy in a tropical downpour.'[1] They crossed the Col de Fenêtre to the Val Ferret and so reached Champex. The party broke up on August 31st at Martigny.

[1] *Mountain Paths* (1948), p. 20.

CHAPTER 2

Mainly Cambridge, 1905–1909

In October 1905 Mallory went up to Magdalene College, Cambridge. The college was small, with perhaps fifty undergraduates; it stood a little apart from the other colleges across the river. Magdalene undergraduates were said to keep their hunters at the gate, never to dine in hall after the Cesarewitch or the One Thousand Guineas at Newmarket, and to translate the motto of their founder, *Garde ta foy*, as 'Mind your liver'. For the Fellows, life was more settled. Arthur Benson, seemingly tranquil at Magdalene after twenty years as an Eton master, had written *From a College Window*: 'I love the youthful spirit that flashes and brightens in every corner of the old courts, as the wallflower that rises spring by spring, with its rich orange-tawny hue, its wild scent, on the tops of our mouldering walls. It is a gracious and beautiful life for all who love peace and reflection, strength and youth.'[1]

On the Sunday before the Michaelmas Term began in 1905, Benson attended Matins in King's College Chapel. He wrote in his diary:[2]

I had noticed in King's in the morning a fine-looking boy, evidently a freshman, just in front of me – lo and behold the same came to call on me, and turns out to be Mallory, from Winchester, one of our new exhibitioners at Magdalene. He sate some time; and a simpler, more ingenuous, more unaffected, more genuinely interested boy, I never saw. He is to be under me, and I rejoice in the thought. He seemed full of admiration for all good things, and yet with no touch of priggishness.

The two became very good friends.

At the end of the term Benson wrote an encouraging letter: Mallory had shown in his essays that he had got a grip of his subjects and might do really well in the Tripos, if he continued

[1] *From a College Window* (4th ed., 1906), p. 13
[2] *The Diary of Arthur Christopher Benson*, ed. Percy Lubbock (2nd ed., n.d.), pp. 126–127.

to work hard; he should take a good holiday, and do as much general reading as possible, and (with an eye to style) have a look at Boswell's *Life of Johnson* and perhaps Trevelyan's *Life of Macaulay*. 'In reading,' Benson advised, 'the best rule is to read what interests one, as long, of course, as the books are good and not merely trivial.' Mallory read good books, and he continued to work very hard over his essays. Often he wrote at such length that he could not finish on time; and once, on reproving him for the belated submission of a bulky essay, so late and so long that it could not possibly be looked at before the hour appointed for supervision, Benson learned that he had worked straight through the night.

For recreation George took to the river, rowing at No. 3 for Magdalene in the Lents and Mays. But it was some time before he could honestly say that he liked Cambridge. After Winchester, he told Benson, Cambridge seemed 'shallow'; and Benson, not without recalling the depth and the intensity of his own boyish feeling for Eton, gently suggested that sometimes the passing years lay bare discrepancies between one's ardent feeling for things and the actual value of the things themselves. 'I won't say I am sorry you still care about Winchester so much,' Benson wrote, 'because I should be much more sorry if you didn't. But you must find room for Magdalene by-and-bye.'

During the second year at Cambridge, Mallory found a number of new friends outside the college. On 6 February 1907 he dined at Christ's College with A. E. Shipley, the zoologist. Among the other guests were Arthur Benson and his brother Hugh; Charles Darwin, undergraduate at Trinity College, son of Sir George, and grandson of the author of *The Origin of Species*; and Charles Sayle, the under-librarian. Sayle, who had recently completed his admirable catalogue of early English printed books in the University Library and his edition of the works of Sir Thomas Browne, lived in a little house in Trumpington Street, with his books, a grand piano, and the photographs of his friends. An amateur of all the arts, he loved to pilot young friends, as Arthur Benson said, 'into pleasant by-paths of literature and art and little humanities which in the crowded atmosphere of Cambridge terms are apt to be overlooked.'[1] Sayle, not yet forty-three, wrote in his diary at this time: 'More and more does it appear to me that all

[1] In *Library*, 4th ser., 5:271 (Dec. 1924).

I have to do for the rest of my life is to stop at home and entertain the next generation. Perhaps this is the inevitable conclusion of middle age. It is ideal enough, God knows.'[1]

Promptly admitted to Sayle's 'menagerie' (as J. W. Clark called it), Mallory met at 8 Trumpington Street several undergraduates with whom he formed enduring friendships. One of them was Jacques Raverat of Emmanuel, a mathematician who later turned to painting, a discriminating reader of French and English literature, a thoughtful host; he would invite friends to stay with his family near Prunoy, on the Yonne, and helpfully explain what one must do to see Paris at its best. Another, very close to George, was Geoffrey Keynes of Pembroke. Lean, intent, and tireless, Geoffrey was reading for the Natural Science Tripos, but found time also for literary studies, in which he had been stimulated by a Rugby schoolfellow, Rupert Brooke of King's.

With Jacques and Geoffrey, George shared two good friends at King's. Hugh Wilson, whose father was a canon of Worcester, was a little older than the rest – already a lively tilter at all the conventions of Philistia. Just before going down in 1907, he wrote to George from Rupert's rooms in King's: 'I hope you two will see a lot of each other next year: he is a quite unique creature, one of the few men for whom I have a profound *intellectual* respect, up here.' George, though never very close, saw a good deal of Rupert, who left to all his Cambridge friends, despite the trying crises he had to endure, the memory of a gay companion, talking brilliantly and bubbling with laughter.

An illuminating account of the group into which George had been drawn was written years later by a friend known to the literary world as Ann Bridge and to British diplomatic circles as Lady O'Malley. Then unknown, except as a mountaineer of some promise, Cottie Sanders met several of the group and thought of them as constituting the 'Cambridge School of Friendship'. Young and older, women as well as men, they were 'conscious or unconscious exponents of an art of life not wholly new but practised in a manner new to their time'; and to the life of their time they were making a remarkable and durable contribution. She recognised that George had been in the middle of all this, an important contributor himself, and that it had left its mark on him in the seriousness and conscientious care with which he treated friendship.

[1] 29 March 1907. The diary is now in the Cambridge University Library.

They held personal relationships [she wrote] as so important that they held only a few other things as being of any importance whatever. Conventional inessentials simply had no meaning for them. They were extraordinarily attached to one another; they stuck closer than brothers; there was, literally, nothing they wouldn't do for one another. They enjoyed each other furiously; delightedly, they examined and explored every means of knowing people better and liking them more, from the simplest pleasures of food and exercise taken together to the final closeness of the common acceptance of some sorrow or some truth. . . . They brought their whole intellectual energy to bear on their relationships; they wanted to know not only that they loved people but how and why they loved them, to understand the mechanism of their likings, the springs that prompted thought and emotion; to come to terms with themselves and with one another; to know where they were going and why. This passion for understanding *was* new; it looked cold-blooded; it shocked people in the poems of Rupert Brooke.

And because of it, and through it, they developed a new technique – an outspokenness which was then extraordinary. There was nothing, whether simple or difficult or disquieting, that they would not express or try to express. They were right, for until a thing is expressed it cannot be understood – often not even by its creator. They ceased to be afraid of words; and this in turn carried their understanding further, since it helped to set them free from the fear of understanding what they might have been afraid to express.

The account suggests, clearly enough, kinship with the slightly older Cambridge men, friends of the Stephens, who contributed to the legend of 'Bloomsbury'.

By 1907 most young Cambridge intellectuals, committed to altogether free inquiry, would have thought it at best eccentric and at worst mindless simply to accept inherited religious beliefs. Leslie Stephen had relinquished the office of priest as long ago as 1875. George's own father had been at Trinity in the Seventies, but had moved in the other direction, taking orders at the age of twenty-three. To George at Cambridge it might well have seemed that his father had surrendered, lamentably early, the privilege of thinking for himself. George criticised freely, indeed, save in his father's presence, what he considered to be the mere trappings of religion; but he always professed belief in the essentials.

G.M. to Edmund Morgan   *'Friday'*

For me, whatever else I may believe, the personality of Christ will live. . . . If all the facts of the Gospels were proved to be false, I should still believe that the figure of Christ was drawn in true characters and that the teaching of the Gospels is, in outline at all events, His teaching.

That there is a God I have never doubted. That conviction seems to be a part of every feeling that I have.

For a while, though conscious that the parson's life would not be his first choice, George thought of taking orders. Rendall had discouraged his hopes for a post at Winchester:

G.M. to A. C. Benson [*1907*][1]

I have at last heard from Rendall, who gives frank advice. He says that, as I have nothing to teach and would probably teach it badly, there is not the least chance of ever getting to Winchester. He thinks it would be a good plan to go to a private school for a year and then possibly to a good country parson as semi-pupil and semi-curate; after which he thinks I should want to go and work anywhere.

I expect this is very good advice. I think it quite likely that I shall some time become desperately keen on parish work of some kind; perhaps the only reason that I am not enthusiastic at present is that I'm at variance with so many parsons that I meet. They're excessively good, most of them, much better than I can ever hope to be; but their sense of goodness seems sometimes to displace their reason.

Politically, the young men tended to support the *Independent Review* in its 'appeal to Liberalism from the left'. George, to his father's dismay, joined the C.U. Fabian Society, founded in 1906; but he concerned himself more actively with votes for women and served, as college secretary for Magdalene, on the committee of the C.U. Women's Suffrage Association. Among the other undergraduate committee members were Cosmo Gordon of King's and Justin Brooke of Emmanuel. The leading elders were A. N. Whitehead and F. M. Cornford, both of Trinity.

An even more active concern was with the arts. One thinks of Mallory and his friends as eagerly awaiting all that would be new and interesting in the years to come – Forster's *Room with a View*, the Post-Impressionist show at the Grafton Galleries, the Russian ballet at Covent Garden. At the same time, they admired William Morris and honoured the octogenarian Meredith as a sage. In their search for the best that had been thought and said and done, as much depended on recoveries by the rear-guard as on discoveries by the van. The poems of John Donne, for example, had yet to be shown at their proper value; and there were old plays that really ought to be seen again on the stage.

[1] Pye, *George Leigh Mallory* (1927), p. 57.

Hugh Wilson read *Doctor Faustus* and expressed his admiration for the play to Justin Brooke. Was there any reason for not trying to put it on? In February 1907 the Marlowe Society was founded; in November, as the first production, *Doctor Faustus* was staged at the A.D.C. Theatre. Justin Brooke played Faustus; Rupert Brooke, Mephistophilis; Geoffrey Keynes, the Evil Angel; Cosmo Gordon, a magician. Mallory took part with enthusiasm as the Pope and as one of the Scholars. 'Crude, awkward, and amateurish, as it all was,' wrote E. J. Dent of King's, the musicologist, 'there was the spirit of true poetry about it. One felt that to these actors poetry was the greatest thing in life.'[1]

According to David Pye, who was at Trinity, reading for the Mechanical Science Tripos, this was the time when George 'took to dressing rather peculiarly in black flannel shirts and coloured ties; and grew his hair long.' But George was never altogether the young aesthete; he never lost his taste for physical activity out of doors. For mountains, Cambridge had only a poor substitute, the Gogs; but there were other possibilities for an oarsman or a walker. George and David made several good excursions in neighbouring country:[2]

One long day we spent on the river at St. Ives. We rowed up a much reed-grown channel to Houghton, and watched a huge dripping mill-wheel, with the sweet scent of the fresh river water all about it. Then we took the other arm of the river, and by dint of carrying the boat round a deserted lock, got to Hemingford Grey and Hemingford Abbots, two quiet villages with fine churches close to the river, and a view over the wide alluvial plain of the Ouse. Other days were spent, more energetically, afoot, tracing the prehistoric earthworks with which the uplands toward Newmarket abound, or following the whole course of the Via Devana where it flings away, a green and crinkly riband over the Gog Magog hills, straight to some forgotten goal.

Pye, at this time, heard nothing of George's Alpine experiences. George was known rather as an oarsman: he had continued to row, very successfully, and became in his second year the Secretary of the Magdalene Boat Club.

At the end of the second year Mallory was placed in the third class of the History Tripos, Part I. 'A worthless performance,' he

---

[1] Quoted by Arthur Stringer, *Red Wine of Youth* (1948), p. 67. For a fuller account of the production, see Christopher Hassall, *Rupert Brooke* (1964), pp. 123–5, 133–5.
[2] Pye, *op. cit.*, p. 24.

called it; but he took some comfort in the thought that his Essay, the part he cared about most, had even surpassed his best hopes. Benson conscientiously assumed responsibility for having allowed him to read widely and to spend so much time over his essays. Perhaps a tighter schedule would make for better results. Anyhow, George must come back from Birkenhead and stay the last week of June at Haddenham, near Ely.

'It is a jolly place to stay,' George reported. Usually he and A.C.B. took lunch to some good place, by motor or bicycle – but A.C.B. always avoided biking against the wind. Once they drove to Cambridge; picked up Benson's brother Hugh, who had left the church of their father, the Archbishop of Canterbury, and become a Catholic priest; and went on over the Gogs to picnic on a grassy bank near Newmarket. 'One generally arrives back in time for a late tea,' George wrote, 'after which A.C.B. produces gems of literature and we both read till dinner at 8:15' – George was reading *Marius the Epicurean* and Benson's own book about Pater. 'After dinner he plays a delightful little organ which he possesses, and I (not at the same time) a pianola. But the joy of the place is that one can do exactly as one likes, and everything is so peaceful and quiet and comfortable.' Poor dear A.C.B.! He kept the gentle good cheer for his friends, and the torments for his diary. Not long after this, he fell victim to acute depression and retired for months from the Magdalene scene.

While George was staying with Benson at Haddenham, Geoffrey Keynes was in the Pyrenees with his family, catching butterflies, climbing the Pic Canigou, and reading *The Ordeal of Richard Feverel*; and Hugh Wilson was at Worcester, dutifully chatting with visiting deans. In July George proposed to them a reading party in North Wales – Ogwen, possibly, for the first fortnight in September. His brother Trafford might come, too, because he was desperately keen to climb in Wales and George had promised to take him if ever he went there himself; and Hugh's younger brother, Steuart, was invited; and Geoffrey was to find out whether Rupert Brooke could join them. Back and forth went the postcards and letters: possible dates, probable expenses, means of transport (bikes useful?), boots and nails, sacks, compass, rope. 'The reading party myth,' Geoffrey remarked, 'is excellent'.

George spent several weeks of August in Aberdeenshire, tutoring a boy at Udny Castle; Geoffrey went off to dig for artifacts at the site of an ancient camp; Hugh at Worcester was trying to work out his plans for the coming year; Rupert crossed the Channel. The Welsh plans changed: not Ogwen but a farm called Gwern-y-Gof-Isaf, near Capel Curig; and the younger brothers would not be of the party. Rupert wrote from Brussels, on the back of a postcard (Rodin's *Penseur*), that he could not come to the 'unpronounceable Welsh cottage' because he had to stay in flat places and work. 'My soul yearns for mountains, which I adore from the bottom,' he said. 'But the pale gods have forbidden it.'

George, Geoffrey, and Hugh arrived at Gwern-y-Gof-Isaf on September 13th and climbed every day for a week – Tryfan, Lliwedd, Craig yr Ysfa, Glyder Fawr. As a guide they used *Rock-Climbing in North Wales* (1906), by the Abraham brothers of Keswick. 'We didn't see the sunrise, I fear,' Hugh told a friend. 'But for seven mornings did we bathe in a mountain stream by the farm house at about 7:15 a.m., start for our mountain [at] 8:30, bathe in some lake before our climb, climb until four or five in the afternoon, bathe on our way back – oh such bathes! and get home absolutely worn out with air and exercise in time for supper at 7:30. Tea at 8:30, bed before 9:00. Isn't it a good life?'[1]

One day, on the Terminal Arête of Lliwedd, the Welsh novices inadvertently contributed to the nomenclature of this great buttress of Snowdon by dislodging a large rock which bounded down the scree. A veteran of Lliwedd, perched on a stance not far away, heard the crash and decided to call the new climb he was making the 'Avalanche Route'. He had a word with the young culprits next day.

On September 19th the party set out by way of Ffynnon Llugwy for the Great Gully on Craig yr Ysfa. They found no need for the rope before they reached the 'Door Jamb Pitch', so named by the Abrahams. George's record of the day, in the Welsh Climbing Diary which the three took turns in keeping, goes on to describe the Central Cave Pitch, 'which dripped abominably with mud and all manner of beastliness':

The leader's coat absorbed moisture most plentifully from a stream which flowed down the left wall, where one's back was 'gripped like a fierce clutch'. The footholds on the opposite wall were good enough, but towards the top one's head seemed to be continually running into

[1] *Letters of Hugh Stanley Wilson to His Family and Friends* (1919), p. 12.

the chockstone and one's weight pressed outwards. The stones, however, afforded good handholds, and near the top the leader untied and passed the rope through a hole behind a small wedged stone. At the top of the right-hand wall (facing pitch), there is a good ledge for one's foot and a spike which affords a left handhold while one pushes off from the opposite wall with the other hand. The grass opposite can then be reached without difficulty. If the rocks had been dry, there would have been little real difficulty about any of this pitch; but as it was it occupied a long time and a great deal of energy, and caused not a few stirring oaths from the second man, who seemed to think the place remarkably like Avernus. The third man was constrained to use the rope as a handhold near the top, owing to the excessive torture of his braces buttons.

H.S.W. then led up two minor chimneys in great form to a point from which the Great Cave Pitch was visible, and here the most hurried and unpleasant lunch on record was consumed. The exceeding humidity of our surroundings did not add to our enjoyment. After this came that 'bloody little chimney' which was shirked by the leader, who preferred a difficult traverse to the right. The two other braver spirits, however, essayed it dauntlessly and, with the aid of a shoulder (G.L.K.) and some tremendous hauling (H.S.W.), scaled its height.

The Great Cave Pitch was now before us and engrossed our attention for the next three-quarters of an hour. G.L.K.'s shoulder was here in great demand, the agony being vicariously increased by the size of the leader's bottom. The final sensational traverse was made more difficult by its wetness, but was safely crossed by the whole party. Goaded by soaked clothes and foul tempers, we hurried up the remaining pitch, oathing at its apparent difficulty. The descent to Ffynnon Llugwy was at once made; and H.S.W. dutifully cleansed himself in its waters, making the hills resound with a magnificent belly-flopper. We then made the best of our way home, convinced that the Great Gully would be a magnificent climb if dry.

Such a mixing of facetious bits with the technical details makes it clear enough that the diarists had read the Abrahams. But the enjoyment shining through is quite their own, compounded of problems confronted and solutions worked out: inconspicuous holds, and the delicately calculated movement of feet, arms, shoulders; fitness, strain, fatigue, and well-earned relaxation; pleasant moments of elation, and now and again a defeat that could not really be thought of as disheartening. Sometimes, paradoxically, the accounts of things that were not quite right, not quite in keeping, suggest with special clarity how happy this time was: the farm hens 'all too irregular in the habit which is the object of their existence'; on Tryfan, the 'party of middle-class climbers who perspired to the refrain of coo-ee'; the lukewarm tea, the loose stone, the rain, the dead sheep in the Bending Gully – 'We reached the top about FED UP.'

But no. Being there in the Welsh mountains was too glorious, and the bathing in Llyn Llydaw was probably the best in the world. Hugh had to leave on the 21st, but George and Geoffrey stayed on until the 25th. Their final effort took them up a buttress of Crib Goch. At first it would not 'go', but they tried again and succeeded. Looking back, Geoffrey thought the ten days had been the best of his life, and Hugh wondered whether such a time could ever happen again.

For the year 1907–1908 George was Captain of the Magdalene Boat Club. The year of his Captaincy, according to the M.B.C. historian, 'throws all other years into the shade'.[1] Long accustomed to being bumped on every possible occasion, Magdalene gained four places in the Lents and five in the Mays, with the Captain rowing No. 7, and performed creditably in the Ladies' Plate and the Thames Challenge Cup at Henley in July. After Henley, George returned to Cambridge and joined the Morris dancers in *Comus*, produced to mark the Milton Tercentenary, with F. M. Cornford as Comus and Rupert Brooke as the Attendant Spirit. Two granddaughters of Charles Darwin, Frances the poet and Gwen the artist, assisted in the staging; and it was announced not long afterwards that Francis Cornford and Frances Darwin were engaged to be married. Then in August, to fulfil a promise, George planned to take Trafford to Wales for ten days of climbing; he hoped for a while that Mary and Avie would come, too – but, though their mother might well have consented, their father would have been shocked.

In the event, the two brothers biked alone to Capel Curig and inhabited a cowshed by the Llugwy, 'a peculiarly pleasant place and always at our disposal in the summer.' It was at this time that George invented the Slab Climb on Lliwedd. 'A difficult and exposed face, with small holds,' says the first guidebook to Lliwedd, published the following year. 'Perfect conditions essential.' There is a story that George made the climb, alone and in failing light, to recover a pipe left on a ledge called the Bowling Green. The editors of a later guidebook (1939) concluded that this was a

[1] *The Magdalene Boat Club, 1828–1928* (1930), p. 43.

'fable', but the repetition of it in George's immediate circle confirms its verisimilitude.[1]

Plans for the last weeks of the summer had to be worked out with Geoffrey Keynes, who had gone to Switzerland with his father and, on returning, immersed himself in Gilchrist's *Blake* and the novels of Jane Austen. Geoffrey hoped to make another trip across the Channel, to Brittany, and then to stay with the Darwins near Montgomery. What could be arranged? The Fabians would be going a Welsh walk late in August, sleeping out and preaching the word in all the villages. Rupert was expected, and Hugh Dalton had assured G.L.K. that the presence of G.H.L.M. would be smiled upon. George, who had been reading Wells's *New Worlds for Old*, thought of himself just now as 'an extraordinarily keen socialist', but could not join the walk.

G.M. to Geoffrey Keynes   *18 August 1908*

If any of your Fabian friends should again mention my name, you might tell them what an enthusiast I am, and how I go about converting business men in Birkenhead, if not to be socialists, at all events to think seriously about the Fabian propositions. I'm afraid I shan't be able to go the Fabian walk, as I believe (though I don't know what they are) that I have made other arrangements.

What worked out at last was another September climbing holiday. George and Geoffrey went this time to the Lakes and stayed nine days at Wasdale Head. Hugh Wilson could not come, but Harry Gibson and Harold Porter joined them on several of their climbs. Much of their time they spent on routes already well known through the writings of pioneers in the district: Napes Needle and Kern Knotts Crack on Great Gable, North Climb on Pillar Rock, Slingsby's Chimney and the Keswick Brothers' Climb on Scafell Pinnacle. But on the 21st, exploring the Ennerdale face of Gable Crag, they made the new routes subsequently known as 'Mallory's Climbs'.

In the History Tripos, Part II, Mallory had risen to the second class. As if in confident expectation that this gain could be consolidated, he returned to Cambridge for a fourth year and settled in new quarters at Pythagoras House, an ancient building near

[1] Pye, *George Leigh Mallory* (1927), pp. 3–4, 43; Robert Graves, *Good-bye to All That* (1929), pp. 48–49. J. M. A. Thomson and A. W. Andrews, *The Climbs on Lliwedd* (1909), pp. 45, 49–50, 99; C. W. F. Noyce and J. M. Edwards, *Lliwedd Group* (Climbers' Club, 1939), p. 144.

the northern end of the Backs. Magdalene was only a short distance away.

Benson had come back, though still suffering from depression and sleeplessness; he managed to get through his work, but shunned society, fearing that his condition would lower the spirits of others. He told David Pye that Mallory was the only one of the younger men who regularly sought him out and tried to help. At least twice a week George would appear soon after two in the afternoon and gently drag Benson out of melancholy indolence for a walk or a bicycle ride. Or he would invite Benson to his rooms to meet an interesting friend – it was thus that Benson first met Rupert Brooke. Or he would come along in the evening and suggest a game of picquet.

Despite the difference in age, despite the difficulty of piercing the cloud that oppressed the older man, Mallory continued to spend hours trying, as Pye said, to lift 'the load of egoism from the invalid by exhibiting it upon his own shoulders'; he would say, 'I have half a dozen things to tell you. You are the only person who really appreciates my experiences.'[1] Benson felt deeply grateful. He took George to stay at Mrs. Benson's house near Horsted Keynes. 'My mother,' E. F. Benson recalled, 'had a discreet passion for so decorative a young man. She wanted to walk round and round him, admiring, and she wanted to call him by his Christian name, but she was afraid that Arthur would think her very daring.'[2]

In December 1908 Mallory experienced a dreary mood, something like the depression he had been trying to relieve in Benson. It was due in part to awareness that he lost patience quickly, in part to a feeling that so far his fourth year had lacked real purpose. To Benson he addressed a self-portrait in which, as Benson thought, the shortcomings were unrecognisably exaggerated; to his mother he confessed that he was 'getting distinctly bored'. This mood was deepened by the family's mourning at the deaths of Grandmother Jebb and of Aunt Ellen Mallory, his godmother. 'You must be tired of hearing about the family "troubles",' he wrote to Geoffrey Keynes, 'but I don't know that I've much else to talk about at this moment.'

The moment was short; the mood passed with the old year, and Mallory's last terms at Cambridge were thoroughly happy.

[1] Pye, *op. cit.*, p. 23.   [2] *Final Edition* (1940), p. 26.

G.M. to Edmund Morgan   *8 February 1909*

I have just been reading a good deal about St. Francis and read a paper about him to our literary society here. I feel quite certain that no better Christian has ever lived. At moments it makes me feel that I must be a parson in spite of my disbelief of some of the Church's doctrines. . . .

I believe it at all events to be a sign of grace that I feel so much joy in the world . . . and all for no reason at all, for I have no more reason to think myself a pleasing object of contemplation (rather less than before), and I have no fewer circumstances to be sad about (rather more). Yet I manage to achieve an almost offensive degree of gladness.

From Charles Sayle came a nudging announcement of the subject set for the Members' Prize Essay in 1909 – James Boswell. Mallory decided to compete. It was Sayle also, an original member of the Climbers' Club, who arranged a meeting between Mallory and Geoffrey Winthrop Young. The second son of Sir George Young of Formosa, Geoffrey had been at Marlborough and Trinity; he had won the Chancellor's Medal for English Verse in 1898 and again in 1899. He had subsequently spent five years at Eton as an assistant master; he was now, at thirty-two, an inspector of secondary schools. He was best known, however, as a strong walker and a superb mountaineer.

Young had made his first climbs in the Alps before the turn of the century. His great seasons began in 1905 when he found a highly skilled and congenial partner in the guide Josef Knubel. In 1906 he made the Charmoz–Grépon-Blaitière traverse and new routes on the Täschhorn, the Dom, the Weisshorn, and the Zermatt Breithorn; in 1907 he traversed the ridge from the Aiguille du Midi to the Aiguille du Plan and made new routes on the Rimpfischhorn and the Zinal Rothorn. He had been a member of the Alpine Club since 1900 and of the Climbers' Club, which centred its activities in Wales, for two years longer. He greatly enjoyed climbing from Pen-y-Pass, in the shadow of Snowdon, and had seen that the inn, called Gorphwysfa, was 'the very place to assemble friends'.[1] Once a year, later twice a year, the band gathered to enjoy the Welsh mountains and one another's company.

Mallory and Young met for the first time on 12 February 1909 at the Charles Lamb Dinner in Cambridge. This was an occasion

[1] *Mountains with a Difference* (1951), p. 18.

which brought together age and youth, the Cambridge past and the Cambridge future; and for many who were present the love of mountains made a strong bond. In the chair was G. E. Wherry (A.C., C.C.), Fellow of Downing and Senior Surgeon at Addenbrooke's. On his right sat the Chief Secretary for Ireland, Augustine Birrell, the essayist; on his left, Sir Clifford Allbutt (A.C., C.C.), Regius Professor of Medicine. Among the other elders were the Regius Professor of Greek, the Professor of Sanskrit, and the Professor of Chinese. At the ends of two side tables were Sayle and A. T. Bartholomew, of the University Library. Mallory sat at Bartholomew's table, with M. A. Bayfield (A.C.), headmaster of Eastbourne and author of *Shakespeare's Versification*, and Dennis Robertson of Trinity, who was reading for the Economic Tripos. Opposite them were Geoffrey Young, Maynard Keynes (who had been a pupil of Young's at Eton), J. T. Sheppard of King's, Rupert Brooke, and the Rev. F. E. Hutchinson, Chaplain of King's.

Between Mallory and Young there might have been uneasiness, for in December Graham Irving had read to the Alpine Club a paper describing his climbs with 'recruits', and Young had joined thirteen eminent fellow-members of the Club in expressing disapproval. In fact, the encounter was entirely happy. 'We became fast friends at once,' Young remembered; 'I invited him to Wales.' Mallory wrote to him on February 16th: 'I am looking forward with unmixed delight to Easter, though I don't expect to fulfil your sanguine expectations. If by chance we may prove that one of the more terrifying places is less difficult than it looks, I shall leap for joy.'

In high spirits, then, Mallory made at Easter the first of his many visits to Pen-y-Pass, on the Pass of Llanberis. For several years Gorphwysfa, under the management of the Rawson Owens, had attracted the climbers who in earlier times would have stayed at Pen-y-Gwryd, a little farther from Snowdon, at the point where the roads from Llanberis, Capel Curig, and Beddgelert meet. At the Owens' table, as at the Lamb Dinner, Mallory encountered both veterans and men of his own age.

Some of the older climbers, already in their fifties, counted among the great Welsh pioneers. J. M. A. Thomson, headmaster of the Llandudno County School, had roamed these mountains since 1894 and devoted particular attention to Lliwedd since 1903. Mallory had met him before: it was Thomson who had invented

and named the Avalanche Route in September 1907. A. W.
Andrews, Thomson's frequent companion, was a University
Extension lecturer in geography; he was also a mile-runner, a
Wimbledon tennis-player, and an explorer of Cornish cliffs.
Thomson and Andrews had just completed the first Welsh
climbers' guidebook, *The Climbs on Lliwedd*. There was a jingle
about it:

> The climber goeth forth to climb on Lliwedd,
> And seeketh him a way where man hath trod,
> But which of all the thousand routes he doeth
> Is known only to Andrews – and to Thomson.

Another veteran was Oscar Eckenstein, whose knowledge of
the mountain world was extensive and peculiar: he had even gone
twice to the Karakoram, with Martin Conway in 1892 and with
Aleister Crowley in 1902. English-born son of a German political
refugee, Eckenstein was by training a chemist, by temperament an
innovator. Early rock-climbers in Wales had generally ascended
the gullies. The techniques which enabled them to emerge onto
the buttresses owed much to Eckenstein's advocacy of 'balance
climbing'. Brown-bearded, incessantly smoking shag, he had
provided his own shelter at Pen-y-Pass in an old mining shack;
he was not at all a clubbable man.

J. P. Farrar, on the other hand, was a devoted member of the
Alpine Club – 'a typically British figure one might have said,'
according to Geoffrey Young: 'soldierly, distinguished, straight-
backed, abrupt, with all the prejudices as also the virtues of its
type, with the rough humour, the impulsive initiative, the essential
dignity.'[1] For service in the South African War he had been
awarded the D.S.O. and the right to retain his rank: he was called
Captain Farrar. Seventeen Alpine seasons had made him a master
of mountain craft.

Of Mallory's doings at this time there is only a scrappy record –
a few notes, a few photographs. One day he joined Young,
Marcus Heywood, and two Dubliners, Page Dickinson and
Edward Evans, in making the third ascent of Route I on Lliwedd
('Only for a thoroughly expert party. Very steep, with hard
chimneys and some exposed situations.'). Another day he set out
with the red-headed 'Bishop' Evans in quest of the Great Chimney
discovered by Thomson. Young Evans was torn, in peculiarly

---

[1] *A. J.*, 41:187 (May 1929).

3. Mallory at Pythagoras House, July 1909

MOUNTAIN HOLIDAYS
4. Pen-y-Pass, 1909: Geoffrey Winthrop Young, J. P. Farrar, Edward
Evans, P. L. Dickinson and George Mallory
5. Mallory at Zermatt, 1910

Irish ways, by conflicting desires: part of him aspired to be a priest, and part loved to ride swift horses, and part made him aware of the spirits in flowers and trees. In Ireland the peasants would kneel down and ask him to bless them; in Wales, at times, he would be carried away into the Celtic mists and see King Arthur's knights riding out across Llyn Llydaw for the final battle. On this day mist made route-finding more than ordinarily difficult; and Mallory and Evans, missing the Great Chimney, invented a climb farther east on Lliwedd. This took them up slabs – but at the start, as Mallory insisted, 'it *looked* quite as much like a chimney.' Naturally, it came to be known as the 'Wrong Chimney'.

During the Easter term Mallory's Cambridge circle continued to widen. Two of his new friends were bibliophiles. Sydney Cockerell, who had acted as secretary to William Morris and written descriptions of mediaeval manuscripts, was the new Director of the Fitzwilliam Museum. Nearer to Mallory in age was Stephen Gaselee, the new Pepysian Librarian at Magdalene. For two years after going down from King's in 1905, he had tutored Prince Leopold of Battenberg; he was by his own account 'a somewhat rigid high tory in Church, Academy, and State'.[1] Arthur Benson could not quite make out what went on inside Gaselee, but thought it must be some sort of ceremony.

As a friend of Geoffrey Keynes and James Strachey, Mallory now got to know their brilliant elder brothers. Maynard Keynes, after two years in the India Office, had returned to Cambridge in November and settled at King's. Lytton Strachey had left Trinity in 1905, after failing in a Fellowship election; he was living in Hampstead and writing for the *Spectator*, but he came up frequently to stay with James. Of his first meeting with Mallory he wrote ecstatically on 21 May 1909 to Clive and Vanessa Bell:[2]

Mon dieu! – George Mallory! – When that's been written, what more need be said? My hand trembles, my heart palpitates, my whole being swoons away at the words – oh heavens! heavens! I found of course that he'd been absurdly maligned – he's six foot high, with the body of an

[1] 'Cambridge Days', in *Arthur Christopher Benson as Seen by Some Friends* (1925), p. 112.
[2] Quoted with the permission of Mrs. James Strachey from Michael Holroyd, *Lytton Strachey: A Critical Biography*, I (1967), 441–442. See the review by Leonard Woolf in the *New Statesman*, 74:438 (6 Oct. 1967); and cf. p. 97, below.

athlete by Praxiteles, and a face – oh incredible – the mystery of Botti-celli, the refinement and delicacy of a Chinese print, the youth and piquancy of an unimaginable English boy. I rave, but when you see him, as you must, you will admit all – all!... Yes! Virginia alone will sympathise with me now – I'm a convert to the divinity of virginity and spend hours every day lost in a trance of adoration, innocence, and bliss. It was a complete revelation, as you may conceive. By God! The sheer beauty of it all is what transports me.... For the rest, he's going to be a schoolmaster, and his intelligence is not remarkable. What's the need?

Mallory, had he known of this effusion, would certainly have felt abashed. Though repeatedly said by his friends to have seemed unconscious of his looks, he had in fact to endure quite enough disconcerting reminders of them; he made clear to one admirer by remonstrance, to another by silence, that he thought of friend-ship as grounded otherwise. The first letter he received from G. Lytton Strachey was so cast as to make a man wonder whether he was being taken up for the sake of his intelligence; it played coyly with the question, What *can* the G. stand for? After that, however, Strachey wrote with much more wit, largely about himself and his ailments, showing his fondness for extreme statement and incorporating every now and then, whether to amuse or to tweak off balance, an irreverent or indecent bit, elegantly formulated and altogether outrageous. George chose to be amused, and he had admiration for Lytton's intelligence and candour; but he could never regard this interesting friend as entirely congenial, well understanding that the very tall and bespectacled Lytton, plagued by ill health, had no use for 'imbecile mountains'. After a visit to Skye, speaking in an emphatic falsetto to Geoffrey Young, Lytton said of the Black Cuillin, 'I think them ... *sim*ply ... ab*surd*!'[1]

Through the Stracheys Mallory met their cousin, the painter Duncan Grant. Grant and Maynard Keynes had shared rooms in Fitzroy Square, not far from their friends Adrian Stephen and his sister Virginia; later they became joint tenants with the Stephens of the house at No. 38 Brunswick Square. The Bells lived in Gordon Square. This was 'Bloomsbury', and it was not so distant from the mountain world as Lytton Strachey's views might lead one to suppose. Maynard Keynes had climbed once in the Alps with Geoffrey Young, and Duncan Grant appeared at least once

[1] Geoffrey Winthrop Young, *Mountains with a Difference* (1951), p. 25.

at Pen-y-Pass. Hilton Young, Geoffrey's younger brother, came often to the Stephens' house in early Bloomsbury days; so did Theodore Llewelyn Davies, whose father had made the first ascents of the Dom and the Täschhorn. And of course the Stephens' own father had been President of the A.C. and author of a mountaineering classic, *The Playground of Europe.* It would have been difficult, in fact, to move for long in any Cambridge intellectual circle without encountering someone who climbed or had a climber's blood in him.

That Mallory's last Easter term was busy and enjoyable is shown by letters delivered at Pythagoras House. From Sydney Cockerell, an invitation to tea: 'We are expecting Burne-Jones's granddaughter, Angela Mackail, who is very charming. . . . You ought not to miss Neville Lytton's picture show in Downing Street this week.' From Geoffrey Young in London to 'Dear Galahad', a report on Pen-y-Pass photographs: 'Heywood has sent me half a dozen very good snapshots: one of our Llydaw bathe, statuesque in its effect. . . . I am just re-reading Milton: curious how completely he bridges to Spenser.' From Edmund Morgan at New College, Oxford: 'I hope you're going to get the 'Varsity Prize. I'm reading Maeterlinck's *Life of the Bee.* . . . I've got a thoroughly good scheme on with the Working Men's College in London. We're going to give chamber concerts there.' From Hugh Dalton of King's, President of the C.U. Fabian Society, in reply to an invitation: 'Rupert shall bring me to you, for I know not your Elysian fields.' From Lytton Strachey, an invitation for a week end in Hampshire: 'This is perhaps a wild project, but it has its points. I'm here by myself with a sister whom I can guarantee you'ld like. . . . You would be as free as in the Garden of Pythagoras, and you could explore the Forest, or you could read the *Faerie Queene* aloud to me in a violet-covered glade.' (This came just as George started training for the May races, in which he again rowed No. 7.) From 'Bishop' Evans in Ireland: 'I would love to help you with your essay on Boswell. . . . I have spent many days since Easter seeking inspiration on the lonely mountains and growing in child-like wonder at the beauty and immensity of Creation.'

A young lady who lived near Birkenhead and well knew George's literary tastes had begun a letter teasingly with 'Mon cher "Henry James" ' – and now came a note from Charles Sayle, who had collaborated with Bartholomew and Geoffrey

Keynes in luring the Master himself to Cambridge for a week end in June: 'I am very anxious to avoid over-crowding James, and I have been obliged to ask senior people tomorrow. But you will be with us on Sunday night, I hope, as well as on Monday.' With others of the 'menagerie', George sat in the garden at No. 8 Trumpington Street on Sunday evening, sipping coffee and listening as James engaged in a discussion of dancing and then talked about the selection of frontispieces for the new edition of his works.[1]

By June it had become necessary to do some hard thinking about the future. George reckoned that, even if he stayed on at Pythagoras House, he could not finish his Boswell essay by the end of July. Then there was August: Geoffrey Young had proposed a climbing holiday, and George had agreed to go; but now Graham Irving wanted to arrange another Alpine meet for the Ice Club, and George could not easily disregard the old alliance and the standing invitation. He had to keep his agreement with Young; he had also to counteract, once he perceived the need, Irving's quite natural regret that old bonds seemed to have been loosened.

And after the climbing season, after completion of the Boswell essay? For a man of almost twenty-three this was an urgent question. Surprisingly, a letter from Winchester raised George's hopes, and his family's, that the happiest possible solution might be near. Dr. Burge mentioned a post at Winchester, to be open next Easter. The teaching would be mainly in mathematics, French, and German. George sat at his desk and took stock. In the higher mathematics he would soon be lost without more calculus; but in geometry and algebra he would probably be quite all right, for he had successfully coached boys for Osborne and Sandhurst. Six months in France, July to December, might give him sufficient preparation in French; but then he would have less than four months, much less time than he needed, to learn German. His thoughts turned to his own subject. 'I do very much want to teach history, sooner or later,' he wrote. 'And I have been so well taught here by Mr. Benson that I believe, if ever it were wanted, I could tell people how to write essays.'

George decided to go down to Winchester, stay with Rendall, and thoroughly discuss the outlook. The results were disappointing.

---

[1] The best account of the week end is by Sir Geoffrey Keynes, 'Henry James in Cambridge', *London Magazine*, 6:50–61 (March 1959).

Mainly Cambridge, 1905–1909

The post Burge has in mind is too mathematical for me, as he pointed out and I clearly see. But there is a chance that I shall be wanted there some time. . . . I want to be wanted; I begin to be a little less sure of the bliss I should feel at Winton. I met a few of the young dons there, and really I doubt if I should have a single real friend in the place. . . . It sounds altogether rather too much as though the place were run according to fixed principles with many of which I should not agree. But then it is probably the same everywhere; I expect one will have to fight some battles.

Anyhow, after finishing his Boswell essay, he would use a modest legacy to go to France and study the language.

From any depression induced by the Winchester interviews George promptly recovered on paying a visit to Lytton Strachey in Hampstead. Duncan Grant joined them, and they made an excursion to Hampton Court. 'It's a surprising thing, I can assure you,' Lytton remarked, 'after the experience of – I won't tell you how many years – to find oneself with someone who really likes things!' Stephen Gaselee wrote from Coburg: he had arrived at Schloss Rosenau, and Prince Leopold was very well. 'You can't think what a difference it will make to me when you are no longer up,' he went on; 'you were the only person I knew in Magdalene when I came (except Dons), and it is through you my first year there has been so pleasant.'

George returned to Cambridge for July. Benson came down from the Lakes for two nights and asked him to dinner. The fourth year, Benson thought, had been good for George and good for the College. 'Anyhow you have enjoyed it,' he later wrote, 'and it is a great thing to have eaten one's cake without too many crumbs. . . . I have not seen as much of you as I might have done and as I had hoped to do, but I have been so dreary and stupid that I have quite put the sparrow on the housetop into the shade. You have been awfully good yourself, about coming to see me and cheering me up; and I have been neither unmindful nor ungrateful – and perhaps some day, when the cloud has flitted on, I may be able to tell you what I feel about it all.'

Happily, a few younger friends had stayed up. Jacques Raverat was there: 'It was much too wet to dream of coming to Sayle's last Sunday so we remained at Grantchester, Rupert and I, talking philosophy.' Rupert wrote: 'My family are taking a Mansion in Somerset in August. Will you be thereabouts, to read, play tennis, walk, etc. ?' Geoffrey Young turned up at Peterborough and wanted to arrange a talk about Alpine plans – it seemed probable now that Donald Robertson would join the party. Edward Evans, over from Ireland, paid a brief visit; and George's sister Avie came from Birkenhead to see Cambridge and meet George's friends. Then suddenly it was over and done with:

Geoffrey Keynes to G.M.   *29 July 1909*

I would have liked to have seen you again, and the Pool would have been a good place for the purpose. Anyway, that's that, and the end of you, from a Cambridge point of view – not a very pleasant reflexion. Do you realise that you've gone down?

CHAPTER 3

Mountains and Charterhouse, 1909–1911

'To see the Alps again!' George wrote to his mother. 'How glorious it will be, after dreaming of them for four years!' And by the end of July 1909 he was really at Bel Alp, looking forward to a fortnight of guideless climbing with Geoffrey Young.

Geoffrey, who had first climbed hereabouts in 1898, well knew the Fusshörner, east of the Ober Aletsch glacier; he was eager to know better the ridges to the west, extending in three directions from the Unterbächhorn. In 1898, when he made the first ascent of a peak which he named 'Dame Alys', midway between the Unterbächhorn and the Gisighorn, to the south, he left unclimbed the northern half of this ridge. It made a good first expedition for 1909. On August 1st Geoffrey and George started from Bel Alp at 5:30 a.m., ploughed across the Unterbächen glacier, found on the ridge a delightfully precipitous bit that made them think of Lliwedd, reached the summit of the Unterbächhorn at 12:35, and took time on the descent to bathe in a cold lake. They made camp on the Unterbächen glacier, intending to reconnoitre the long ridge between the Unterbächhorn and the Nesthorn. A party had descended the southeast arête of the Nesthorn in 1895; none had ever ascended it.

Donald Robertson joined them. A grandson of Robertson of Brighton, the great preacher, and a kinsman through his mother of the Bismarcks, he had distinguished himself at Eton and Trinity and then accepted a clerkship in the Treasury; and he had recently become, at thirty, Secretary of the Royal Commission on Electoral Systems. His scholarly concerns – metaphysics, comparative religion, music, architecture, poetry – might well have induced him to stay at Trinity as a Fellow. Once an Italian priest identified him as 'clearly an Englishman by his size and silence, but with a smile stolen from Leonardo.'[1]

[1] *A. J.*, 25:143 (May 1910).

Bad weather drove the party from the glacier camp to the Ober Aletsch hut and then back to Bel Alp. On the night of August 3rd conditions were still so unsettled that it seemed wise to include a guide in plans for reconnaissance of the Nesthorn ridge on the morrow. But no willing guide could be found; and at 3:00 a.m. on the 4th, determined to do something, but aware that the weather might prevent them from doing much, the three set out again for the Unterbächen glacier. It was not a very hopeful march: first rain, then hail and snow. At dawn the prospects improved a little; and at 7:00, despite fresh snow and glaze, the Unterbächhorn looked possible. Why not go up?

At 9:00 they stood on the summit, above the storm-mists, and saw the long ridge leading northwestward to the Nesthorn. This, as Geoffrey remembered it, was irresistible: 'Think of it! – two and something miles of selected ridge climbing: pinnacle and tower and wind-balanced knife-edge, notch and comb and up-ended slab.'[1] Geoffrey led off; and the three moved rhythmically and speedily, as if they had always known the exact tempo for climbing together, along the crest to Point 3617, then down to the col beyond which rose the southeast arête of the Nesthorn itself. By now it was 12:30: they must consider the mountain, the weather, the time of day. On they went. Finding their way past four great gendarmes took them until 4:00 p.m. Above, the rocks were steep, some of them nearly perpendicular; but most of them could be climbed direct, on good holds.

There was one unforgettable contretemps. At the last dark tower, Geoffrey and George changed places on the rope; and George, seeking a way up vertical slabs and past an overhang, came off. He fell some forty feet and swung in mid-air, but lost neither his ice-axe nor his composure; and he climbed back so rapidly that Donald Robertson had no inkling of what had happened until he was told. Geoffrey found another route up the tower and then put George in the lead again, confident that of the three George could best set the pace they would all have to maintain. At 7:00 p.m. they reached the summit of the Nesthorn.

By way of the western arête they made the descent to the Beichfirn and, after darkness had fallen, commenced the long trudge down the Ober Aletsch glacier, and then up the zigzags to the Aletschalp, and finally, after midnight, to the hotel. 'We were out twenty-one hours,' George wrote to his mother, 'and

[1] *On High Hills* (1927), p. 178.

were altogether rather pleased with ourselves, as we started in bad weather which afterwards cleared up beautifully. The sunset from the Nesthorn was the most wonderful I have ever seen.'

From Bel Alp the party went up to the hut by the Concordia, where tributary glaciers converge to feed the Grosser Aletsch glacier; and on August 7th they crossed the Grünhornlücke and mounted from the Fiescherfirn to the southeast arête of the Finsteraarhorn. The day was sunny but very cold. 'Every notch was snow-crested or corniced,' G.W.Y. remembered, 'and every pinnacle so deeply flounced with ice and snow-frond that we had to smash a way into it with arm or leg before we could embrace its solidity.'[1] It was not a day for lingering on the summit, but the three unroped. Then Mallory led down, chopping minute footholds as he crossed a glazed slab.

Young suddenly saw that Mallory had not re-roped. Speaking softly, to avoid giving any sign of alarm, Young told Mallory just to hold still, and asked Robertson to climb down and tie him in. But Robertson slipped a little, and the sound made Mallory 'spin round like a flash on his one-foot ice-nick'. It looked a desperately perilous stance. Mallory, however, kept his balance; and the party resumed the descent to the Hügisattel, whence they returned to the Concordia. The way seemed very long and fatiguing. Two days later, they climbed the Jungfrau, descended the Ewige Schneefeld, and continued down the Grosser Aletsch glacier to Bel Alp, planning to go to Chamonix on the 11th.

The guide Josef Knubel joined them; and on the 13th they traversed the Aiguille Verte, descending by the Moine ridge. They meant next to explore the precipitous walls of the aiguilles rising above the Mer de Glace; they had hopes of climbing to the Col des Nantillons, between the Grépon and the Blaitière. Two parties had climbed down from the col, one in 1875 and the other in 1904; they had reported that ascent would be practically impossible. On the 15th, therefore, accompanied by a porter, the hopeful four made camp on the moraine by the Trélaporte. For three nights, waiting for the weather to improve, they endured remarkable discomfort.

At last they were able to start. For a while, the discouraging reports seemed altogether just. Then Knubel led brilliantly up a 100-foot cleft, of which, as Young thought, thirty feet were harder than the Grépon crack. This lead raised hopes again; but

[1] *Ibid.*, p. 173.

early in the afternoon a hailstorm glazed the rocks and poured icy water down the crevices, making further ascent unthinkable. 'In a breath a climb, difficult, but sound enough to leave us a margin of safety,' Young wrote, 'had been changed to a dangerous cling, with chilled extremities, upon treacherous holds.'[1] They descended as rapidly as possible, most of the way by doubled rope. Mallory and Robertson led down and, by showing firm confidence, helped to steady morale; Knubel came last, shepherding the porter, whom Young counted among 'unsuccessful experiments'. Though frustrated, this expedition took its place in memory with the climb on the Nesthorn.

A few days later, Mallory, Young, and Robertson made their last climb together, a traverse of the Aiguille du Chardonnet. They found a perfect ledge for breakfast, in full view of the Droites and the Verte; enjoyed a cloudless day; and came down by the Col du Passon. G.W.Y. had an appointment with Oliver Perry Smith to try the north face of the Weisshorn, and George accompanied him to Zermatt.

It was at this time that George first met Miss Cottie Sanders, who later recorded her first impressions:

At the end of August 1909, a young man was sitting on an iron chair before a round iron table in front of the Monte Rosa Hotel at Zermatt, reading Galsworthy's *The Country House* in a Tauchnitz edition. Around him the tide of plans and gossip and guides and climbers – the whole *va-et-vient* of a summer's day at Zermatt – ebbed and flowed; but he sat in a sort of oblivion, never looking up, only sometimes raising a hand to push back the shock of brown hair which fell constantly over his forehead. He was picturesque and untidy, in loose grey flannels with a bright handkerchief round his neck; but the things which chiefly aroused attention were his good looks and his complexion. It was a bad season, with a good deal of new snow; and faces hideously disfigured by sunburn were the rule. But this young man's skin was clear and fair as a girl's. Presently another man came out of the hotel and roused him for an introduction. He got up at once, and went through it adequately, but with a sort of restive shyness, carefully controlled; the moment that courtesy permitted, he relapsed into his iron chair and his book. This was George Mallory, and the man who was with him was Geoffrey Young.

They had arrived at Zermatt after some sort of a season – pretty strenuous, one gathered. . . . Rumour had preceded them, and comment flowed about them. Geoffrey Young's paper on his Chamonix climbs,

[1] *On High Hills* (1927), p. 129.

'Two Days with a Guide,' had appeared in the *Alpine Journal* shortly before [May 1909]; *Wind and Hill* was just out. . . . Everyone was curious about Geoffrey. Climbers do gossip; it was surprising what an amount of information or invention was going that August on the subject, from the times in which he had gone up various peaks to where he had bought the straw-coloured corduroys which so much shocked the sense of propriety of the old gentlemen at the Riffel.

They were at Zermatt for about a week, during which time Geoffrey Young and Perry Smith brought off their climb on the Weisshorn. George was not very much in evidence – his taste for his kind had perhaps not yet developed. He appeared to spend a good deal of his time looking at books at the Wega, and a good deal more in his tin chair with a Tauchnitz. . . . But he was not wholly unsociable and not in the least difficult to make friends with. We had a good deal of talk, generally about mountains and the quality of their beauty; and he made one feel at once that here, in him, was the authentic thing, the real flame and passion. His talk, in his beautiful voice, with the very careful choice of words, in its quality stood out extraordinarily from the ordinary run of conversation at the Monte Rosa – the topography and personalities. And on the whole he seemed to enjoy himself hugely. . . . He was charming with Geoffrey Young – happy, equal, generously admiring. He was very intolerant of the potterers and gossip-mongers, very modest about his own performances; but he did not mind, in fact rather enjoyed, confessing with a half-shamefaced, half-whimsical amusement to some of his more desperate escapades. . . .

He was very vague and ramshackly about everything practical. We travelled down to Visp with them when they left, and derived great amusement from Geoffrey Young's efforts to get George packed and breakfasted and off in time. They galloped to the bus at the last second. When we got to Visp, George was sent to buy food while Geoffrey saw to the luggage. I met him in the restaurant, on the same errand. Something made him notice my alarm watch; he had not seen one before. 'Work it!' he said in his eager way. So we sat down at a table to make it work. Food and time were at once forgotten; and, when the express came roaring in, nothing had been bought but a packet of Basler Leckerli, which I had got before I met him. We went out to the train; but he was still chiefly concerned to press on me the importance of going to Wales in September, and the value of Peck's Hardening Lotion for the feet. He gave us Peck's address – by which we guessed that he was, or had been, at Cambridge – but not his own, though there was a loan of books or maps to be returned to him. And should we be at Zermatt next year? Because –. But the train bore them off; and the last we saw of him was his vivid face framed in the darkness of the carriage window, calling out something about a mountain.

That was all for 1909. We knew nothing of him but his name – and that Geoffrey Young had plucked him as a brand from the burning of guideless climbing and hoped everything of him as a mountaineer. And that it was his third season, so that he could not be eighteen, which was what he looked. And that one hoped, of course, immensely to meet him again. I clearly remember that a very dreary walk down the Rhone valley and up to Ried was gilded and comforted by the thought that there *were* such delightful people in the world and that sooner or later, among mountains, one was bound to find them again.

In September Mallory had an accident more damaging than the fall on the Nesthorn. Walking near Birkenhead with his sisters and Harold Porter, he came to a sandstone cliff in a disused quarry. There was no need whatever to climb it, but George naturally made for it and started up. The top proved to be quite insecure. He had to throw himself outward and downward, and he landed with one foot on a rock in the long grass. His ankle seemed to have been sprained, and for a long time it refused to get better. George confessed that he 'hobbled about shamefully'.

Nevertheless, he finished his essay on Boswell and prepared to leave in October for the south of France; he was to stay several months at Roquebrune with the Bussys. Simon Bussy was a painter, a friend of Renoir; Dorothy Bussy, a sister of Lytton Strachey, translated André Gide. On the way, George stopped in Paris and called on M. Hovelaque and M. Legouis, to inquire whether he might be admitted to work at the Sorbonne. Hovelaque seemed to think he could become a lector if he wished – but 'M. Legouis, who evidently took me for a schoolboy and didn't inquire my age, thought otherwise.' How very young George looked, to other French eyes, is suggested by the portrait painted soon after by Simon Bussy and now deposited in the National Portrait Gallery.

At Roquebrune George thought of himself as an exile, but found much to enjoy; he missed Cambridge, but delighted in the unfamiliar place and in the company of people who, for all their intellectual gifts, lived a life of unaffected simplicity.

G.M. to his sister Avie   [*Before Christmas 1909*]

La Souco is a very small villa; my bedroom is about the size of a grand piano. We all live for the most part – except Monsieur, who has his studio – upon a large balcony which lies between the front door and the garden. . . . The whole concern, you must understand, is upon a steep hillside; the garden is a series of terraces. There is another balcony higher up, which has to my mind an even more glorious view than the lower one, though both look out in the same direction, southwestwards, over a little bay in the sea to Monte Carlo. To this I retire when I wish to be solitary, and I feel sometimes as though I could leap from it straight into the clear sea down below. . . .

George read French; he bathed, most days, in the Mediterranean; sometimes, although his ankle was far from well, he walked on the hills. To write about the country, he feared, would make him turn poetical – 'a dreadful quality in a letter'. For his sister, however, he tried to describe Roquebrune:

In all but the fact that it is actually in France, it is an Italian village; it might have been taken out of a picture by Filippo Lippi and planted up there among the rocks. . . . I think what I like best is a certain flavour of the East. The olive trees and the cypresses, the white houses, the deep orange tints of sunset, and the contrast of all this richness with the bare rocky hills remind one continually that the ships one sees sailing by are on the way to Asia. . . .

From Cambridge came word that essays submitted for the Members' Prize had been adjudged: G. H. L. Mallory, *proxime accessit*. 'I was disappointed, of course,' George wrote. 'It is rather desolating to be deprived of a hope one has cherished for half a year or so. But through some fortunate arrangement in my disposition, I am not troubled for long by that kind of grief, and easily forget it in the occupations of the moment.' At the end of February 1910 he left Roquebrune to make a pilgrimage to Italy. 'It is rather a wicked expedition, under the circumstances,' he admitted to Geoffrey Keynes. 'One doesn't learn much French in Italy, and one doesn't fill one's pockets. But then it was impossible to make up my mind to leave the Italian frontier without a dash across the border.' The dash inspirited him – 'Genoa, Pisa, Florence: I have really seen them at last.' To travel northward again was not easy. George stopped in mid-March at Basel to see Hugh Wilson, who was learning German; he went on to stay a few days with the Raverat family at Prunoy, before returning to Paris for the final month of his Continental sojourn. 'The days in the country,' he wrote, 'seem to have done me good – mentally, I mean – for I now face Paris with a proud and cheerful heart.'

Mallory in Paris felt duty-bound to work hard at his French, by conversing, by listening to lectures, by going to the theatre, by reading. Lytton Strachey recommended going to the Comédie and 'facing out something infinitely classical'; Jacques Raverat supplied the names and addresses of booksellers. 'It is a curious life,' George wrote: 'a poky little room over a large street, lonely strolls in the Tuileries or the Jardin de Luxembourg, which is near by, and visits to the museums and other sights and sounds. I know very few people here at present. The man I see most of is a poet and literary critic and is very interesting on these subjects. He was a great friend of one Jean Moréas, who died just lately and is said to have been the greatest French poet of the nineteenth century. Unfortunately my friend is blind.'

Easter had come and gone. George missed the climbing party at Pen-y-Pass; he heard about it while he was still in France. Donald Robertson had gone up on the night train and set out immediately after breakfast the next morning, Good Friday, to lead up the Eastern Gully of Glyder Fach. At a difficult over-hanging pitch he fell and fractured his skull; he died soon after midnight in the Bangor infirmary. Geoffrey Young was preparing to lead a party up Tryfan when news of the fall was brought to him across the slopes. An eye-witness remembers him 'running along the tiny path like someone blinded or demented, throwing his scarf back as it blew across his face.'

What would George do after his return to England? It was high time for a decision. His father pointed out that he could not seriously plan to use up his funds, and then write something and sell it, and spend the proceeds, and then write something else and hope to sell it. He must have a proper career. Teaching continued to attract him, despite the disappointment at Winchester; and a temporary job at the Royal Naval College, Dartmouth, gave him a first brief taste of the schoolmaster's life. On 20 May 1910, as the appointment was coming to an end, he wrote:[1]

Lord! how pleasant it has been! I have even learnt to enjoy my 'Early Schools' – five in a week! and out of bed at 6:15 punctually. I expect I have been a failure: it is almost impossible to be serious with youth. But it does everyone good to be merry.

In June, after discussing the future with friends at Cambridge, George went to several schools for interviews. At Haileybury he had a glimpse of his brother playing cricket, but most of the impressions he carried away and conveyed to his friends were somewhat disheartening. As individuals, schoolmasters might be quite all right; as a group, they made him impatient. 'They must

[1] Pye, *George Leigh Mallory* (1927), p. 61.

be a very rum lot,' Hugh Wilson sympathetically conceded. Wilson, who held that Mallory should aim at a university lectureship in history or English, wrote at this time to Sayle: 'What cynicism he has to arm him does not seem to help him in his direct relations with unsympathetic men; and all public schools have a majority of masters whom we young people regard as fools.'[1] The older friend who best understood George's traits carefully restated a suggestion he had already offered:

A.C. Benson to G.M.   *29 June 1910*

I have *often* found your directness and frankness a *real* compliment, as proving that I was not getting so elderly and portentous as I sometimes fear. . . . What I believe is merely that you are rather combative, and execute a war-dance rather easily. A man at Eton once said to me, when I wrote him what I thought was rather a sparkling letter, 'You have cracked the literary whip so long that you forget how much it may sometimes hurt.' I have often thought of that; and it is the injection of a kind of rhetorical contempt for your adversary into what you say that is what may be amiss, I think?

George had gone north, for the wedding at Mobberley of his sister Avie and Harry Longridge; he went on to Pen-y-Pass for a bit of climbing with Edward Evans. Then, during the first week of July, the path into the future became clearer. George heard of a job for August, taking a boy to the Alps; and he received from the headmaster of Charterhouse the offer of a probationary appointment at £270 a year.

G. H. Rendall to G.M.   *5 July 1910*

The work will be mainly or wholly upon the Modern side. I cannot foresee the exact distribution of history, French, Latin, and maths., but shall do my best to accommodate these to your own preferences, and hope that it may be possible to place in your hands some at least of the higher teaching of history to candidates preparing for scholarships.

So the question of a career was settled, and the time came for escorting John Bankes-Price to Switzerland. The thought of George Mallory 'bear-leading' was too much for Lytton Strachey to cope with. 'The imagination cannot create,' he wrote; 'it can only reconstruct and on this occasion mine has no materials, except a snow mountain, laziness, energy, George, and a perfectly

---

[1] *Letters of Hugh Stanley Wilson to His Family and Friends* (1919): Wilson to G.M., 22 June 1910, p. 102; Wilson to Sayle, 23 June 1910, p. 104.

absurd companion aged 15½ – and I can make nothing out of them.'

The season, which must have been the most trying that George ever spent in the Alps, began with a week at Bel Alp. 'We pitched the tent for two days above snow very successfully,' George reported, 'but afterwards my pupil hurt a knee, and we've had a very slack time in consequence.' On August 17th they arrived at Zermatt, where George found a number of friends. Geoffrey Young had just made noteworthy ascents of the Dent d'Hérens and the Dent Blanche; Cottie Sanders had come to Zermatt with her mother. The 'bear', Miss Sanders observed, had no desire to climb; he did not even enjoy a picnic in the fields towards the Gorner gorge. Mallory discharged his responsibilities with admirable conscientiousness, cajoling and ragging the boy, never openly losing patience though 'he found it much harder than most people to make any allowance for apathy'. That he had to repress irritation was no secret from his friends. Once, leaving John in their care, he dashed off to make an unsuccessful attempt on the Arbengrat.

Mallory and the boy finished the season with a week at Arolla. W. H. Beveridge, recently appointed Director of Labour Exchanges under the Board of Trade, saw Mallory walk into the Hôtel du Mont Collon 'looking like a Greek god'.[1] The weather turned bad; but Mallory took great satisfaction in traversing the Collon, and John managed to get some pleasing photographs of a crack on the Aiguilles Rouges. Indeed, the season seems ultimately to have been more of a success than Mallory's friends could have guessed at the time. John wrote in October to say that he had never enjoyed a holiday so much: 'I shall certainly go climbing whenever I can now.' He had read George Abraham's *Complete Mountaineer*, started Martin Conway's *Alps from End to End*, and subscribed to the *Alpine Journal*; he wondered whether he might be able to climb from Davos or Klosters that winter. August had undoubtedly been a trial; but the boy had learned something about mountains, and George had made use of an excellent opportunity to develop some patience.

As an assistant master at Charterhouse, he had to develop yet more. He arrived on 21 September 1910 and took up residence in Nercwys House with two colleagues, Lancelot Allen and Norman Chignell.

[1] Lord Beveridge, *Power and Influence* (1953), p. 96.

6. The Nesthorn from the Ober Aletsch Glacier

7. On the Moine Ridge of the Aiguille Verte, 13 August 1909

G.M. to his mother   *25 September 1910*

I am enjoying life here, though there are moments of doubt. My work is a good deal with small boys, who are much more difficult to teach and to control; but it amuses me, and that is the great thing. Dreariness is fatal to success in teaching, and if I escape that I may learn to be of some use.

A. C. Benson to G.M.   *26 September 1910*

I hope you won't go on thinking boys beastly. They are very limited and very conventional. . . . I don't think I should care much to live amongst them now; but if one can only be both strict and kind they *do* respond – and some of them are quite delightful.

'To teach and to control': for a new master who looked no older than the oldest boys, these were obligations that seemed full of problems. How could he keep discipline without acting like a drill-sergeant? How could he transmit his intellectual enthusiasms to young pupils without violating accepted pedagogical conventions and losing authority altogether? The problems were aggravated by the state of the school. Dr. Rendall, a kindly man, had let things get rather out of hand: there had been a relaxation of discipline and a general lowering of tone. It was not easy for a newcomer to find the way.

By November Mallory felt somewhat happier. He had found Allen congenial and several pupils promising; he was learning to bear irritations with patience and to ward off ennui by reminding himself that it is always one's own fault. As a teacher, he depended rather on enthusiasm than on authority. Being accustomed to heady talk with Cambridge friends, he naturally hoped to teach in a civilised way; he wanted to treat all questions as open and to share with his pupils the difficult and exciting effort to attain the truth; he tended to become discursive, following lines that struck him as interesting. The trouble was that boys generally know how to start a hare and then relax while someone else chases it. On hearing that Mallory had not stuck to the approved scheme for teaching English grammar, a senior colleague entered a friendly but firm remonstrance; and Mallory, without admitting that this was a moment for contrition, thanked him for his words about the common good – 'I think you need not be troubled by the matter any further.' No one, after all, could count on inspiration every day of the week; no one could expect to make real progress by rambling.

E   *65*

It would be impossible for me to say that you had *improved* by being at Charterhouse, but in the spirit of the hymn which says 'new graces ever gaining,' &c., I may say that I was considerably struck with the fact that you seemed more contented and tolerant, and with something about you which you had not got before: call it, like John Stuart Mill, a healthy objectivity. I think it does people like you and me good to have a definite job, and definite people to have the anxious care of – or even the amused care of! It is a great thing to deal with realities, not with only theories; and to *have* to be in relations with people whether one likes them or not.

Towards the boys whom he liked Mallory adopted a manner more avuncular than schoolmasterly. A Cheshire boy named Rooper pleased him by reading Wells and Belloc, and by suggesting that *The Knight of the Burning Pestle* would be fun to put on at Charterhouse. A remarkably inquisitive and articulate young cosmopolite named Raymond Rodakowski, son of a Polish father and a Scottish mother, engagingly professed the belief that a man's first duty is to be happy and that one of the greatest pleasures in life is to be skilled in physical activity. Sometimes Raymond would be driven by his uncompromising rationalism into a fit of melancholy; but he could always recover his *joie de vivre* by sparring, or playing real tennis with Neville Lytton at Crabbet Park, or riding in the ring where the Lyttons trained their famous Arab horses. It was unconventional, no doubt, but hardly surprising, that before the year was out these two boys, Rooper and Rodakowski, addressed their letters not to 'Mr. Mallory' but to 'Uncle George'.

Throughout the year, Mallory kept in close touch with his older friends. Gaselee came for a night just two weeks after Mallory arrived. He had recently edited the *Satyricon* of Petronius, and he had just attended the Church Congress; he probably talked of both. Ten days later, Lytton Strachey reached Godalming for a week end, apparently without difficulty, despite his qualms over a venture into the unknown. 'I wonder where Charterhouse is,' he had written; 'I think probably in some semi-detached Surrey region.' Mallory's friendliness so touched him that he had trouble finding the words for his 'Collins'. He and his brother James thought of taking a house together somewhere and wondered whether one could be found in Surrey: 'Couldn't we have the other half of your house? That would be perfect.' But it did not work out: Strachey went off to stay with the Bussys, who sent their love to the 'beau Mallory'; then he returned to London and had mumps. Meanwhile, Geoffrey Young had appeared at Charterhouse; and Geoffrey Keynes had run down for a week end from St. Bartholomew's Hospital, where he had won the senior entrance scholarship.

Mallory had been proposed for the Alpine Club by Young and Graham Irving; he was elected on December 5th and promptly went up to London for the A.C. reception at the Grafton Galleries. As usual, he gave little or no thought to his attire; his habitual carelessness once made his father exclaim, 'Do you realise that George has come through London in carpet slippers and no hat?' On this occasion, Miss Sanders had invited George to tea:

My brother Jack and I [she later wrote] had found that we could manage New Year in Wales, and we wanted to make plans. That was a very characteristic episode altogether. George's simplicity in the matter of conventions was extreme. He came up fully purposed to go to an evening reception of about a thousand people in a very nice, old, comfortable greenish tweed suit and the very odd-looking porridge-coloured felt hat which was then his favourite headgear. It never occurred to him to bring any evening clothes. He explained to me after-wards that it was, after all, an Alpine Club reception – a gathering of climbers! – so who *could* have presupposed evening dress?

He came, as I say, to tea; and we promised ourselves a thoroughly good evening among the pictures, for the Grafton Galleries were then housing the first Post-Impressionist Exhibition. I had danced among them several times and thought them very comic, but I was quite pre-pared to be taught better by George. We arranged, then, to meet under a certain picture at a certain hour and then plan for Wales. I was taking a party to the Ladies' A.C. for dinner and had to go off to dress. I don't know who it was that enlightened George in the matter of the dress suit; but when I came down I learned that he had been enlightened, had been filled with dismay, had rumpled his hair – and fled.

He came to dine once before Christmas, and either then or later we did go to the Post-Impressionists. He tried with great patience and eagerness to make me see the point of Cézanne and Matisse and – what I found more difficult – of Gauguin. But what he did do for me was to make me look at them, and go on looking, seriously, and not treat them as a huge joke; and so in time I came to see something of what there was. In the face of his enthusiasm it was impossible not to try at least to understand them.

George paid a Christmas visit to the Longridges at Mobberley and then, as Cottie and Jack Sanders had suggested, began the

New Year at Pen-y-Pass. Geoffrey Young had stayed on, after the Christmas party; and among the others present were H. O. Jones, Ralph Todhunter, Leonard Noon, and Geoffrey's cousin Norman Young. The first expedition was a memorable failure. Miss Sanders had strained her right side and left shoulder, and she had caught a chill –

I felt very unlike doing anything, but consented to walk up to Lliwedd with Geoffrey and George to see them start. I had my first experience that day of a certain inexorableness there was in George if he thought one ought to climb – and Geoffrey was worse. 'The rocks look bone dry today, Mallory. I think we ought to have a very pleasant day, Miss Sanders, if you feel inspired to it when you get there.' But I didn't, and said so – and that I would watch them climb. It was no use. They were full of consideration. 'But you must climb *something*, Miss Sanders,' from Geoffrey. 'Something quite short, of course,' from George. Then both: 'Seriously, it isn't any particular pleasure to either of us to do one of these things together again. We'll do something with you; we don't mind a slack day.'

The slack day resolved itself, I found, into the Girdle Traverse when we were half-way up the Far East Buttress. But that was too much. I was bitterly cold and feeling rather ill and completely off climbing; in fact, I was frightened out of my wits at being on rocks at all in such a state. I asked to be taken to the top. I was, by devious routes, but with a certain silence in front and behind. We lunched on the top; and Geoffrey went on up Snowdon, while George took me home in sad disgrace. He was kind, but a little mocking, and inquisitive as to why I should have been frightened – it clearly was something he had no experience of whatever. But when he saw that I was really unhappy over it he left off teasing and saw to it that I got a huge tea and afterwards offered to take me up to the little lake behind the hotel, which I had expressed my intention of seeing. . . .

Geoffrey left next day; and George took Norman Young, my brother Jack, and myself up the Central Buttress of Tryfan. This was our first climb under George's sole guidance. It was a cold, disagreeable day; we had started rather late and were chilly and discouraged when we tackled our climb after lunch. The first fifty feet took us forty minutes – we chose the hard way, certainly; and the rope was too short for comfort. I muttered to George that we should never finish by daylight, at that rate. But George wasn't going to have any nonsense or any more failures. I can see him now, moving about over the rocks like a great cat, scolding, exhorting, encouraging us. . . .

He was never a showy climber; he did not go in for the minute precisions of style at all. On the contrary, he seemed to move on rocks with a sort of large, casual ease which was very deceptive when one came to try and follow him. When he was confronted with a pitch which taxed his powers, he would fling himself at it with a sort of angry energy, appearing to worry it as a terrier worries a rat, till he had mastered it. Geoffrey Young once said, watching him, 'George always looks as though, if he couldn't get up, he would destroy the climb!'

From Pen-y-Pass George went to Ogwen, for a few days of climbing with Graham Irving. On January 14th he called at a London nursing home to see Edward Evans, who had suffered a breakdown; then he proceeded to Cambridge, where he saw Benson, Gaselee, and Sayle. It was his habit to plan every vacation, every journey, in such a way as to include all the friends he possibly could. By January 20th he had returned to Godalming – Evans came for a week end and talked hopefully of entering a holy society of friars. Even after the term began, George managed to get about a little. In February he gathered up flannels and tennis shoes for a week end with Beveridge at Shottermill.

The Easter party at Pen-y-Pass again included a number of veterans in their forties and fifties – Andrews and Thomson; K. J. P. Orton, F.R.S., and O. K. Williamson, F.R.C.P.; and Oscar Eckenstein and his Austrian guest, Karl Blodig, who had almost completed his ascents of all the 4000-metre peaks in the Alps. It was at this time that Mallory first climbed with H. V. Reade, the Squire of Ipsden, a financial expert serving H.M. Customs. The party at Gorphwysfa had expanded by now, in accordance with Geoffrey Young's belief that 'good society is composed of three elements, men, women, and children'.[1] Mrs. Reade, with the assistance of Young's cousin Edith Stopford, chaperoned the young ladies.

On April 12th two ropes started up the Great Gully of Craig yr Ysfa: H. O. Jones, Blodig, Mrs. Orton, and Leonard Noon; Mallory, Reade, Miss Sanders, and G.W.Y. Dr. Blodig, when he recorded his impressions of the day, frankly admitted that an iced chimney had made him uneasy:[2]

I favoured going back and finding another route, but that did not please the second party at all. Mr. Mallory climbed up, turned his back against the block of ice, wedged himself in the chimney as best he could, and brought Mr. Reade up. Then Mr. Mallory used him as a

[1] 'An Impression of Pen-y-Pass, 1900–1920', in *The Mountains of Snowdonia*, ed. H. R. C. Carr and G. A. Lister (2nd ed., 1948), p. 78.
[2] 'Ostertage in North Wales', *Climbers' Club Journal*, Feb. 1912, p. 55.

human stepladder and, with the greatest dash and marvellous skill, worked his way up the smooth surface until he disappeared from our view. Unanimous cries of 'Hurrah' and 'Bravo' hailed this extraordinary performance.

Three days later, Mallory and Reade took Dr. Blodig up Route I on Lliwedd and made the Girdle Traverse with him. The visitor wrote:[1]

Mr. Mallory led; I brought up the rear. If I may venture to express an opinion, the coolness with which Mr. Mallory showed his mastery of the hardest pitches was really astounding – but then Mr. Reade kept impressing on me from first to last the conviction that this man 'couldn't fall even if he wanted to'.

At the end of the day, Blodig had spoken more ominously, shaking his head: 'That young man will not be alive for long.'

Poor George, Miss Sanders observed, was quite upset. 'He always used to defend himself vigorously against any suggestion that he was not a perfectly prudent mountaineer,' she wrote, 'and looked almost comically dismayed and surprised over this dictum':

He *was* prudent, according to his own standards; but his standards were not those of the ordinary medium-good rock-climber. The fact was that difficult rocks had become to him a perfectly normal element; his prodigious reach, his great strength, and his admirable technique, joined to a sort of cat-like agility, made him feel completely secure on rocks so difficult as to fill less competent climbers with a sense of hazardous enterprise. But he was very careful of unskilled performers, and very down on any clumsiness or carelessness. I never saw him do a reckless or ill-considered thing on steep rocks. He hated the irresponsible folly and ignorance which led incompetent people into dangerous situations, and so brought mountaineering into disrepute.

On Easter Monday George and G.W.Y. turned out to perform a rescue on Clogwyn y Person, where a German from Bradford, wearing ordinary shoes, a long mackintosh, and reversible vulcanite cuffs, had rashly attempted a route of his own up some wet, mossy slabs. Once out of danger, the man offered his rescuers a sovereign – which, as Geoffrey said, they of course refused, laughing a little. Blodig then bestowed on them red paper medals inscribed 'For Live Safing'. But George was too indignant to see much fun in the episode.

On the damp evening of Easter Sunday, in the smoking room at Gorphwysfa, George had become involved in a long discussion

[1] 'Ostertage in North Wales', *Climbers' Club Journal*, Feb. 1912, p. 59.

of ethics. Miss Sanders found him an impressive disputant:

Owing to the death of someone's grandfather, the usual sing-song was not taking place; the old gentlemen were doing feats of strength with Geoffrey and Owen in the hall, and the younger members gathered rather *désoeuvrés* round the fire under Mrs. Reade's presidency. George and one of the Irishmen were the protagonists, and the subject was whether one should or should not have principles. George held that one should – at least one or two fundamental ones – and keep as close to them as possible. The Irishman had no objection to one's having principles, so long as he was prepared to break them. Mrs. Reade pronounced herself to have none. Here were the makings of a famous ethical row – and we had it!

The Irishman had really all the cards in his hands: he was quick, he was witty, his mind was rather deadly in its keenness, he was exceedingly well informed, and he was taking the side easiest to defend – the broad-minded, airy, tolerant point of view. It was not difficult for him to make George's insistence on the importance of thinking right and doing right look pedestrian and priggish, and he was very unsparing. And the sense of the meeting was on the whole against George – at the start, anyhow. George stood up to it superbly, really: no irony, no dialectical skill, would budge him from his position – that it might and must be necessary to alter the letter of principles to suit fresh facts as they entered into a person's experience, but that the spirit informing them would remain the same. There *was* a right, and if you wanted to you could find it, and it was supremely important. The discussion grew very heated. George was really outmatched; but the thing that gradually emerged most, for me, was the practical demonstration he was giving of living up to the principle of keeping one's temper in an argument – in spite of shrewd blows given and received. And his extraordinary insistence on purity of motive.

I have a picture of the group now: Mrs. Reade on one side of the fire; the Irishman opposite, with his feet over the arm of his chair, mowing down opposed theories with the skill of a good fencer; George on the floor between them, his hands round his knees, unclasped now and then to throw back his hair, stammering a little with his eagerness and impatience and the difficulty of getting out what he had to say, but getting it out all the same; while in corners pairs expounded *their* views to one another or put in a quick word, and a big black-haired Munsterman drummed with his fists on the book-case and talked about Bentham.

George went from Pen-y-Pass to Birkenhead, to see his parents; on to Oxford, to stay with 'Sligger' Urquhart at Balliol; and so to London, where he saw Jacques Raverat and Gwen Darwin, who were engaged to be married, and attended the meeting of the

Alpine Club on May 2nd. He stayed three nights with the Sanders family. Miss Sanders wrote:

We spent most of our time in the British Museum. The collection of Chinese paintings had been opened fairly recently; I had never seen them, and of course I must. We spent hours there, George fairly intoxicated with their beauty. . . . The simplicity, the assurance, the consummate perfection of design, the exquisite economy of line and still more of colour: beauty and the most vivid portraiture pressed in close between the framework of a rigid convention and flowering out from it – they took one's breath away at first. And what a field of speculation they opened up! Exactly why did they make the composition of European artists look almost childish? We hurried to the National Gallery to see. We compared the great *Earthly Paradise*[1] with the *Primavera*. I had been reading Aurel Stein's books; and George must read them, too. What was there in the theory of the relation of Chinese to Greek art? We had to consider this among the Elgin marbles, and George decided that he must in any case have a cast of the Hypnos for his rooms at Charterhouse.

He stayed an extra night to go with us to hear Debussy's *Pelléas et Mélisande*, though it involved a start at 6:00 a.m., and breakfast first, to get back to Charterhouse in time for some school or chapel. That was a good evening. Donald Tovey was sitting a few seats off and began to give us a résumé of the play and the music; he stood up to do it and forgot everything but his thesis, as his habit was. The lights went down, the overture began, while he was still pouring out criticism in his high level voice – till he was hushed and pulled down into his place by his indignant neighbours. That sort of thing began an evening well, for George; he was delighted by human oddity. It waked in him a sort of mischievous amusement that he didn't really indulge nearly enough. From this point of view, the evening was a success. I cried, as often happens at an opera. More human oddity! George was enchanted.

In June Maynard Keynes came down to Charterhouse from King's; and then, 'to avoid the terrors of the Coronation', Lytton Strachey reappeared, wearing now (as he had warned) 'a red-brown-gold beard of the most divine proportions'. Summer in the Surrey countryside was irresistible, and the outlook in school was not altogether bad.

G.M. to Miss Sanders   *2 June 1911*

Lord, it is good about here, particularly as I spend many glorious nights under the stars. I expect I told you about the proposed site for

---

[1] A painting of the paradise of Avalokitesvara, brought by Aurel Stein from Tun-huang to the British Museum.

my camp. It has been rather a success. My brother comes over from Guildford, and one of the beaks from here (not very beaky); a farm supplies bread and eggs and washes up our messes. A night jar perches in the Scotch firs a few yards away and makes thrilling music; the mist is white in the valleys; and there is no hill between our heathery couch and Hindhead ten miles away. The sun gives the signal for our uprising (in theory), and one often gets an hour's work done before early school.

G.M. to A. C. Benson   [*24 July 1911?*][1]

Things go fairly well here, but it is very uphill work, and there are a good many horrors when one sees people getting visibly worse through being at school. However, this last term has been very agreeable; several things got better. I got less irritable and found it easier to be severe without being angry. Also, the other ushers seemed to be more friendly. There is only one common task I really dislike. Imagine me tomorrow morning teaching the smallest boys about the fall of man! What the devil is one to say?

Until the last moment, Mallory's plans for the summer of 1911 remained uncertain. He hoped to revisit the Alps, but he had very little money, and his heart seemed to have developed a worrying click. By the end of July, however, to the relief of family and friends, he had been declared physically fit; and he made ready for a climbing holiday with Graham Irving and Harry Tyndale, of the old Ice Club.

The three went first to the Graian Alps and crossed the passes from Bonneval-sur-Arc to the Valsavaranche. At the end of the day, they came to the Nivolet glen, the steep descent to Valsavaranche, and the inn at Pont. Later, in moments of disquiet, George found that he could regain something of peace by remembering this scene, one of the 'pleasant and comfortable Gorphwysfas, so well known to us by now that we make the journey easily enough with a homing instinct':[2]

An infant river meanders coolly in a broad, grassy valley; it winds along as gently almost as some glassy snake of the plains, for the valley is so flat that its slope is imperceptible. The green hills on either side are smooth and pleasing to the eye, and eventually close in, though not completely. Here the stream plunges down a steep and craggy hillside far into the shadow of a deeper valley. You may follow it down by a rough path, and then, turning aside, before you quite reach the bottom of the second valley, along a grassy ledge, you may find a modest inn.

[1] Pye, *George Leigh Mallory* (1927), p. 67. Dated by reference to A.C.B.'s letter of 26 July 1911.
[2] 'The Mountaineer as Artist', *Climbers' Club Journal*, March 1914, p. 35.

They stayed three nights in the Victor Emmanuel hut and, for training, climbed the Gran Paradiso and the Cima da Ciarforon. It was a cold morning on the Ciarforon, but the warm afternoon sun gave promise of glorious weather to come. On August 9th, a day of brilliant sunshine, they ascended the Herbetet by a route, probably new, on the western arête. Tyndale remembered that the 'passage from ledge to ledge, the smooth, almost unconscious progress across the cliff face in the peace of Italian sunshine, was like the development of a melody in some stately chorus where each part takes up the theme in sequence.'[1] This was a day for a long rest on the summit, with a clear view of the great southern precipices of Mont Blanc. At last the three descended to Valnontey and in the evening came by pleasant paths to Cogne.

Here, as Tyndale thought, was lotos-land; but Irving had not had enough of action. After a day of walking about the flowered meadows, he proposed a midnight start for the ridge extending southwestward from the Col des Sengies. This unfrequented course led over the Cima Ouest de Valeille and the Punta Scatiglion to the Ondezana, from which the descent took them by way of the Monei chalets to Valnontey. Next, on the 13th, with the good wishes of George Yeld, bearded doyen of English mountaineers in the Graians, they went up to the Pousset huts; and on the 14th, another day of bright sun, they climbed the Grivola by the north ridge. Mallory enjoyed this day enormously. Tyndale never forgot the sight of him leading on steep ice:[2]

> He cut a superb staircase, with inimitable ease and grace and a perfect economy of effort. In watching George at work one was conscious not so much of physical strength as of suppleness and balance; so rhythmical and harmonious was his progress in any steep place, above all on slabs, that his movements appeared almost serpentine in their smoothness.

From Cogne the party moved on to Courmayeur, where they heard talk of great achievements. Geoffrey Young and H. O. Jones had climbed on the ridges of the Grandes Jorasses; Dr. Blodig, in their company, had completed his list of *Viertausender*; the brothers Finch, George and Max, had traversed Monte Rosa. Such reports gave added stimulus to the Ice Club in its own next project, the ascent of Mont Blanc by the eastern buttress of Mont Maudit. Remembering in wartime this 'culminating event for three fit men in the splendid August of 1911', Mallory wrote his

[1] *Mountain Paths* (1948), p. 68.   [2] *Ibid.*, p. 73.

most interesting essay for the *Alpine Journal*.[1] Since his purpose in that essay was not to record bare facts but to express remembered thoughts and feelings, using the third person, it is necessary to fill out the account with details gleaned elsewhere.

On August 17th, having gone up to the Col du Géant, Irving, Mallory, and Tyndale supped at the hut and found places to sleep. At 3:30 a.m. they left for the Col des Flambeaux, whence they made for a point west of the Fourche de la Brenva on the frontier ridge between France and Italy. They reached the bergschrund at 5:00 a.m. and climbed in an hour to the top of the ridge. After advancing a few hundred feet toward Mont Maudit, they stopped for a hot breakfast, with a splendid early-morning view of the Brenva face. By now it was evident that George was not going well. At the hut he had drunk a half-glass of sour Chianti; he was now struggling, in consequence, against a stomach disorder and an almost immobilising fatigue. He fell asleep and kicked over the porridge, thus compelling Graham to start a fresh brew of snow and oats. Graham, as George said in his essay, was rather annoyed; Harry, however, expressed his sympathy for human frailty –

But there was more comfort than that. There was rest, not the least of the rewards. And there was beauty. He didn't precisely feel that these places were more beautiful than others. What use in comparing absolutes except to appreciate quality? This was conspicuously unlike many of the most beautiful mountain scenes, which are often dominated by the sheer lyrical force or the rugged magnificence of a single peak – so that one *must* look at the Weisshorn, it may be, or the Matterhorn, or the Dent Blanche. Here an enchanted host surrounded him. Probably everyone who knew them had a place apart, as he had, in the imagination for the great members of Mont Blanc; their spell captured and held his mind during the first halt; not only the impression of what he immediately saw, beautiful as it was, but the sense of all that was suggested and could be said actually to be present because there seemed to be no limits. Therefore, so long as he had stayed just looking and wondering, feeling breadth and height and space, the personal question had been put aside. The end was still unthinkable; he had banished all agitating speculation on that head, not caring to be perplexed. To be there! nothing else mattered. And though no hope of the expedition

[1] 'Mont Blanc from the Col du Géant by the Eastern Buttress of Mont Maudit,' *A.J.*, 32:148–162 (Sept. 1918). See below, pp. 120–121. Cf. R. L. G. Irving, 'Mont Blanc by the S.E. Ridge of Mont Maudit', *A.J.*, 25: 749 (Nov. 1911), and 'Mont Blanc', *Ten Great Mountains* (1940), pp. 104–118; H. E. G. Tyndale, 'Mont Blanc', *Mountain Paths* (1948), pp. 75–85.

had been born then, he had received an assurance of the day. The great thing had happened; the spirit had its flight; and the rest must take care of itself.

Irving led up steep rocks, and occasional patches of hard névé and ice, to a huge gendarme which blocked progress for another half-hour. Again Mallory fell asleep for a few seconds, to his great consternation; thereafter, as the party climbed higher and higher on Mont Maudit, he gradually recovered his powers. Continuing up steep rocks, the party reached the skyline at 2:00 p.m. and the summit of Mont Maudit at 3:30. All three were feeling tired. They descended to the Col de la Brenva for a long rest, rejected their chance to go down at once by the Corridor to the Grands Mulets, started at 5:00 up the Mur de la Côte, and at 6:30 stood on the summit of Mont Blanc. George's essay reads:[1]

A breeze cool and bracing seemed to gather force as they plodded up the long slopes, more gentle now as they approached the final goal. He felt the wind about him with its old strange music. His thoughts became less conscious, less continuous. Rather than thinking or feeling he was simply listening – listening for distant voices scarcely articulate. . . . The solemn dome resting on those marvellous buttresses, fine and firm above all its chasms of ice, its towers and crags; a place where desires point and aspirations end; very, very high and lovely, long-suffering and wise. . . . *Experience*, slowly and wonderfully filtered; at the last a purged remainder. . . . And what is that? What more than the infinite knowledge that it is all worth while – all one strives for? . . . How to get the best of it all? One must conquer, achieve, get to the top; one must know the end to be convinced that one can win the end – to know there's no dream that mustn't be dared. . . . Is this the summit, crowning the day? How cool and quiet! We're not exultant; but delighted, joyful; soberly astonished. . . . Have we vanquished an enemy? None but ourselves. Have we gained success? That word means nothing here. Have we won a kingdom? No . . . and yes. We have achieved an ultimate satisfaction . . . fulfilled a destiny. . . . To struggle and to understand – never this last without the other; such is the law. . . . We've only been obeying an old law then? Ah! but it's *the* law . . . and we understand – a little more.

They took time for coffee at the Janssen observatory, not yet buried in the snow, and then hurried down the Bosses du Droma-daire as the sun was setting. They reached the Grands Mulets after dark and persuaded a reluctant cook to make a late supper

[1] The dots in this paragraph are Mallory's; they do not mean that words have been cut.

for them. Sixteen and a half hours, they had been out: a long day, especially for a man poisoned by bad Chianti; a day made unforgettable by the holding-on and the winning-through. George and Harry shared a room with a little Austrian who had a most unusual snore. Graham could hear the two of them laughing themselves to sleep.

George's Alpine season ended with a climb on the west side of Mont Blanc, from St. Gervais to the Col de Miage, along the ridge to the head of the Trélatête glacier, and up the Tête Carrée in a thunderstorm. The three friends descended by the Col du Mont Tondu to Les Mottets; Graham and Harry went on to Courmayeur and the Val d'Isère, and George set out for home.

There was still time for a little more climbing. Early in September George and his sister Mary went to the Snowdon Ranger at Quellyn, and for a week George climbed with Harold Porter. The best of it, as Porter wrote in his diary, was a long day, gloriously fine and hot, on Lliwedd – half a dozen routes, 'climbing very fast and mostly unroped'. Never had Porter enjoyed a day of rock-climbing more thoroughly. It was exciting to perform up to the standard set by Mallory, who 'climbed with that miraculous ease and grace which I had already learnt to admire'.

CHAPTER 4

Godalming, 1911–1914

In 1911 a new régime began at Charterhouse: G. H. Rendall retired, and Frank Fletcher succeeded him as headmaster. At Marlborough since 1903, as the first lay headmaster of a great school, Fletcher had made a reputation for toughness. 'I was surprised to learn,' he wrote, 'that school rumours at Charterhouse credited me with having in my first two years at Marlborough expelled forty boys.'[1] Blunt and occasionally tactless, he understood that at Charterhouse, as one of his friends said, he would have to be, like the wild west wind, 'destroyer and creator'. He was a mountaineer and a member of the Alpine Club, but George Mallory took some time before admitting his virtues.

On returning to Charterhouse in September, Mallory faced his own double task: to teach his pupils, and to revise his Boswell essay for publication as a book. John Murray had politely returned the manuscript; Smith, Elder and Co. had undertaken to publish it, but asked for careful revision before the end of December. This request was no surprise; Mallory himself recognised the need. 'It seems to me a very curious hotch-potch from a literary point of view,' he wrote to Benson; 'I imagine that I have been learning to write while writing it and that it contains a series of experiments in expression.'[2] He asked one or two other friends for their opinions.

Lytton Strachey to G.M.   *25 September 1911*

I think you seem to be rather anxious to include too much, both in the sentences and in the general scheme. A good many of the sentences appear to me overloaded. I think it's usually better to sacrifice comprehensiveness to lucidity, especially in prose. One can only hope at best to say a part of what one thinks, and so one may as well make up one's mind to choose the part that's simple.

Mallory saw that Boswell deserved fuller and more sympathetic

[1] *After Many Days* (1937), p. 153.   [2] Pye, *George Leigh Mallory* (1927), p. 56.

attention than he had yet received. Macaulay's famous essay had acknowledged that the *Life of Samuel Johnson* is the most interesting biographical work in the world, but left the impression that the biographer was an impossible person; it had not tried to explain how a man who nursed vain ambitions and often behaved foolishly could produce a masterpiece. Mallory conscientiously studied the materials in print, old and new, and concluded that Boswell would have dropped into oblivion, with others who aspired merely to be gentlemen in society, had he not been moved by an insistent desire to understand himself, to see other men truly, and to speak honestly. Candour lifted Boswell far above the rest:[1]

> Herein lay the essence of his genius. The story of Boswell's life is the story of a struggle between influences and ambitions which led him towards the commonplace, and the rare qualities grafted deeply within him, which bore him steadily in an opposite direction.

John Murray, who had been consulted by a representative of the Boswell family, had an inkling that masses of journals and letters might turn up before long; but Mallory, unsuccessful with his inquiries, had to finish his work in ignorance of the undiscovered treasures. At any rate, with help, he tried to make it readable. After the New Year, staying a week end with the Lyttons at Crabbet Park, he met Edward Marsh, who was serving at that time as Winston Churchill's private secretary at the Admiralty. Generous with his time, Marsh sometimes helped a friend by removing stylistic blemishes from a manuscript or proofs; and in March he undertook, at George's request, to 'diabolize' *Boswell the Biographer*.[2]

Neville Lytton, younger son of the first Earl of Lytton, had been encouraged by his father to study painting; he had adopted traditional techniques because he found them healthier than new, and he held toward the Post-Impressionists an attitude of disrespect which Mallory could not share. On modern education, however, the host and the guest agreed; for both believed that schools too often produced either a 'brainworm' or a 'muscle fiend', too seldom a man with balance approximating that of an ancient Greek. Never quite accepting the public school as it was, sometimes wondering whether work at a university might be

---

[1] *Boswell the Biographer* (1912), p. 39.
[2] Edward Marsh, *A Number of People* (1939), pp. 336–339; Christopher Hassall, *A Biography of Edward Marsh* (1959), pp. 181–182.

happier, Mallory nevertheless devoted his energies to the job in hand, gradually ascertained what a schoolmaster could do and not do, and developed unselfconsciously a balance of his own: aestheticism without softness, honesty without priggishness, sportsmanship without heartiness.

'He was full of ideas about the teaching of history,' David Pye wrote, 'and about the value of bringing humane letters to their proper place in education as its liveliest and most enduring part.'[1] Once he had finished *Boswell the Biographer*, he could spend more time in the preparation of lectures, and he took pleasure in doing so. When he gave his form the topic for an essay, he would try his own hand at it; he simply could not expect the boys to write on 'Candour' or on 'Hope' without sorting his own thoughts. If he read an interesting book, like Jusserand's *English Wayfaring Life* or Graham Wallas's *Life of Francis Place*, he immediately asked himself what the boys might gain from it. At Nercwys House he held play-readings for them. Miss Sanders described the scene:

> Friends visiting him at Charterhouse in the little house which he shared with one or two other masters, found the room a litter of books and papers – books in French and English, modern plays which were being examined with a view to readings with his brighter spirits, Fabian tracts, reproductions or photographs of Greek sculpture or modern French paintings – all more or less drowned in a sea of essays from his form.

Sometimes George persuaded his friends from London and Cambridge to advance the cause of education in their own special ways. 'Duncan Grant stayed with me last week end,' he wrote, 'and is to paint two pictures for my classroom!' Whenever he had guests, he saw to it that a few boys were invited to meet them. At twenty-six he still felt close to the boys: the one good thing about his own youthful appearance, he said, was that it reduced the gap. Robert Graves, ten years younger, wrote of him:[2]

> From the first he treated me as an equal, and I used to spend my spare time reading books in his room or going for walks with him in the country. He told me of the existence of modern authors. My father being two generations older than myself and my only link with books, I had never heard of people like Shaw, Samuel Butler, Rupert Brooke, Wells, Flecker, or Masefield, and I was greatly interested in them.

George's friends thought that at Charterhouse George had not

---

[1] *George Leigh Mallory* (1927), p. 62.   [2] *Good-bye to All That* (1929), p. 80.

8. Mont Blanc and Mont Maudit

PEN-Y-PASS,
1913
9. Mallory and
Herford

10. Gorphwysfa after Easter: Standing, Geoffrey Winthrop Young, Lloyd Baker, Geoffrey Keynes, Geoffrey Madan, Mrs. Slingsby, Cecil Slingsby, George Mallory; seated on the wall, Robert Mühlberg, Conor O'Brien, Eleanor Slingsby and Hugh Heber Percy

enough room to be himself and attain his proper stature. He alienated some of his colleagues and puzzled many of his pupils by refusing to accept the tradition of hostility between masters and boys; he was much more interested in raising intellectual aspirations than in imposing discipline; he freely criticised such conventions as he found stultifying; he cared little for the usual sports. 'George was wasted at Charterhouse,' Graves wrote – but added that he 'always managed to find four or five boys in the school who were, like him, out of their element, and befriended them and made life tolerable for them.'[1] Miss Sanders had much the same opinion: 'He was, as has been said, working perhaps too much outside the ordinary scholastic framework of a public school to be a very successful schoolmaster, but he must have been a rather exciting one.' A Norfolk vicar, father of a boy at Charterhouse, said, 'Like everybody else, we loved him.'

Soon after Christmas 1911 George and Trafford went on together to Pen-y-Pass. The weather was splendid for climbing; and in the evenings, as Geoffrey Young wrote in the Gorphwysfa Visitors' Book, the band of friends 'set a record for talent'. These were halcyon days; this was one of the meets that G.W.Y. kept always apart in memory – crags to explore and cold llyns to plunge in, and Gorphwysfa filled in the evening with 'rhymesters, wits, singers, players on many and unknown instruments, all at the top of their form and spirits':[2]

> There are days upon Lliwedd beyond all desire,
> And conflict with cavern and crack.
> There are thoughts of the songs by the smoking room fire,
> And talks after twelve in the Shack. . . .

The Reades were there again, and H. O. Jones with his sister Bronwen, and Cottie Sanders. From Ireland came Page Dickinson and Conor O'Brien; from Oxford, Hugh Rose Pope, tall and Etonian, and Trevenen Huxley, brilliant brother of Aldous and Julian. Hilton Young and Alexander Lawrence, a cousin of the Youngs, were of the party; and so was Geoffrey's great friend at Trinity, George Trevelyan.

Returning to Pen-y-Pass at Easter, George and Trafford found among the newcomers David Pye, Raymond Bicknell, and the

---

[1] *Ibid.*, p. 92.
[2] Geoffrey Winthrop Young, 'An Impression of Pen-y-Pass, 1900–1920', in *The Mountains of Snowdonia*, eds. H. R. C. Carr and G. A. Lister (2nd eds., 1948), p. 78.

Australian George Finch. The weather was chilling, and the rocks were white with snow. A note by Geoffrey Young reads: 'G.W.Y. and Mallory took Charles Trevelyan, then President of the Board of Education, up the Far East Cracks on a blasting wet and cold day. It cured his acute lumbago.'

The weather in the Alps that summer was as bad as anyone could remember. Mallory went out with Porter and Pope; Geoffrey Young, with Josef Knubel, joined the party for a week in the Valais. 'One hardly talks of the mountains,' Mallory wrote after a few days; 'they're in disgrace just now.' So far, the party had made two passages of the Furggjoch and 'spent one pleasant day wandering in the mist'.

On August 6th all five went up to the Schönbühl hut, and on the next day they crossed the Col d'Hérens in a mist which made everything around them – snow, mist, and sky – look the same. Most uncharacteristically, Knubel stepped into several crevasses; Young took over the lead and had the same experience. There was nothing the leader could focus his eyes on. They turned, therefore, and found their way to a point under the col; and thence they aimed at the rocks of the Dent Blanche. Young led, trying to compensate for the well-known tendency to bear leftward; Mallory, carrying the compass, shouted directions from the rear.

At length they sighted their landmark and descended to the Alpe Bricolla.

G.M. to Miss Sanders   [*6 and 9 August 1912*]

It *was* dreary. I felt as though I were being extinguished: the cold bareness of it! No sign of warmth or comfort, and the white mist all around, and slushy snow on the ground; finally, an insufficient supply of mostly wet clothes. How could one have been such a fool as to be there? For half an hour we tried to play bridge with a pack of thirty-six cards; the only hope would have been a desperate gamble, and the others were too nice to do that. We had to retire to bed to pass the two hours before we could decently eat dinner. The other sturdy mountaineers tried to read. I don't know how they fared – there were only four books to be had, and the most interesting appeared to be *La Première Prière de Marguerite*, in the most sentimental French style. I relieved my feeling by writing some expletives on the subject of boredom.

Enfin, I woke yesterday morning [8th] at about 5:00 and saw the clouds still encircling the peaks; and then I thought the moment had come for serious action and I must firmly and decisively abandon the Alps. An hour later I saw the top of the Dent Blanche. At 8:00 G.W.Y. went off to join Jones in Chamonix, and we three started for a peak.

Happily accepting the possibility of a night out, which (as George noted) 'always adds a certain cachet', they traversed the Pointe des Genevois and the Dent Perroc; and by hurrying they managed to get down to the Hôtel du Mont Collon at Arolla before dark.

Snow fell in Arolla on August 9th. At 3:30 the next morning, the party set out by lanternlight for the steep north face of the Pigne d'Arolla. By noon, all three had begun to suffer from the effects of hot, dazzling sun-glare on the fresh snow; but they went on to the summit, descended to the Col de la Serpentine, and trudged on up the snow slopes of Mont Blanc de Seilon. At 3:00 p.m., from the top, they started for La Ruinette; but, seeing that time was short, they turned down to the Col de Seilon and descended by the Pas de Chèvres to Arolla. Neither glasses nor grease had protected them adequately against the glare. In the morning George awoke with eyes so painfully swollen that Dr. Wherry, who happened to be at Arolla with A. D. Godley, forbade him to read or write or go out. During the night, anyhow, the weather had turned bad again.

By the 15th the swelling had gone down, and the barometer up. On a traverse of the Douves Blanches, Mallory led Canon Harford, a veteran who had climbed in the Eighties; Pope and Porter escorted Miss Mabel Capper, who had only recently started. On the next day, intending an ascent of the Dent Blanche, Mallory, Pope, and Porter returned to the Alpe Bricolla.

The 17th began auspiciously at 2:00 a.m. – 'a cloudless sky and a night such as must have been the rule on Olympus, calm and undisturbed by any wind.'[1] But what evil conditions might they encounter, after a fortnight of bad weather, on the mountain itself? Laboriously they made their way up loose moraine to an offshoot of the Ferpècle glacier, under the Ferpècle ridge, and by lanternlight threaded among the crevasses to a steep rock wall which rose 600 or 700 feet above them. Just as dawn touched the peaks, they stopped for their first meal. Then Pope led up the wall. 'The lower rocks were very steep,' Mallory wrote, 'but a series of chimneys somewhat upon the left-hand side took us up in the

[1] H. E. L. Porter, 'A New Climb on the Dent Blanche', *Climbers' Club Journal*, Feb. 1913, p. 40.

most delectable fashion without any serious difficulty.'[1] After another breakfast at the top of the wall, they made a line for the southern arête (10:00 a.m.), which they followed to the summit. 'A whiff of tobacco and we were off again,' Porter wrote, 'slightly uneasy as to the state of the gendarmes and the snow below. All went well. The first gendarme took time, but was vanquished by Mallory's skill and a plentiful supply of spare rope.' From the Wandfluh they descended to the Schönbühl hut (4:45 p.m.) and finally arrived at Zermatt (7:30 p.m.). 'Seventeen hours,' as Porter said, 'had compensated us for seventeen days of gloom.'

Meanwhile, Young and Knubel had crossed the Col du Géant from Chamonix and gone up to the Gamba hut with H. O. Jones, his bride of a few weeks, and the guide Julius Truffer. Young and Jones together made a first ascent on the Peuteret ridge – the Pointe Isolée of the Dames Anglaises. Then Young and Knubel went down to Courmayeur. The Joneses and their guide stayed at the Gamba and on August 15th set out with a distinguished young Austrian climber for the Monts Rouges de Peuteret. When Young and Knubel returned to the Gamba that afternoon, hoping to make another climb next day, they learned that Jones, his wife, and the guide had been killed; they found their bodies that evening.

A few days after the funeral at Courmayeur, still heavy with the sense of loss, Young, Mallory, and Pope stood at sunrise under the Tête du Lion, expecting to traverse the Matterhorn and go down to Zermatt. So much snow had fallen, and so much ice began now to clatter down under the sun, that they decided rather to go straight up the rocks of the Tête du Lion and then to cross the Col Tournanche. Young wrote:[2]

Mallory overwhelmed the first little overhang with wave-like ease. His movement in climbing was entirely his own. It contradicted all theory. He would set his foot high against any angle of smooth surface, fold his shoulder to his knee, and flow upward and upright again on an impetuous curve. Whatever may have happened unseen the while between him and the cliff, in the way of holds or mutual adjustments the look, and indeed the result, were always the same – a continuous undulating movement so rapid and so powerful that one felt the rock either must yield, or disintegrate.

At the top they turned westward to the Col Tournanche, with Mallory still in the lead, and then descended to the lower glaciers

---

[1] 'Dent Blanche: Ascent by the W. Face and Traverse', *A.J.*, 26:462–463 (Nov. 1912). [2] *On High Hills* (1927), p. 218

and the dark valley of Zermatt. A week later, they recrossed the Channel. Hugh wrote to thank George for his 'introduction to the Alps'. George lent him an ice-axe to take to the Pyrenees.

George, Trafford, their sister Mary, and several friends spent five enjoyable September days at the Snowdon Ranger, Quellyn. With Ralph Todhunter, one of Young's companions in the great climb on the Mer de Glace face of the Grépon in 1911, George explored Craig yr Cwm Dhu, Craig Cwm Silin, and the Eastern Gully of Clogwyn du'r Arddu. On the way back to Charterhouse, he stayed a couple of days with Duncan Grant at 38 Brunswick Square; they dined in Soho on the 17th with Eddie Marsh and Rupert Brooke.

Three weeks later came word of Hugh Pope's death on the Pic du Midi d'Ossau.

Remembering how Graham Irving had taken his 'recruits' to the Alps, Mallory had started inviting Charterhouse boys to join him – with parental permission – in Wales. One boy had come to the Snowdon Ranger in September 1911; two more in September 1912. In April 1913, after Easter, Robert Mühlberg and Hugh Heber Percy accompanied Mallory and Geoffrey Keynes to Pen-y-Pass. Geoffrey Young had stayed on after the Easter party, with the Cecil Slingsbys and their daughter Eleanor; Todhunter and Conor O'Brien were also there. From Gorphwysfa Mallory led his contingent across the mountain to the Snowdon Ranger where Robert Graves joined them, taking Mühlberg's place. Conditions were blizzardy.

G.M. to Miss Sanders   [*9 May 1913*]

Wales was specially jolly. Three of the best boys effectively prevented any grain of seriousness for the most part of the time; they did not, however, though never more than two were there together, have a stimulating effect upon climbing. The snow-balling of Todhunter was a good incident. Much singing of folksongs made the atmosphere emphatically non-musical.

Robert Graves to G.M.   [*Late April 1913*]

I never remember enjoying myself so much as at Quellyn. It was an experience to me in dozens of ways. I fear Hugh and I went rather too far in our festivity, for which apologies. But you will have the whip-hand of him next quarter, and I will be wonderfully humble and dutiful. The rafters of this house have been continually ringing to the strains of the enthusiastically adapted 'Green grow the rushes, O!' and the mournful history of the venerable and lamented episcopal personage who recollected that it was the Sabbath.[1]

After this, both Hugh and Robert called Mallory 'Uncle George', until they dropped the 'Uncle'.

As the spring came on, George felt very much on top of things. 'My life even now,' he wrote, 'is the most agreeable I know of. When we see the sun again in this green paradise, I shall effervesce into a spirit.' In this happy state of mind he worked with Robert Graves, Raymond Rodakowski, and Cyril Hartmann to bring out a new school magazine called *Green Chartreuse*. 'It was only intended to have one number,' Graves explains; 'new magazines at a public school always sell out the first number and lose heavily on the second.'[2] *Green Chartreuse* appeared on Old Carthusian Day, advertised by a large poster on the cricket pavilion – a vivid green monk with uplifted glass, painted by Duncan Grant. This episode, according to David Pye, created 'some flutter among the decorous upholders of public school proprieties.'[3]

Instead of going to the Alps in 1913, Mallory went camping in Cornwall and cruising off the coast of Ireland. He met Geoffrey Young and Conor O'Brien at the foot of Mount Brandon in County Kerry and sailed with them, in O'Brien's ketch *Kelpie*, along the coast between Valentia and Tralee. On hearing of the cruise, Lytton Strachey professed a secret longing to sail Oriental seas as master of a sloop: 'Can anything be more bitter than to be doomed to a life of literature and hot-water bottles, when one's a Pirate at heart?' Only a humdrum heart could have been unexcited by an Irish adventure with Conor, a man of remarkable gifts. In Wales he would climb the rocks in bare feet, with a pipe in his mouth. One of the versifiers at Pen-y-Pass caught in two lines both his appearance in a crottle-dyed homespun suit and his descent from the kings of Thomond:

[1] Robert Graves writes: ' "Festivity," a technical term at Charterhouse, meant being cheeky to one's seniors; in this case to George, our "Beak". I can't recall how "I'll sing you one, O" and "I'll sing you two, O" were changed by us. The second reference is to one of the "Clerihews" we used to sing to a mournful Gregorian hymn tune:

> Archbishop Odo
> Was just in the middle of "Dodo",
> When he remembered that it was Sunday.
> "Sic transit gloria mundi." '

Dodo, the popular novel by E. F. Benson, A.C.B.'s brother, had appeared in 1893; E. C. Bentley's *Biography for Beginners*, in 1905.
[2] *Good-bye to All That* (1929), p. 81.   [3] *George Leigh Mallory* (1927), p. 67.

Red as a rose the clothes he wore;
His secret name was Conchubor.

As a yachtsman, he was already famous; it was a piece of uncommon good luck to have this chance to sail with him.

On returning from Ireland, George spent a long week end in
Wasdale with Alan Goodfellow, of Charterhouse. They rambled
up the Mosedale beck, they bathed, they climbed. With Harold
Porter and Nigel Madan, they enjoyed a day on Scafell, climbing
up and down Deep Ghyll and Moss Ghyll. By themselves, they
made two new routes still called by Mallory's name: one on the
west side of Low Man, Pillar Rock; the other on the upper part
of the Abbey Buttress, Great Gable. On the day of the Great
Gable climb, George planned no more than a gentle scramble;
but he spotted an interesting line and started to climb. Half-way,
on a small ledge covered with bilberries, the two stopped to
consider their situation: going back would be extremely difficult;
going on would mean risking an unprotected traverse, because
the rope was not long enough to permit a belay. Alan Goodfellow
writes:

It must have been a very anxious moment for George, faced with the
responsibility of an inexperienced schoolboy climber as his only
companion; but he showed no trace of it and quietly suggested that
we should eat all the bilberries before we went on. Then we effected the
traverse unbelayed, with George leading the way and instructing me
exactly where to put my hands and feet. He was quite the finest rock-
climber I have ever seen, with a wonderful sense of balance.

Soon Mallory was deep in Charterhouse routine again. 'How
am I to read *Paradise Lost* with a form of thirty boys?' he wrote on
September 21st. 'I'm perplexed day and night by considerations
of that order.' He felt that most of the boys were deficient in
understanding, and he disliked the 'mechanical atmosphere' of the
school. His publishers reported that sales of the Boswell book had
not reached 'a point affecting his pecuniary interests'. And yet
this winter turned out to be highly enjoyable.

On December 26th Mallory and Porter left Birkenhead, met
Siegfried Herford at Bangor, and drove up to Pen-y-Pass in a
violent storm. On arrival, George felt tired and feared that he
would be a difficult companion; but, as he later exclaimed,
'What a kind and agreeable party it was!' George Trevelyan was
there, and Claude Elliott, then Fellow of Jesus College, Cambridge;

George Mallory

and Geoffrey Young, who had come to Wales from Italy, reported the usual 'musical, controversial, and surprising' evenings at Gorphwysfa.

This was the time when Mallory, Young and Herford made the first Double Girdle Traverse of Lliwedd. The single traverse, across the north face from the Far East Buttress to the Slanting Buttress, had been described by Andrews and Thomson as 'presenting problems so numerous and varied in character that they feed the appetite for novelty with perpetual gratifications'.[1] It was all so gratifying, indeed, that Mallory, Young, and Herford could not bear to come down from the West Peak at lunchtime:

> Why make an end? We dropped down a ridge to a promising level, and then re-crossed the whole face once more, on a higher and even more exacting line, over bastion, wall and chasm. . . . We travelled on the return even faster, and in a rhythm which I never remember attaining again on stiff rock with a rope of three.

Years after, Young could still recall his 'view either way across the Lliwedd precipices storming up the sky under ghostly downfalls of ice, forward and back to the agile figures in white sweaters, swinging, turning, belaying in a counterpoint of precision and force, as the occasional sun-gleam glinted from one or other of the rough fair heads white-rimed with frost from the shadows.'[2]

Mallory enjoyed equally a long ramble in the snow and frost, 'exquisitely beautiful':

G.M. to Edward Evans   *13 January 1914*

On one superb day, the last for me, four of us walked over Crib Goch and Llechog down to Quellyn and back by the Zigzags, starting about 4:00 with the sunset and lit by the young moon over the pass as we came down the snow to Glaslyn – Snowdon and Lliwedd more wonderful than I've ever seen them, with a sort of divine Chinese mysticism.

Quite aware that his experience of the mountains was largely aesthetic, he had begun work on an essay entitled 'The Mountaineer as Artist', addressing himself to these questions: 'To what part of the artistic sense of man does mountaineering belong? To the part that causes him to be moved by music or painting, or to the part that makes him enjoy a game?' For himself Mallory had an answer: he took 'a high line about

[1] *The Climbs on Lliwedd* (1909), p. 88.
[2] *Mountains with a Difference* (1951), pp. 24–25.

88

climbing' and treated his responses to it as analogous to delight in music:

Climbers who, like myself, take the high line have much to explain, and it is high time they set about it. Notoriously they endanger their lives. With what object? If only for some physical pleasure, to enjoy certain movements of the body and to experience the zest of emulation, then it is not worth while. Climbers are only a particularly foolish set of desperadoes; they are on the same plane with hunters, and many degrees less reasonable. The only defence for mountaineering puts it on a higher plane than mere physical sensation. It is asserted that the climber experiences higher emotions; he gets some good for his soul. ... What are these higher emotions to which he refers so elusively? And if they really are so valuable, is there no safer way of reaching them? Do mountaineers consider these questions and answer them again and again from fresh experience, or are they content with some magic certainty born of comparative ignorance long ago?

It would be a wholesome tonic, perhaps, more often to meet an adversary who argued on these lines. In practice I find that few men ever want to discuss mountaineering seriously. I suppose they imagine that a discussion with me would be unprofitable; and I must confess that if anyone does open the question my impulse is to put him off. I can assume a vague disdain for civilisation, and I can make phrases about beautiful surroundings, and puff them out, as one who has a secret and does not care to reveal it because no one would understand – phrases which refer to the divine riot of Nature in her ecstasy of making mountains.

Thus I appeal to the effect of mountain scenery upon my aesthetic sensibility. But, even if I can communicate by words a true feeling, I have explained nothing. ... We do not think that our aesthetic experiences of sunrises and sunsets and clouds and thunder are supremely important facts in mountaineering, but rather that they cannot thus be separated and catalogued and described individually as experiences at all. They are not incidental in mountaineering, but a vital and inseparable part of it; they are not ornamental, but structural; they are not various items causing emotion but parts of an emotional whole; they are the crystal pools perhaps, but they owe their life to a continuous stream.

It is this unity that makes so many attempts to describe aesthetic detail seem futile. Somehow they miss the point and fail to touch us. It is because they are only fragments. If we take one moment and present its emotional quality apart from the whole, it has lost the very essence that gave it a value. If we write about an expedition from the emotional point of view in any part of it, we ought so to write about the whole adventure from beginning to end.

George Mallory

A day well spent in the Alps is like some great symphony. Andante, andantissimo sometimes, is the first movement – the grim, sickening plod up the moraine. But how forgotten when the blue light of dawn flickers over the hard, clean snow! The new *motif* is ushered in, as it were, very gently on the lesser wind instruments, hautboys and flutes, remote but melodious and infinitely hopeful, caught by the violins in the growing light, and torn out by all the bows with quivering chords as the summits, one by one, are enmeshed in the gold web of day, till at last the whole band, in triumphant accord, has seized the air and romps in magnificent frolic, because there you are at last marching, all a-tingle with warm blood, under the sun. And so throughout the day successive moods induce the symphonic whole – allegro while you break the back of an expedition and the issue is still in doubt; scherzo, perhaps, as you leap up the final rocks of the arête or cut steps in a last short slope, with the ice-chips dancing and swimming and bubbling and bounding with magic gaiety over the crisp surface in their mad glissade; and then, for the descent, sometimes again andante, because, while the summit was still to win, you forgot that the business of descending may be serious and long; but in the end scherzo once more – with the brakes on for sunset.

Expeditions in the Alps are all different, no less than symphonies are different, and each is a fresh experience. . . . But every mountain adventure is emotionally complete. The spirit goes on a journey just as does the body, and this journey has a beginning and an end, and is concerned with all that happens between these extremities. . . . The glory of sunrise in the Alps is not independent of what has passed and what's to come; without the day that is dying and the night that is to come the reverie of sunset would be less suggestive, and the deep valley-lights would lose their promise of repose. Still more, the ecstasy of the summit is conditioned by the events of getting up and the prospects of getting down. . . .

It seemed perfectly natural to compare a day in the Alps with a symphony. For mountaineers of my sort mountaineering is rightfully so comparable; but no sportsman could or would make the same claim for cricket or hunting, or whatever his particular sport might be. He recognises the existence of the sublime in great Art, and knows, even if he cannot feel, that its manner of stirring the heart is altogether different and vaster. But mountaineers do not admit this difference in the emotional plane of mountaineering and Art. They claim that something sublime is the essence of mountaineering. They can compare the call of the hills to the melody of wonderful music, and the comparison is not ridiculous.

This essay appeared in March 1914, in a remarkable number of the *Climbers' Club Journal* edited by Trevenen Huxley. Among the other contributors were W. P. Ker, the editor's brother Aldous, Katherine Cox, and Mary O'Malley – the Cottie Sanders of earlier years, married in 1913 to Owen O'Malley, of the Foreign Office. George Mallory's essay seems to have stirred the liveliest interest. The next *Climbers' Club Bulletin* included a rhymed critique: the Mountaineer as Artist had put two Scherzos in his Alpine symphony!

> A climb, wherein perhaps may lie its worth,
> Resembles nothing else at all on earth.
> The Mountaineer, thrice Artist though he be,
> Should not compare it to a Symphony.

Mallory could afford to smile, for the essay had elicited another comment of quite different sort:

Geoffrey Winthrop Young to G.M.   *30 March 1914*

I liked your paper, specially the end . . . but it will read well all through. You can't think what it is to have someone else active on *this* side of the mountains, too! I hate being treated as 'old' or an authority – and you alone run out and hit and give one a rowing time in talk.

After Christmas in Wales, G.W.Y. had returned to a house in the hills near Fiesole, 'one of the loveliest places in the world'. He shared the house with Will Arnold-Forster, 'the best company and one of the quickest and most sympathetic temperaments conceivable'. On the terrace at Monte Fiano, in the sun, while Will painted and talked, Geoffrey worked on a book to be called *Mountain Craft* and on the poems for a volume entitled *Freedom*. Occasionally they would go down to Florence and look at pictures or talk with friends. 'Altogether, the world is smiling,' Geoffrey wrote, 'and I am getting as brown as an old bear and feeling like a god'. George must come: Monte Fiano, the new poems, and 'Will the genius' would be exactly right for him.

Eddie Marsh, now deep in his venture as editor of *Georgian Poetry*, came down to Charterhouse for a week end and met Graves for the first time. Geoffrey Keynes, in London, was combining surgery at St. Bartholomew's with work on his bibliographies of John Donne, Sir Thomas Browne, and William Blake. It was George's good fortune to have interesting friends who continued to make themselves interested in whatever he was doing.

He took great pleasure at this time in giving a series of lectures at Charterhouse on Italian painting. By this enterprise he hoped to encourage the response to beauty; he felt content when he seemed to have opened the eyes of fifteen or twenty boys in the top parts of the school. His opening remarks suggest how much art meant to him:

Art matters supremely because it is entirely disinterested; and, as I suppose we are all agreed, it is only when we are disinterested that we have got beyond circumstances. At all other times, however our vanity may attempt to conceal the fact, circumstances have the best of us. Furthermore, Art is to be enjoyed. The response to beauty is in itself a pleasure, and no little part of our happiness. . . .

After warning the boys that they must not expect all art to imitate reality, Mallory went on to talk about Botticelli. Nothing in his jottings for later lectures on Raphael and Michelangelo has in it so much of enjoyment. Flora in the *Primavera* is 'triumphant with fresh vitality'; she shows 'a sparkle of mind as well as a joy of lithe vigorous limbs'. She makes one think of the girl in *Love in the Valley*: 'Certainly she's "wayward as the swallow" 'and probably as heartless'; but the heartlessness one can explain as Meredith did:

Deals she an unkindness, 'tis but her rapid measure,
Even as in a dance.

In speaking of the *Birth of Venus*, Mallory essayed a Pateresque flight, stimulated by a re-reading of *The Renaissance*, which Benson had given him in 1907, and by his own love for sunlit places and for grace in action:

And then Venus herself: a stray lock floats gently in the breeze, and no more than in so much is she perturbed by life. A strange thrill (you see it in the right hand) and a gleam of wonder: that is all of the deep disturbances of life – less than the faintest shadow on the calm surface of a sunlit pool. Surely she will forget even this light care when she steps ashore with the perfection of graceful balance.

During the early months of 1914, George felt more happiness than he could at first explain. In retrospect, the reasons for it are clear: the lectures, the climbs, the good friends, and – most important of all – the Turner family. Hugh Thackeray Turner and his three daughters lived at Westbrook, on a hill west of Godalming, across the Wey valley from Charterhouse. George met the Turner girls when he played Cyril in a garden performance of *The Princess*; the Turners took part as Ida's maidens. Before long, there arrived at Westbrook an invitation to a Shakespeare reading at Charterhouse; and then George began to appear at Westbrook,

to go walking from there or to play billiards with Mr. Turner.
Mr. Turner practised architecture, in partnership with Eustace
Balfour; he had built Westbrook himself in 1898–1900. Both the
house and the garden suggested the planner's admiration for
William Morris. Indeed, he had worked closely with Morris and
succeeded him in 1883 as Secretary of the Society for the Protec-
tion of Ancient Buildings. His brother Laurence Turner was, like
Morris, a designer-craftsman; another brother, Hawes, was
Keeper of the National Gallery. Their father, for many years vicar
of Wroughton in Wiltshire, was a grandson of the John Turner
who had kept a private school at Chiswick and there instructed
his wife's young grandnephew, William Makepeace Thackeray.
Thackeray Turner was born in the year when the first parts of
The Newcomes appeared, 1853.

As a young architect, living in Gray's Inn with his brothers,
Thackeray Turner had met the Powell family, of Piccard's Rough,
Guildford. Thomas Wilde Powell, a stockbroker of considerable
means, had nine children. The eldest, Christiana, married Wilmot
Herringham, a young physician at St. Bartholomew's, and later
translated Cennino Cennini's *Trattato della Pittura*. Another
daughter, Rosamond, married a son of Sir Alfred Wills, Justice of
the Queen's Bench and a renowned pioneer in the Alps, often
counted as one of the founders of mountaineering as a sport.

The second Powell daughter, Mary Elizabeth, despite her
father's misgivings over the young architect's worldly prospects,
became Mrs. Turner. She bore three daughters, Marjorie, Ruth,
and Mildred, who in due course attended Prior's Field, the girls'
school recently founded by Mrs. Leonard Huxley. Mrs. Turner
was a gifted artist in embroidery; she was also, according to a
friend at Prior's Field, 'one of the finest and noblest women I have
ever known, as well as the most unselfish'. She died in 1907, when
her daughters were seventeen, fifteen, and fourteen.

The Turners were going to Venice in March 1914; they invited
George Mallory to join them, and Marjorie and Mildred wrote
from Italy to confirm plans. The Trevelyans expected to stay with
Will Arnold-Forster at Monte Fiano just before Easter; George
Trevelyan hoped that George Mallory would come for a week's
walk in the Apennines. – Italy in the spring, with such companions!

G.M. to F. F. Urquhart   [*March 1914*]
I have been drinking streams of delight this term – and yet I can't

say why. (Here follows a considerable period of reflection, just because the matter is so entirely puzzling.) Why in the name of all true usherdom, beakism, pedagoguery, pedantry, and routine discipline? I can't believe that it depends much upon activities, and I put my money on states of mind. . . .

George Mallory and the Turners met at Verona on April 3rd; they spent the ensuing week in Venice, and George quite lost his heart to Ruth. One day they went up to Asolo, where Pippa sang:

> Overhead the tree-tops meet,
> Flowers and grass spring 'neath one's feet. . . .

Then the Turners returned to England, and George took the train to Florence and made his way to Monte Fiano. He felt at once that he could talk with Will; they went up on a hillside and sat in lavender, and George told of 'finding' Ruth in Venice. On the 11th he wrote to his sister Avie: 'I had a glorious time in Venice and left it with much regret. It *is* a wonderful place – and then my companions were perfect.' On the 12th, Easter Day, he composed a sonnet 'To Ruth'. On the 13th, with George Trevelyan and Stephen Tallents, a colleague of Beveridge at the Board of Trade, he set out on foot for Arezzo and Perugia. Ruth wrote to him from Westbrook: 'How wonderful it was that day among the flowers at Asolo! I hope you are having a lovely time among the mountains, little towns, and flowers.'

It was no wonder that George fell in love with her. Ruth was beautiful – the poor word *pretty*, George insisted, had nothing to do with her. *Botticellian* would be more apt. And when he called her 'true', he meant much more than that she told the truth: she saw with great clarity the things that mattered, and she spoke with sometimes startling honesty; she was by nature true in every thought and act. Her sense of humour worked perhaps a little slowly, and she had never learned to spell; but these faults (so to call them, quite without conviction in her case) simply had to be accepted. George loved everything about her. On May Day 1914, at Westbrook, they became engaged.

G.M. to his mother   *1 May 1914*

I'm engaged to be married. What bliss! And what a revolution! *Ruth Turner* – she lives just over the river from here in a lovely house and with lovely people, and she's as good as gold, and brave and true and sweet. What more can I say! I fixed it up this morning. It was with Ruth and her family that I was staying in Venice, and it was there my own mind became resolved.

Geoffrey Young came down from London to meet her – and found that his first cautiously worded congratulatory message to George had been altogether inadequate:

Geoffrey Winthrop Young to G.M.   *5 May 1914*
I have never met anyone who brought such an atmosphere of reality, such a certainty of a true nature. . . . It is *big*, just *big*, that nature. And I felt it enough to feel a sort of breath of what you know to be there; and so, as a side joy, I know just a bit what you must be feeling. I could *shout*.

Ruth's Aunt Rosamond wrote to a friend who happened to know George well:

Mrs. Wills to Mrs. O'Malley   [*May 1914*]
My niece, Ruth Turner, is engaged to be married. She is one of the 'twice-born': a soul of the most crystal wisdom, simplicity, and goodness – pure gold all through. She is going to marry a young Charterhouse master, George Mallory – I hope he is good enough for her, but it is hardly possible.

Mrs. O'Malley replied that George was one of the rarest spirits of his generation, and that it sounded, on the whole, as if *she* might be nearly good enough for *him*.

Mr. Turner would not be rushed into giving his final consent to the marriage. Like his father-in-law before him, he wondered about money. How would a young schoolmaster manage? Did he expect to rely on his wife's income? The very idea bewildered the impecunious and romantic George: 'Oh, I couldn't possibly marry a girl if she had her own income!' The girl's father, though quite appeased, responded rather gruffly: 'You couldn't possibly marry her if she *hadn't*.'

It would be just as well, Mr. Turner thought, for George and Ruth to exist apart for a while, and he took his daughters with him for three weeks near Gartan Lough in Donegal, where he liked to fish. George and Ruth wrote almost every day; each felt stricken if the other missed a day.

George to Ruth   *14 May 1914*
My sweet Ruth, I've done very little pining today, I freely confess; it's sadly improper of me, but you see it's impossible to imagine that it ever should be in any way painful for you to come into my mind; and, when you do, I'm just too infinitely content to begin cursing that you aren't there. . . .
A long morning in school, with much *Lear* and some history and

some Carlyle. What a bore Carlyle can be! Do you know *Heroes and Hero-Worship*? It would be such a good book if it were compressed into a quarter its length; I felt this morning that I knew exactly what he was going to say at every moment. . . . I hope this isn't very tiresome; it's very odd for me to be writing it. I never should think of talking about such things to any of my friends. You must rebel at once if I make a target of you.

Ruth to George   *14–15 May 1914*

My dearest, we have got here. It is really beautiful. I have been looking for some time at the hill I want to go up. I can't call it a mountain while I am reading *Scrambles amongst the Alps*. It isn't very far off as the crow flies, but I shall have to go a long way round a lake that lies along the foot of it. There is another more distant one that looks better still, but I suppose they always look more thrilling when they are far off. . . . I do wish you were here and we could go off and explore the very wildest parts. We might go on from place to place and stay a night or two away – but we will do that sort of thing some time.

George to Ruth   *17 May 1914*

If only I could walk those hills with you! But, as you say, we shall; we shall before so very long. It *is* good that you love the hills, and I'm glad you're interested by Whymper's *Scrambles*. The more I think of it, the more convinced I become that we ought to have a proper climbing season this year in the Alps. . . .

My sister Mary comes on Tuesday, and her man, too. He is an instructor at Woolwich, and therefore both a schoolmaster and a soldier. For which shall I dislike him most? Well, anyway, he used to be very nice. . . . I'm rather behindhand with my work and rather worried over the Shakespeare paper, most of which is now corrected. They don't appreciate Cordelia, blighted little asses!

George to Ruth   *16 May 1914*

Tennis at the Headmaster's – the Friday levee, where a dozen or so pedagogues contend. Mrs. Fletcher asked questions about our arrangements for the future – too many questions, I thought, but I suppose women can't help being like that, however nice they are – e.g., what colours our rooms were to be, black or purple or anything of that sort? A reference, I suppose, to my Posty tastes, and quite typical of the world's way of classifying such things. Mrs. Fletcher, like almost everybody, has divided them into proper and outré; and mine are outré, and therefore probably I like black rooms. . . .

Let's be really high-toned and have an emerald room and a sapphire room and an amethyst room! Or really Romantic and have a room like Monte Cristo's cave and a room like the bottom of the deep green sea, with mermaids sitting on the mantelpiece, an octopus in the corner, and seats of sponge and coral! Or shall I take orders, and we'll go in for mid-Victorian culture and get me made a headmaster in no time and then a bishop? If life is meant for fun, then a bishop I would be – if only for a week or two.

Ruth to George   *18 May 1914*

I think that an Alpine room would be more suitable for you than a deep sea one – a glacier, a mountain. And the chairs could simply be boulders, which would be cheap. Then we will ask Mrs. Fletcher to dinner. . . . I read yesterday afternoon of the ascent of the Pointe des Ecrins. It must have been awful. Well, even the writer thought it too bad, so I suppose people don't often do things like that.

George to Ruth   *19 May 1914*

My sister and her man are in the room, talking. It's been very agreeable seeing Mary so happy, and today has been rather a success because *he* played [for I Zingari] against the School and made a century. Wouldn't you like me to be a hero like that? I like him very much, and I think you will; we shall have to get them to stay with us.

Ruth to George   *22 May 1914*

Marjorie and Mildred, and to a certain extent me, have been discussing the wedding today; and it seems generally decided that your clothes are much more difficult than mine. Mildred seems to think that white tennis flannels and scarlet sash would look the best; I still rather incline to brown corduroys. It is a shame to tease you about it; I won't say a word more today.

George to Ruth   *23 May 1914*

I've just finished [Arthur Clutton Brock's] *William Morris*. I am delighted and much moved. We owe that great man a vast amount. . . . Of course I always connect you and yours with W.M. Incidentally, Brock's book contains a very nice reference to your father's work for Anti-Scrape. . . .

I am expecting a friend to arrive shortly to stay the night – one Lytton Strachey. He is very, very queer – not to me, of course, because I know him as a friend, but to the world. He must be very irritating to many people. My profound respect for his intellect, and for a sort of passion with which he holds the doctrine of freedom, besides much love for him as a man of intense feelings and fine imagination, make me put up with much in him that I could hardly tolerate in any other.

George to Ruth   *24 May 1914*

I wasn't up till 9:00. Some talk with Lytton afterwards, and reading of poetry, particularly W.M.'s 'The Message of the March Wind', which I must show you if you don't know it – about young love in the country and thoughts of poor people in towns. . . .

Lunch (just over) and breakfast have been rather trying. Lytton doesn't like boys; and I imagine he is very shy, because he talks in a falsetto voice very often. At all events, he says almost nothing in this sort of company and yet looks very striking – a man you can't ignore.

Ruth to George   *28 May 1914*

I was reading some of Keats's letters yesterday. I particularly loved one of his endings: 'In the name of Shakespeare, Raphael, and all our saints.' I wouldn't put Raphael in myself, but perhaps Botticelli. Just now you would put William Morris, wouldn't you? For us, for me, he has done an infinite amount. Just think: I have lived my whole life surrounded by his designs and actively taking keen interest in them. I can never remember a time when patterns did not mean a good deal to me. . . .

We have just had lunch, and Father and Uncle Hawes and Captain Morgan are all smoking cigars. I suppose they will go on fishing presently. . . .

George to Ruth   *30 May 1914*

Perhaps that old saying that sounds so trivial contains some truth. At least, if I don't actually love you more, dear Ruth, I know better how much I love you, how much I want you to love and to be loved by and to live with. . . . It is easy to think oneself into a romantic and heroic frame of mind, and sometimes I distrust the reality of all I feel. But no! It *is* real. You are you, the only possible you that can matter to me; and the only illusion was that life could be good without you. . . .

Tomorrow and the day after tomorrow – and then! It's a short time before Wednesday. Good night, Beloved.

> Your loving
> George

Plans were made for a wedding in July. Mary was to be married on the 22nd to Ralph Brooke, of the Royal Artillery; George and Ruth would be married at Godalming on the 29th. For the honeymoon George wanted to take his bride to the Alps. David Pye would be in Savoy during July and might join them; and perhaps they could take on Knubel, if he happened to be at liberty. George discussed the idea with Ruth, with Dr. Wills, with Mrs. Reade, with Geoffrey Young.

Geoffrey Winthrop Young to G.M.   *[June 1914?]*

Now look here: if you mean by 'climbing' a respectable journey in a jolly district with decent passes and small excursions when found attractive – yes. But if you mean real climbing, in a big district, or long days for her – then absolutely *no*. You simply must put it out of your mind, for this year. . . .

Remember – I must recall it – I saw H.O., one of the coolest and most balanced of minds, distinctly overdoing it.[1] His wife was physically and emotionally overdone those days, *not* by big climbs. He had to take the more care for her; both of them were steeped in the double romance of themselves and the mountains. And the accident came of his over-care for her, his distraction from the single eye of the mountaineer, that he *must* have, and that he *cannot* retain if he is throwing himself into someone else's being, outlook, and performance.

Now – forgive my going on, but I feel this sincerely – your weakness, if any, is that you *do* let yourself get carried away on occasions in the mountains. . . . I think that it is your failing, the consequence of your combination of extraordinary physical brilliance in climbing and of power of mental absorption in it, that you do not, or at least have not, held back from allowing yourself to sweep weaker brethren, carried away by their belief in you, to take risks or exertions that they were not fit for, and which, had the crisis come, neither you nor any man in climbing could have the margin to cover for both. . . .

All I ask is, think it over. There is always time to begin climbing. The whole weight of stupid old tradition is against you in making anything but a quiet time of these weeks. . . . This is all to my loss, and horrid hard to say; but, if I've got anywhere, it is to seeing that human relations are more precious than mountains.

The wedding took place on July 29th. George's father performed the ceremony, and Geoffrey Young was best man. The bride and groom looked, as a complete stranger later said of them, 'too good to be true'. An Alpine honeymoon was out of the question now, for hostilities had broken out on the Continent. Instead, George and Ruth went first to North Devon and then camped along the coast of Sussex –

> Iuppiter illa piae secrevit litora genti,
> Ut inquinavit aere tempus aureum. . . .

No peace, even there. In the crazy first weeks of the war, the sight of campers-out aroused suspicion; and George and Ruth, of all people, were held briefly as German spies.

[1] See p. 84, above.

CHAPTER 5

The War, 1914–1918

Before the Charterhouse term began, George and Ruth went up to the Lakes and stayed six nights at Row Head. George took Ruth on her first rock climbs, with Harold Porter as third on the rope. It was a strenuous novitiate, including the Napes Needle and Kern Knotts Chimney, the New West Climb on Pillar Rock, and the West Wall Traverse and Jones's Pinnacle on Scafell. Porter noted with admiration that Ruth showed great confidence, complete freedom from any trace of beginner's nerves, and remarkable enthusiasm. The Friday was so threatening that Porter expected to take the day off, but the Mallorys would not hear of such a thing; and they all went up Esk Hause in a howling gale, danced a Morris dance to warm themselves after a very cold lunch, plunged down Long Strath to Seatoller for tea, and then made their way back by Sty Head. The weather continued wet; and on Monday, when the Mallorys left for Godalming, the clouds hung lower than ever.

For a young couple living in a rented house in war-time, there could be no normal settling-down to married life. Ruth went to work in the hospital at Godalming. George, with a growing concern for the moral lessons in history, lectured at Charterhouse on the causes of the war; he enjoyed hearing the boys cheer when he finished, but felt profoundly discontented. 'It becomes increasingly impossible to remain a comfortable schoolmaster,' he wrote to Geoffrey Young in November 1914. 'I read this morning the dismal tale of wet and cold, which made my fireside an intolerable reproach.' Sometimes he would go down to the hospital and talk with the Tommies.

In the mountains there was still some sort of peace. The Mallorys spent a December fortnight at Pen-y-Gwryd with David Pye – 'a time of gales and snowstorms', David remembered, 'enough to daunt any but the stoutest-hearted novice.' One day, after climbing the Parson's Nose, George, Ruth, and David set out over Crib y Ddysgl toward the summit of Snowdon:[1]

On the ridge the gale was of hurricane strength, screaming and whirling the snow in all directions so that not a word was audible even when shouted in the ear. On our left was the snow slope down to Llyn Llydaw, and once over on that side there would be comparative shelter from the gale. But the slope in the driving snow and mist looked precipitously steep and terrifying. We were roped, Mallory in front, then his wife, myself last. When the wind at length became so fierce as to make breathing difficult and steady walking impossible Mallory decided that we must get down on to the sheltered side of the ridge.

Explanations were impossible. I saw him point down the horribly steep looking slope and urge her in pantomime to take the plunge. From this, lacking our knowledge that it was in fact perfectly safe, she very naturally recoiled. And then there was enacted the most perfectly staged scene of mountaineering melodrama. Taking his wife by the shoulders, Mallory simply pushed her forcibly over the edge! I meanwhile, guessing what he was up to, stood down on the windward side to hold her rope. Next he jumped over also and soon we were all gasping in comparative peace while the wind still roared overhead.

New obstacles to settling-down arose with the New Year. Since the rented house had to be vacated in December and the new house, the Holt, would not be ready before March, the young couple stayed at Westbrook. Living there, two miles by bicycle from Charterhouse, on another hill across the river Wey, George saw distressingly little of the boys. 'Nor was I completely happy to be living with my wife's people,' he wrote to Benson. 'They are very good people, but one doesn't want to live that way when one is married.' When at last the Holt was ready, it became clear that Ruth, who was expecting her first child in September, should have a thorough rest, away from the smell of fresh paint. She went to a nursing home and then back to Westbrook for several weeks, while George coped as best he could with all the questions brought to him by the builder. He rather enjoyed talking with the builder's men, but felt bitterly disappointed that Ruth was not with him. As a companion, he had David Pye, who planned to fill a teaching post at Winchester, being barred by his then state of health from more active service.

George's own inquiries about joining up met the firm resistance of the headmaster. As chairman of a committee of the Headmasters' Conference, Fletcher had asked the Government for a

[1] Pye, *George Leigh Mallory* (1927), p. 75.

George Mallory

policy on the release of schoolmasters; and Kitchener, replying from the War Office on December 9th, had encouraged headmasters to use their own judgment in deciding 'who can be spared without impairing the work of these schools and the training of the O.T.C.'.[1] George thus missed a chance to work with Will Arnold-Forster at the Admiralty:

G.M. to his sister Avie   *22 March 1915*

I did feel sick the other day. I was offered a commission by the Admiralty to help with the contraband business, under a friend – a most thrilling job, involving the commerce of all the world. Of course it wouldn't have been risking one's life, but it would have been wearing the King's uniform. I have an almost childish feeling for the virtue of that. However, there was no serious question of my being allowed to go. . . .

As if to assure himself that the schoolmaster's role in wartime really had importance, Mallory composed a pamphlet entitled *War Work for Boys and Girls.* The ideals he held in mind were international understanding and the 'good life', for nations as well as for individuals of all classes; and these ideals, he thought, could not possibly be attained without an education which fostered both self-discipline and growth of the spirit. War not only set the nations at odds and literally destroyed good lives; it threatened also, by stirring emotions and evoking floods of propaganda, to overwhelm clear thought. To boys and girls who wondered how they might assist the war effort, Mallory addressed the exhortation: 'Besides trying harder to live well and strenuously in your part of life, which is the first duty for all of us, *you can think*':

We must think with all our minds; think hard and clean and straight; think with labour and with pain – all the labour of discovering the truth, and the pain of knowing it; think with imagination and sympathetically; think passionately and, not less, think calmly, without prejudice and critically – think and, when we think, devote ourselves to learning what is right for England.

When Ruth, quite well, returned to the Holt, and friends came to see them, and the house began to look thoroughly their own ('a blend of Morris and Omega', Geoffrey Keynes called it[2]),

---

[1] Frank Fletcher, *After Many Days* (1937), p. 196.
[2] In 1913 Roger Fry had founded the Omega Workshops, in Fitzroy Square, to produce well-designed articles of daily use.

George felt an excess of happiness. Instead of persuading him to
stay at home, it made him think of friends in uniform:

G.M. to A. C. Benson   [25 *April* 1915][1]
    To 'settle down', that is what one wants; it sounds dull; in reality,
it's a sort of deliberate adventure. It's not that one wants to be a fixture
in one of two easy chairs or perpetually to rub noses over the hearth,
but rather to turn freely and curiously about with the chosen companion
in chosen spheres until a new way of life is evolved. . . .
    It is true, I'm afraid, that I've been too lucky; there's something
indecent, when so many friends have been enduring so many horrors,
in just going on at one's job, quite happy and prosperous. I hear this
morning that Rupert Brooke is dead of blood poisoning. I expect my
friends to be killed in action, but not that way. It seems so wanton, and
somehow it's a blow under the belt. He was a lovable person, and besides
he had gifts. I never much believed that he had it in him to be a great
poet, but after all he might have become one.

G.M. to Geoffrey Winthrop Young   31 *May* 1915
    This is quite a charming little place. I spent most of yesterday sitting
in our loggia, a place divinely sheltered from this keen north wind, just
caught in the sun's warm comfort. It has a tiled floor and a low brick
wall to lean your elbow on and support the posts that take the roof.
The centre of our life, as you may imagine: the drawing room and
dining room both give onto it.
    Below the house we have a strip of copse. The domain goes down
far enough to provoke a question as to where it ends; it has a number of
winding paths and certain flower beds carved out of the jungle, though
the bottom is still practically unreclaimed copse; the proper wild
spring flowers have been blooming all about – primroses, daffodils,
celandines, bluebells, anemones. It is a steep warm bank and very green.
Above it, a low terrace wall with breadth of three tiles to sit on,
guarding our little lawn and a small formal garden you go up steps to.
And a glorious view of the Wey valley from everywhere.
    Add that Ruth, after two miserable months, has been living here just
expanding her absolute plumbwellness . . . and you can imagine what
life ought to be like. But I expect my turn will come in August, if the
bloodshed continues to be as heavy (I quote from *The Times*) as this.
I'm putting out feelers for the Royal Flying Corps. . . .

    Will Arnold-Forster and Eddie Marsh came down to Godalming
that week end; and Marsh encouraged Mallory, though over age,

[1] Pye, *George Leigh Mallory* (1927), pp. 81–82 – undated there. Brooke died on 23
April 1915; Edward Marsh wrote to Mallory on the 24th. On the 26th, in a letter to
Mallory, Benson referred to the letter here quoted.

to try for the Royal Naval Air Service. So many friends were already seeing action and taking on their share of the danger. Geoffrey Young had been through the battles of Ypres and was soon to join George Trevelyan in the First British Ambulance Unit for Italy; Hilton Young was about to go with a Naval Mission to Serbia. Hugh Wilson was serving with the Worcestershire Regiment, and Geoffrey Keynes with an R.A.M.C. ambulance train. Porter planned to leave Rugby at the end of the term. The boys were going, too. Trafford had been in the trenches since March. Robert Graves had joined the Royal Welch Fusiliers, and Rodakowski the Irish Guards; Alan Goodfellow would soon be at Hendon, training for the R.F.C. But Mallory again encountered opposition:

Frank Fletcher to G.M.   *7 June 1915*

I was told the other day that you were 'going to take a commission in the Flying Corps'. I certainly never gave my consent to this; I only agreed that there would be no harm in your making enquiries, so that in case the War Office asked us for more officers you might be ready among others. Till they do, in view of Kitchener's answer, I cannot consent to your going.

Ruth perceived George's restlessness and, being unable now to take an active holiday herself, packed him off to Wales and then to Yorkshire for three weeks. Pen-y-Pass was far from normal – the military had tried to bar the way to Lliwedd! But on the first evening George sat with a mug of beer by the fire, played a game of picquet with Hugh Heber Percy, and read a chapter of *The Ambassadors* in bed; and on the following day he climbed the South Buttress of Tryfan with Hugh and a congenial stranger, rescued a small lamb, and carried it down to safety in his rucksack. After the arrival of the O'Malleys, Ursula Nettleship, and Bertie Graham, the days of not too strenuous walking and climbing ended pleasantly with singing.

Yorkshire, too, despite reminders of the war, was highly enjoyable. George met his father at Ripon; then from Pateley Bridge in Nidderdale, where the only available accommodations were compartments of a railway carriage drawn up in the hydro garden, father and son prowled the dales on bicycles and looked at the old abbeys. Without really communicating much, save about the family, George's father managed by saying outrageous things to be an amusing companion. Trafford had announced his intention to be married to Doris Sawyer while he was home on leave. Ruth wrote of Mildred's engagement to Major Robert Morgan. As an already married man, soon to be a father, George naturally was thinking of Ruth at the Holt.

Their first child, Frances Clare, was born on September 19th. For about three months George stayed at home, working out a new, more flexible programme for the teaching of history at Charterhouse and finding intellectual refreshment in conversation with the Brocks, who lived near by. He admired Arthur Clutton Brock's far-ranging thoughtfulness, which seemed even more stimulating in his talk than in his essays; and he discerned in Mrs. Brock something of that transcendental sanity which he admired and loved in Ruth.

But how could he feel settled when friends were dying? Jack Sanders had fallen in April, in the first German gas attack; Harry Garrett had been shot through the head in August, fighting the Turks; Hugh Wilson had been killed at Hébuterne in September, when he stood up and told a German patrol to surrender. 'And how many more will there be?' George wondered. 'My Charterhouse friends don't and won't leave such big gaps; but the loss of them is more tragic in a way, like cutting off buds.' In December, with the help and advice of Ralph Brooke, then an instructor at Woolwich, George made inquiries about a commission in the Royal Garrison Artillery. Miraculously, Fletcher happened to hear of a man who could take George's work in history at Charterhouse; and the War Office forwarded Second Lieutenant Mallory's commission.

G.M. to his sister Avie   *13 December 1915*
Whether I should have taken French leave I can't really say. I was as keen as possible to become a soldier, and now I am one I feel really happy. R. is perfectly happy, too, and wants to make her part of the sacrifice, which indeed is far the largest. The first rub is making itself felt already: we are trying to let our house.

After Christmas, between visits to his parents at Birkenhead and to the Longridges at Mobberley, George had a last fling in Wales with Herbert Reade and Conor O'Brien. The weather was wet and cold, bad enough to make George wear two shirts; but the climbs on Lliwedd and Clogwyn y Ddysgl were glorious.

George to Ruth   *1 January 1916*
We made a new climb on the West Peak of Lliwedd yesterday. My

lead: you may imagine if I enjoyed it! There were some very good bits, especially one near the bottom . . . which proved too big a step for H.V.R., who had to take a handhold on the rope (climbing has just enough of competition about it for the leader to enjoy such moments), and also one near the top, where we were confronted by an overhanging wall. Standing away from it was a spillikin of ten feet having an extraordinarily sharp edge. To kneel was too painful, and there was nothing at a higher level to pull on, so that to attain a standing position was really difficult; and then came a very stiff struggle to get up the wall – altogether quite exciting.

In January George began a special course at Weymouth for subalterns who might prove eligible for further training at Lydd in the Siege Artillery (Heavy Howitzers). As a friend of Ralph Brooke's explained in a letter from Weymouth, the carefully selected group was expected to include two *Punch* artists, editors of the *Illustrated London News* and the *Sporting and Dramatic*, and a master from Repton – 'the idea being that genius should be combined with gentility'. Ruth came down and stayed at Abbotsbury while George was in training at Weymouth, and at New Romney while he was at Lydd.

Just before going to France, George wrote: 'I can't pretend to be bursting with joy at this moment; the personal tie is too great. But I believe I'm completely happy in the insidest part of me and the thinking part.' He crossed to Le Havre on the night of May 4th; and for nearly a week at No. 1 Base Depot, B.E.F., he underwent the final preparations for active service – listening to a colonel hold forth on 'The Soldier's Character', learning to put on a gas mask (rather unpleasant), and shooting his new revolver, with which he thought he might hit a German twenty yards off, if the German gave him plenty of time to aim. One fine afternoon he walked alone through the countryside to Montvilliers, where he stopped to admire the church and to count the names on a list of dead from the town. For Ruth's sake, he felt somewhat depressed by the thought that he might be assigned to trench mortars.

From Rouen, where he had time to visit the church of St. Maclou, he rode a very slow troop train to Armentières.

George to Ruth   [*Ca. 12 May 1916*]

To feel that one is 'in for it' at last! Things get stirred up and raked over. The irreconcilable wrongness (in a general sense) of war has come very strongly upon me. When I have looked upon the good

green and blossom of spring in this beautiful country and seen beautiful buildings, war has seemed more than ever inconceivable and
monstrous. . . .

And then, my dear, I have actually turned over and weighed (I
suppose this happens to everyone) my own personal courage. Curious
how I have found myself going back for reassurance to old football
days at Winchester! I have found myself repeating words from one of
the little red volumes of Artillery Training – 'such a complete absence
of self-interest that he will do his duty in the hour of danger *coolly and
accurately*'.

On reporting to headquarters, Mallory learned that he had been
assigned to the 40th Siege Battery, operating north of Armentières,
in the direction of Ploegsteert. The officers were quartered in a
town street which they called 'Red Slum'. Captain Lithgow,
Lieutenant Glen, and Lieutenant Bell had been there since
February; they seemed a very decent lot. Bell and Mallory had
charge of No. 4 gun detachment and shared a cottage.

George to Ruth   *14 May 1916*

[Bell] is very studious this evening, sitting up at the table (I in my
camp armchair) with my French dictionary and scratching his head
over the famous passage in Pascal's *Pensées*: 'L'homme n'est qu'un
roseau.' The humour of it to me is that the light dawns so gradually,
and in the end he'll appreciate it so well. As I see nothing, practically
speaking, of anyone else, it's very lucky I like this man – and that do I.

Curious that I've met now three men of this métier – men who've
started life in the Gunners as boys of fourteen and fifteen and taken
commissions during the war or a little earlier – and find them wonderfully alike in having the most uncommon qualities: all quiet, observing
men with a marked refinement of feeling, and living in harmony
with life in some queer rare way quite their own; all three so competent
(so far as I can judge) and yet apparently so easy-going. Bell hasn't
in the faintest degree any of the hardy-driving manner which is associated particularly with schoolmasters and Prussians, and I'm afraid
also with soldiers in general, though for the most part I suspect
undeservedly. He doesn't shout or swear or drill the men, but they
know very well what they have to do and do it keenly; they would be
gently and firmly admonished if they didn't. One doesn't often meet
real competence so well combined with real Christianity. . . .

I've spent some time in an observation post. Plenty of 'em round
here: merely high places in the town. We use others nearer the enemy,
too. Nothing to be seen of Fritz, but one knows where he is on the
map and in a good light could see his trenches. I played the game, on
my way to the O.P., of shell-dodging for the first time. Quite an

amusing game, given as much protection as we have here – you hear them coming and get out of the way. Under these circumstances, one would be very unlucky to be hit. Stones falling in a gully might be much more dangerous. But the danger to a battery is that it will get 'spotted' by an aeroplane. . . .

Nothing about bullets. Weeks later, George confessed to Ruth that on his first night at the O.P. a bullet passed between him and a man walking a yard in front. 'But we settled long ago,' he added, 'that there's no reckoning with Death.'

At the end of May, 40th S.B. moved southward. Mallory found the moving and the camping-out quite tolrable; he regretted only that he had just planted seedlings from Westbrook in the forsaken garden at Red Slum. On June 10th the battery occupied a new position in Picardy, near Albert, between the Ancre and the Somme.

George to Ruth   *11 June 1916*

Personally, I get some fun out of this sort of performance – a fun that fits in with Clutton Brock's explosion of the absolute, for it depends on the complete evaporation of all elements of comfort. I went round the camp before the men turned in last night and found myself quite merrily ragging them about the opinions they had expressed on leaving the last position. Many of them were glad to go because they expected that any other quarters would be more pleasant than those; you see, they're mostly townbred men with no experience of camp life. But those expectations have not been fulfilled. They were quite jolly about it; and we came to the agreeable conclusion that nothing matters very much so long as you are doing something worth doing with the right companions.

Vast forces were gathering thereabouts. 'I'm feeling tremendously strung up now for great things,' Mallory wrote on the 22nd; 'I hope they'll begin soon.' The bombardment preliminary to the Somme offensive began two days later. For a week the battery fired pretty continuously, most of the time at a slow rate but on occasion taking part in furious shelling of particular villages and trenches. The greater part of the shooting was observed; it was known to have done a lot of damage. 'I want to feel that we're some use,' Mallory wrote, 'and I can feel certain we are.'

At 7:30 a.m. on July 1st the infantry of the Fourth Army, and of the French Sixth Army, to the south, attacked the German positions. The function of 40th S.B. was to fire a lifting barrage. At intervals during the first twenty-four hours, while standing by for orders in the map room, Mallory composed a long letter to Ruth about religion and the religious education of children. It was impossible to know how the battle was going until the wounded and the prisoners began to pass by. Then the reports, though various, indicated clearly enough that the British attack had been held up by machine-gun fire. 'To me this result, together with the sight of the wounded,' Mallory wrote, 'was poignantly grievous'.

A thunderstorm broke on July 4th, and the weather turned chilly. The Fourth Army's advance continued to be distressingly slow, and the battery no longer operated according to preconceived plan. Orders to open fire came frequently at very short notice; sometimes, once started, the firing went on all day long. On the 5th a picture of one of the guns appeared in the *Daily Mail*. 'This is evidently the advertising centre,' George wrote. 'O God! O Montreal!' He asked Ruth to send out bundles of *The Times*.

On July 11th, just before the second phase of the offensive began, Mallory went up for a three-day spell in an O.P., with two Scottish signallers as his companions. As always, he enjoyed finding his way and studying the terrain. From a flat hilltop he could look out over the bare rolling country, intersected by the white lines of trenches cut in the chalk, and broken here and there by little woods. But this land was now a desert; the trees had only ragged remnants of branches. It was Mallory's job to register one of the guns on a windmill at 8500 yards, east of Pozières. 'The holes in its well-battered sides,' he said, 'give me a queer mixture of pain and satisfaction.'

For his physical comfort at the O.P., he had only a pipe, French coffee brewed over a Tommy's cooker, and a bed of rabbit wire in a wet clay hole; but he kept up his daily letters to Ruth, who had spent a day in London at the end of June and gone to tea with Mrs. Reade.

George to Ruth *13 July 1916*

I am very glad you saw Mrs. Reade; I am sure she is one of the best of women. You told her that I 'like the life out here', and she was surprised by that. I wonder what she understood by it. It's not a style of existence I particularly care about, and I would never choose the soldier's profession. Probably campaigning is more tolerable than the artificial peacetime interests of the barracks – the hot-bed *esprit de corps* and diverse forms of purblind eyewash. But no: I wouldn't choose the life for its own sake, even as I find it at its best out here.

Like the life? I prefer to say that I like living. To be in a state of mind that won't say so much is to be defeated; and the most degrading condition of that defeat is boredom, its most usual companion 'self-pity'. No! I'm not bored, and I don't intend to be; nor have I the faintest degree of pity for myself, who have so much more to be grateful for than the great majority of men. . . .

The battery moved up to positions taken from the Germans in the second phase of the offensive. George now occupied a captured dug-out.

George to Ruth   *20 July 1916*

It's rather a smelly part of the world; the trench has been knocked to pieces, and the floor of it must be two to three feet higher than it was – I wouldn't care to dig there. . . .

The journalistic capital which the halfpenny press is making out of the war just now – well, 'I have a sort of disgoost for it, like for vomit and such.' Lord Harmsworth passed in a car today and got out to look at one of our guns which was firing at the time. . . . Probably if I had been out on the gun, instead of in the tent drinking tea, I should merely have felt impressed by the fact that I was talking to an important man. O what a peasant slave am I! And how different from you, dear Ruth, who would so readily give him one of your direct hits, no matter who he might be!

George to Ruth   *25 July 1916*

I was thinking yesterday when I finished reading *The Wings of the Dove* how glad I am that you are so pure and true. You don't wobble. I think I wobbled much more without you. It's chiefly because you're like that there can't come any real shadow between us – unless you consider it a shadow that you can't spell?

Thoughts of home usually turned into visions of Ruth playing with Clare, or painting a china bowl, or moving among the flowers at Westbrook. It pleased George to know that Ruth and her father were seeing old friends and keeping up the hospitable tradition. Sydney Cockerell came to Westbrook and sent messages to George. When Ruth heard that Robert Graves had been wounded, she planned to invite him to stay as soon as he could come.

George spent all his days in the front line, helping to straighten out difficulties over communications. 'Happily, my nerves are quite unaffected by the horrible,' he wrote. 'But oh! the pity of it!'

The War, 1914–1918

George to Ruth   *29 July 1916*

I had a horrible experience yesterday: two of my party killed by a shell on the way back from the trenches. They were walking a little way behind the rest of us, carrying a reel of wire between them on a stick. No doubt this burden prevented them diving into the communication trench beside which they were walking when they heard the shell coming.... I had no clear idea where the shell exploded (what we know as H.E. shrapnel), but looked back to see if the two were all right and saw the reel of wire by the side of the trench – but, as I saw no sign of them, I supposed they were safe.

After that, during the next two or three minutes, about half a dozen 5·9's came over into the same area, quite uncomfortably near us, so that we remained crouching in the trench. Then one of the signallers whistled for the two left behind. There was no response for a minute or so. I became anxious and, leaving the trench, walked back in their direction. I had not gone many paces when I saw that they were both lying face downwards. They seemed to be dead when we got to them; but we got stretchers at once and, with the aid and advice of a R.A.M.C. sergeant, carried them down to the nearest dressing station. They were very nice fellows – one of them quite particularly so. He had been with me up in the front line all day and proved the most agreeable of companions. . . .

George to Ruth   *2 August 1916*

The heat has been trying, but I am getting used to it. I always walk up with a rucksack on my back which contains chiefly a large water-bottle and serves also to carry my coat. Really these expeditions aren't so bad. The point is, I suppose, that they *are* of an adventurous nature and that one has companions. It is curious how often I am taken back to the Alps, partly through an association in the code of conduct. . . .

Heartening reports from the infantry, seemingly confirmed by the sight of German prisoners, induced the men to predict that the war would be over in a fortnight. Mallory, though he could not share their optimism, let his imagination play with thoughts of home and his return:

George to Ruth   *4 August 1916*

I wonder if you'll find me different. I think not. Slightly more self-indulgent perhaps, a bit easier-going: I was wanting to be that before ever I came out here. But I don't think I shall ever be a person to let myself off easily, because if ever I'm finding excuses for myself I'm desperately unhappy, and that gives the show away. Lazy: you may find me very lazy. I hope not.

One thing has come upon me lately: it's no good pretending I can be satisfied with life if it offers too few opportunities for deep thinking. Nothing annoys me more than not to be efficient, and yet I perceive a real opposition between what is usually meant by efficiency and the experience of thought as I understand it. . . . I can very often get myself to do correctly a number of little things which efficiency demands (I'm not only referring to the soldier's life), but they give me no satisfaction when done. My mind is in a state of constant rebellion. I believe that always will be so.

In mid-August Lithgow took to his bed with a chill, Glen went to hospital for an operation, and Bell left for four days of rest. Mallory found himself in charge of the battery. Three new officers reported for duty, none of them altogether prepossessing; and a visit to the trenches on the 13th deepened a melancholy mood.

George to Ruth   *15 August 1916*

The trenches were in a filthy state, owing to a more or less futile attack made by our men the night before. I don't object to corpses so long as they are fresh. . . . With the wounded it is different: it always distresses me to see them. . . .

Yesterday I was superintending works in the battery and generally running round after one thing and another; and in addition I had to square my canteen and mess accounts, which were sadly behind after our disorganised life lately. How I hate accounts! But I feel sure after doing them that I shall go to Heaven.

His immediate reward was a ten-day sojourn in 'rest camp' at La Houssaye, not far from Amiens. He lived in a tent and joined a number of A.S.C. officers in their mess. The first day was blissful:

George to Ruth   *18 August 1916*

I lay idly in a lovely field and after tea walked into one of two convenient valleys. It was a perfect day. There was corn standing and corn in sheaves all over the rolling country, and a valley full of trees. The colours were deliciously fresh in the pleasant breeze. You may imagine how I sought the stream which I knew must be winding somewhere among the green glades, how suddenly I came upon it . . . and all the rest.

I wondered when I felt so divinely happy what the further bliss of your presence could have done, or what sort of joy I should feel if I were at home with you. My belief is that, when that does happen, I shall simply burst with over-fullness.

With time to think about problems of education, Mallory

decided to start a book; he planned it as a journal showing how a father presented to his son Geoffrey the idea of the Good. Geoffrey would learn to perform habitually, with no great effort of the will, his duty with respect to such irreducible obligations as cleanliness and promptness; he would learn further that, in every moment of life which allowed him a choice between one action and another, he must keep spiritually and intellectually alert. He would be considered 'a good boy' not for mere avoidance of naughtiness, but only for receptiveness to spiritual promptings and for decisions well considered; he would be punished only for showing boredom, which 'means the complete breakdown of spiritual life'.

Ruth wondered whether Geoffrey's father, like Richard Feverel's, would seem excessively concerned with education; George himself regarded his notes 'alternately as a sacred store-house of accumulating treasure and as a vastly growing and illimitable rubbish-shoot'. One day the notes could not be found:

George to Ruth   *27 August 1916*
My condition has been perfectly pitiable. For nearly an hour I have feared, or felt convinced, that the notes for the Book of Geoffrey were utterly lost. It was quite decided that my man Symons, the model valet, who has the detestable habit of shuffling papers away into holes and corners and other damned tidy places, should never touch my things again. Rather than see his fine fingers wandering over my possessions with infernal deftness, I was resolved to have no servant. And now I have just pulled the lovely sheet of paper, neatly folded, from an unsuspected pocket.

Unfortunately, the service which was being decently conducted near by (my scene of anguish hid the while within a tent) has ended, or I shouldn't be writing to you but mingling my music with the band and singing a hymn, even if it were 'Onward, Christian soldiers' – much more if it were 'All people that on earth do dwell', which the first hymn *was*. Would the parsons agree that the next best way of praising God was to write to my wife?

Mallory returned to the battery on August 27th. Torrential rains made a morass of the track used by the ammunition wagons and flooded the drainage system around the dug-out, which Mallory now called 'Fathom Five'. The ankle injured in 1909 began to trouble him again; it felt as if the bone had developed a sharp corner. The men were plagued by lice picked up at La Houssaye, and the whole place swarmed with rats and mice. Mallory bought traps for his own dug-out and persuaded Lithgow to send to Corbie for as many more as could be found. A trap in the officers' cookhouse caught six rats in an hour.

When the weather improved, and word came that the French had taken Combles, the world of war presented itself as somewhat less dismal.

George to Ruth   *9 September 1916*

I have recently read a little volume by Henry James called *The Coxon Fund* – not by any means one of the great novels, but sufficiently amusing. I was delighted by one phrase about women: 'the unfastidious sex.' You'ld endorse that, wouldn't you? Or at least you'ld make the corresponding statement about the male. I have been thinking I shall be more than ever so *p.b.* (please adopt this convention for 'post bellum'). The effort to make life decent makes one so jealous of the little decencies.

In fact, I expect I shall be quite intolerable. . . . You'll be expected to walk the garden with the daintiness of a Watteau lady and move about our drawing room with an exquisitely polished and distant manner, casting an occasional pearl for me to set before the swine chew it up or, if they aren't swine, tossing the fine sparkle of conversation about as the diamond reflects the light.

I had quite a thrill in the trenches yesterday on seeing a really beautiful face. . . . This R.F.A. man was sitting quietly beside his signaller, waiting on events. He had a rare dignity; for him clearly there were things beyond his surroundings. He had beautiful visionary eyes which looked at me thoughtfully before he answered my remarks; and I felt that, if I had timidly asked him, 'Do you hate it all very much?' he would probably have replied with infinite reserve, 'Why, yes; sometimes I hate cheese without bread, tea without milk, and meat without potatoes.'

The battle of Flers-Courcelette began on September 15th, and the taking of a crest between Martinpuich and High Wood made it possible at last to see the land sloping down on the far side. Boggy though it was, and ploughed up by shell-fire, this was a prospect to make an artillery officer cheerful.

George to Ruth   *23 September 1916*

As I look at No. 4 gun sitting under her camouflage of wire netting, she looks quite a pleasant object. And yet Dante, if he could see some of the terrible monsters out here, would beam with pleasure and say to himself, 'Why, here's just the thing I'm wanting for my Inferno,' and make accurate drawings in his notebook. It's a curiously distinct impression I have that Dante was a notebook man. . . .

You know, for I think I have mentioned it before, that Hell is peopled by bores; everyone in Hell is a bore. There's no disputing this, because it has been revealed to me. Well, Ruth, I make out now that the bores of Hell are of two kinds and only two. The first have harsh, insistent voices; their speech is virulently offensive, like the choice worst of the Cockney accent. The rest have polished manners, so polished, so irreproachable, that it's impossible to be rude to them. And there's no escape from either sort, only change from one to the other; and each change brings regret.

As the advance to the Flers Line continued, Mallory spent as much time as possible in a forward O.P.; he saw very little of the other officers in the battery. If the weather had been less bad, all the officers might have moved up to new quarters; as it was, they went up to the guns by car and to the O.P. on foot, through seas of mud. Mallory would have liked to see Bell more frequently. 'The others,' he said, 'I put up with quite well, with no sense of martyrdom – much better than they put up with each other.'

George to Ruth   *8 October 1916*

I suppose I'm the only officer who has any pleasure in our O.C.'s company. . . . He's too much the business man driving his team, all for efficiency and nothing for sympathy, and doesn't know how to correct people or to get them to work for love of their work or for any higher end than to avoid being 'strafed', as he would say. He's really a very difficult person to work under; he worries and fusses far too much. My method is to preserve an unruffled dignity which is above being hustled, and that method is fairly successful. Bell's way is to be obstinate as a mule, and I can be that too on occasions. But they are very few, on the whole; and I prefer to be polite, reassuring, imperturbable, and cheerful.

The weather began to behave, as Mallory said, like a personal devil. In a chilling rain, the battery finally moved on October 18th to new quarters taken from the Germans. The first frost was observed on the night of the 19th, and thereafter the daytime temperature seldom rose above 40°. The cold, pitiless rain cut artillery action to a minimum; at the same time, it compelled action to make life tolerable through the winter. One of Mallory's friends in a neighbouring battery, Austin Earl, reported that on a trip to the trenches he and another man had tried for fifteen minutes to pull an officer out of the mud and succeeded only after help came. On the afternoon of October 30th rain flooded Mallory's own dugout.

George Mallory

George to Ruth   *1 November 1916*

I went to sleep doubtfully that night and woke up to the sound of fast-dripping water – another leak beside my bed, the result of another deluge. Shortly afterwards, I was aware of confused shouting. Our Irishman was rushing wildly about, crying out that nine tons of earth had fallen upon him. The wall of a dug-out had collapsed, and in point of fact quite a considerable amount of earth had fallen in. If it hadn't been so humorous, it might have been rather alarming.

Of course it meant that everyone turned out to dig. Mallory wrote that he had developed a quite special feeling about men digging; he would have liked to be able to draw them, like Millet's figures, only 'more *there*': 'You would feel all the stiffness of the clay and the spiritual comfort of getting the better of it.' With some difficulty, he found a stove for his dug-out; and he asked Ruth to send out woollen things and climbing boots.

George to Ruth   *14 November 1916*

I have not been very content with myself just lately. One falls into the way of making so many arrangements for avoiding discomfort that one gets into the habit of thinking too much about comforts altogether and living in a spiritually lazy fashion all round.

By ordinary standards, Mallory fell into no culpable idleness. In one week he read *The Woman in White*, Kipling on the battle of Jutland, George Eliot's *Felix Holt*, and Renan's *Life of Jesus*; and he took considerable trouble to get better acquainted with his brother officers and to see friends in other batteries. In addition to Austin Earl, these included a young Winchester master named Maurice Platnauer[1] and two Carthusians, Chamier and Shepherd, who had been in Mallory's Modern Sixth.

George to Ruth   *20 November 1916*

Last night I was much cheered by the appearance of Platnauer; Yeo, his brigade doctor; and Falconer, the doctor who is with Chamier. . . . I found myself quite gay, talking about books and art to some extent; and yet I had been so depressed before that when I heard they were coming I was annoyed. Is it that I have a very ready response to the presence of fresh people? Or that it is almost a necessity for me to have a certain kind of mental excitement if I am to keep in spirits? In any case, it seems feeble to be so dependent on anything exterior. I suppose in common parlance I'm 'wanting leave'.

[1] Fellow of Brasenose College, Oxford, after 1922; Principal, 1956–1960.

Leave came through, marvellously, after maddening uncertainties and delays, in time for George to be at home with Ruth over Christmas. The few days together at Westbrook seemed dreadfully short. When George had to go, on Boxing Day, Ruth walked a little way with him:

Ruth to George   *26 December 1916*

I went up the steep way, through the little gate I showed you, after I left you. I could cry that way; I simply had to a little, you know. Then I leaned against the ivy wall and looked through tree twigs into the mist; and I tried to pray in silence, just getting near to God and to you and to everything. I don't think I did it very well, but I did feel wonderfully soothed and better. .... I do so want to become a brave, strong person; and I suppose it may grow better in adverse circumstances than in ones that are always favorable. All the same, I don't want them to go on.

Mallory spent the first weeks of 1917 as orderly officer at 30th H.A.G. headquarters, some three miles behind the front. With little to do but look after an ageing colonel, pleasant enough but rather deaf, he felt out of the war – 'Damn it all, I'm not a valet!' At the beginning of February, he was recommended for a staff lieutenancy, which he did not want, and sent to work for a brief spell as liaison officer with the French. Snow lay on the ground.

George to Ruth   *4 February 1917*

I'm sitting by a very warm stove in a wonderfully white little room. A couple of maps are pinned to the walls, and a few cuttings from an illustrated paper, *La Vie Parisienne*. What a change of scene! To be comfortable and alone: I like that. And what a change of companions! Yesterday my English colonel – Hullo, aeroplane bombs quite near, and I can hear the Boche's engine. I hope he won't drop any here, damn him! – who, on reflection, seems to be more like a Gilbert and Sullivan Chinese mandarin than any other figure I can think of; a typical smart young man of the most respectable kind; a typical North Country engineer; and a typical deliberate Scot. Today three Frenchmen, Latin to the core. ....

I'm bound to say I feel somewhat of a stranger in a strange land. .... This afternoon some of our infantry acted in an almost incredibly foolish fashion. It concerned the people here to some extent, and I heard them talking of the incident ('Ces messieurs anglais,' etc.) with more than a shade of contempt for our nonchalant way of doing things. Later I heard one of them talking on the telephone; I heard him say, 'Ils sont grotesques'; and I was aware that he referred to the English.

Mallory described the army of France as 'braced to a state of fine efficiency beyond what the British Staff has been able to imagine'; and in due time he found the young artillery officers to be intelligent and ready for good conversation.

When he rejoined 40th S.B., the Western Front was relatively quiet. The principal news was rather of the campaign in Mesopotamia, the revolution in Russia, and the reaction in Washington to the German declaration of unrestricted submarine warfare. In mid-March sunny days held out a hint that the long winter might be over. The Germans began their withdrawal from the Somme to the Hindenburg Line; and on March 17th British forces occupied Bapaume, long an objective desperately and bloodily fought for. Mallory walked into Péronne, where (as he knew from reading *Quentin Durward*) Louis XI had been imprisoned by Charles the Bold; and with Lithgow and Glen he made a twenty-mile reconnaissance of the countryside. All the recovered area, he found to his dismay, was dotted with booby-traps. One of the most beautiful old houses in Péronne was burning as he approached, and the orchards in the countryside had been wantonly cut down. Angered by this incomprehensible 'frightfulness', Mallory felt as never before a desire to kill Germans.

He had little time for the working-out of his vengefulness. The ankle again became troublesome, making it painful for him to get about in boots. When at last he had it examined, the doctor concluded that the injury in 1909 had been a fracture and that, untreated, it had failed to heal properly. Mallory was sent home and operated on in London at the end of May. His life was thus reserved for other risks than those encountered by an artillery officer in France.

With Clare so young and a second baby on the way, Ruth stayed at home through the summer of 1917; but by August George was fit enough for a holiday in Scotland. He went first to Kintyre and stayed with Cosmo Gordon's in-laws at Skipness. Then he crossed from Carradale to Arran. He arrived late for a rendezvous on top of Cir Mhor with David Pye and Will Arnold-Forster, but from the col between Glen Sannox and Glen Rosa he could hear them shouting on Goat Fell. They stayed at Corrie, and George and David had an afternoon of strenuous climbing – 'about 200 feet in four hours'. The ankle behaved very well, and the day was clear. 'All the strange islands and tongues of land were lying about in the sea like gems.'

At the end of August Mallory was ordered to Avington Park Camp, near Winchester. As usual, he found it hard to make a start in a new place. 'The English coldness is so overwhelming,' he wrote. 'Dinner the first night was the solemnest meal imaginable. I addressed one remark to each of my neighbours and one to the man opposite, all of which had the same fate, like dropping stones into the ocean.' Furthermore, he had been transferred from the Siege Battery to a Heavy Battery, but could not discover what his new duties would be – only that it might be a good idea to ride a bit, because a Heavy Battery had well over a hundred horses but there was a little difficulty in that a new order prohibited the use of riding horses by subalterns.

For a Wykehamist there were compensations. After the dull dinner on the first evening, Mallory walked to the top of a hill he knew, and looked out on one of the loveliest views in England. In the morning he spent some time in Winchester Cathedral and then took his favorite short walk to the Hospital of Saint Cross. The next day, he walked twenty-two miles from Itchen Abbas up the river to Swarraton and Brown Candover, and back by Old Alresford, Tichborne, and Cheriton – 'not bad for a crock like me'.

George had very little to report from Avington, except when he was snapped at by the colonel's horse. Everything that really mattered was happening elsewhere – to friends fighting the war, and to Ruth at Westbrook, only thirty miles away, awaiting the arrival of 'Edwin-Arabella', who was sure to be a beautiful baby because 'any baby of yours must be beautiful'. George sped away to Ruth on week ends, travelling part of the way by motor bike, part of the way by train. Their second daughter was born on Sunday, September 16th. It was a little time before they chose her name: not Arabella, not Althaea, not Veronica; but Beridge Ruth, after her grandmother and her mother. Her godfather was Geoffrey Young.

This was a time of anxiety about Geoffrey. On the last night of August, in the battle for Monte San Gabriele, he had been severely wounded; and his left leg had been amputated above the knee. Did this mean an end to all the marvellous activity? George wrote to Geoffrey's mother:

G.M. to Lady Young   *16 September 1917*

I never believed in Geoffrey so much as now. He'll be fine in his misfortune – finer than ever. There'll be a gesture to rise above it, still gracefully. He'll be more distinguished, too – not by the fact itself but by his beautiful attitude towards it. The greatness of him will be seen more than ever in his spiritual endowment: he'll be wonderful always with that. And won't he – alert, imaginative, and profoundly interested – be happy, too?

As soon as he had an address, he wrote to Geoffrey himself; and Geoffrey, replying, protested that 'dear Galahad' almost made him see himself as a pathetic heroic figure – which would not do at all.

Geoffrey Winthrop Young to G.M.   *26 September 1917*

I am frankly diverted with the prospect of seeing how far I can work up to my old standard of motion with the aid of a sham leg and my trusty old right! I couldn't, at forty-two, have *bettered* my old hill-going. Now I shall have the immense stimulus of a new start, with every little inch of progress a joy instead of a commonplace. I count on my great-hearts, like you, to share in the fun of that game with me.

In October, as a newly promoted first lieutenant, Mallory began a senior officers' course at Avington; but on the 8th, returning by motor bike from Westbrook, he swerved into a post at the entrance to the camp and crushed his right foot. He lay in hospital for a full week, planning a series of articles on education. When he was released, he heard that Raymond Rodakowski had been killed at Cambrai. This was a hard blow, but not unexpected.

George to Ruth   *16 October 1917*

He was a wonderfully innocent creature, and I haven't a doubt devotedly brave. I doubt if any boy I have known has ever quite come up to him for unconscious natural enjoyment. And he was extra-ordinarily kind and thoughtful. . . . There's no one in the world it would have surprised me more to see again. I'm glad you were fond of him, my dear; you *are* good at loving my friends.

Once the course at Avington was over, Mallory had time to see old friends at Winchester, principally Rendall and the Irvings. Graham Irving had written for the *Alpine Journal* a reminiscence of his crossing of the Col du Géant in 1914 with two young friends since killed in action. Now Mallory decided to rewrite his account, begun a year before in France, of the climb on Mont Blanc in 1911 with Irving and Tyndale. On a week end early in November, kept at Avington by a cancellation of leaves, he nearly finished the job. 'Last night I hated it and was in despair,' he told Ruth; 'but I have now decided that, if I cut out a whole host of pure Henry James phrases, I can make it do.' Quite aware that it would still seem different from most articles on climbing, he forwarded it to the editor of the *Alpine Journal*, George Yeld, whom he had first met at Cogne.

G.M. to Geoffrey Winthrop Young   *5 December 1917*

I sent it up to Yeld the other day; and he sent it on to H.V.R., who is now I suppose making up his mind what he shall say to me about it. . . . I fear it's a wild performance, an attempt to treat an expedition as a spiritual experience, with a great deal about states of mind and very little about the physical details. The spiritual thread, however, is itself greatly spun about the physical conditions of a disordered stomach; and I fear the patient reader may be inclined to ask whether the disorder has yet been cured.

The final version appeared in the *Alpine Journal* for September 1918: 'Mont Blanc from the Col du Géant by the Eastern Buttress of Mont Maudit.'[1]

Meanwhile, Mallory had been passed as fit for general service, posted to a newly forming battery, and sent to a gas course at Aldershot. 'I seem to be frittering away days and weeks in England as one only can do in the Army,' he wrote, 'and that irks me. And the ever-lengthening war is a gloomy business for us all. Still, I find plenty to amuse me and plenty to make me happy.' In January 1918 he and Ruth went up to London for the wedding of Robert Graves and Nancy Nicholson; Robert had asked George to be his best man. Only a few weeks later, on Easter Day, George had the great pleasure of congratulating Geoffrey Young on his engagement to Eleanor Slingsby.

Most of that summer Mallory was doing a course under Ralph Brooke at Lydd and assisting in the trials of a new big gun at Newcastle, but at the end of July he had a short leave and headed for Skye with Ruth. David Pye and Leslie Shadbolt joined them, and for five days the party enjoyed quite perfect weather in the Black Cuillin. From Sligachan they traversed Sgurr nan Gillean and made a new route on Sgurr a' Mhadaidh. Then, moving westward to another base, they crossed the ridge of Druim nan Ramh to the shore of Loch Coruisk, struck up the face of Sgurr Coire an Lochain and reached the col between Sgurr Alasdair and Sgurr Mhic Choinnich, and thence descended to Glen Brittle.

The three men fixed their attention on Sron na Ciche, a precipice mostly of rough gabbro, about a mile long and 1000 feet high in the middle. After a leisurely ascent of the great projecting rock

[1] See the excerpts above, pp. 75-76.

called the Cioch, while Pye basked in the sun, Mallory led Shadbolt straight up the buttress behind and, from above, studied the curving fissure known as the 'Crack of Doom'. Later, they made a new route right up from the screes to the ridge of Sron na Ciche. Described in 1920 as 'probably the finest buttress climb in Skye', and classified by the Scottish Mountaineering Club as 'severe', this route has been remembered also as 'Mallory's Climb'.

Mallory crossed to Calais on September 23rd and spent the last weeks of the war near Arras with the 515th Siege Battery. The major was Gwilym Lloyd George; another officer bore the name Wilson. The battery expected to work with an aerial observer, but found little scope for activity. The capture of Cambrai ended the battle of the Hindenburg Line, and news of the German note to President Wilson stimulated hopes for an armistice. On November 3rd the major received orders to join his father at Versailles. 'Lucky dog!' George wrote. 'I wish my papa were P.M.' A week later, on the 10th, he walked and talked all the afternoon with Geoffrey Keynes, who was a surgical specialist in a Casualty Clearing Station beyond Cambrai; and that night, hearing shouts before he fell asleep in Geoffrey's bell tent, he concluded that news of an armistice had really come.

No sooner had George returned to the battery on November 11th than Trafford rolled up, to carry him off by car to an aerodrome south of Cambrai. Trafford had been flying since 1916. For almost a year he had commanded No. 8 Squadron, showing great enterprise and resourcefulness.

George to Ruth   *12 November 1918*

I was delighted to see T. He was in tremendous form, happy and gay and full of life. He gives me the impression of success, not merely from the fact that he affects magnificence, rushing about in a splendid Crossley car and giving orders with the curt assurance of an Alexander the Great, or Lord Northcliffe or Rockefeller, but because he so evidently enjoys every detail of successful action and has such a wonderful singleness of forward-looking conviction. . . .

We celebrated peace in Cambrai last night at the Officers' Club, five of us from here, a very agreeable little party. It was a good evening altogether, of the kind one would expect from the public school type of British officer, and good of that kind, with much hilarity and no drunkenness. The prevalent feeling I make out, and in part my own, is simply the elation that comes after a hard game or race of supreme importance, won after a struggle in which everyone has expended himself to the last ounce. . . .

What a wonderful life we will have together! What a lovely thing we *must* make of such a gift! I want to lose all harshness of jagged nerves, to be above all gentle. I feel we have achieved victory for that almost more than anything else – to be able to cultivate gentleness.

George to his father   *15 November 1918*

Life presents itself very much to me as a gift. If I haven't escaped so many chances of death as plenty of others, still it is surprising to find myself a survivor, and it's not a lot I have always wanted. There has been so much to be said for being in the good company of the dead. Anyway, it's good to be alive now, partly because this gigantic struggle has been worth while. We haven't fought for any flag-wagging jingoism nor for any remote and material political aim, but simply to have a better world to live in. . . .

You see, my generation really grew up with a disgust for the appearances of civilisation so intense that it was an ever-present spiritual discomfort, a sort of malaise that made us positively unhappy. . . . It wasn't that we simply criticised evils as we saw them and supported movements of reform; we felt such an overwhelming sense of incalculable evil that we were helplessly unhappy. Civilisation will leave us plenty of evil appearances and realities henceforward; but the world will seem to have a chance, and western civilisation may be brought into line with Christianity.

George could not be home for Christmas, but during a rather lonely short leave in Paris he resumed his peace-time interest in books and pictures. A friendly librarian allowed him to hold in his hand the manuscript of *Figaro*; a bookseller had for him a beautiful old edition of Beaumarchais, complete, at five francs. In a shop window he saw a picture that he liked and wanted to buy for the Holt. From a Posty point of view, everything was against it; it was simply an interior, with the artist's mother standing in calm stillness; but, said George, 'it happens to be alive'.

George to Ruth   *19 December 1918*

I must send you my Christmas wishes tonight or they may not reach you for the Day. Firstly: my love to you, in fullest measure . . . strong enough and deep enough to cover the space between us. Secondly: my love to our children, to mingle with yours and shine radiantly upon their lives to make them good and happy. And thirdly I wish for you love for our brothers and sisters (in the Christian sense), and their love, and love of Truth and Beauty. . . , and 'the peace of God which passeth all understanding'. And so there is no need to add happiness. . .

CHAPTER 6

Post Bellum, 1919–1920

Mallory returned to Charterhouse as soon as possible. 'Whenever you come,' the headmaster had written, 'you will be welcome.' Both the Fletchers seemed now to be, and perhaps always in fact to have been, on the side of the angels. The teaching, partly in history but mostly in English, placed Mallory in the fields he most enjoyed; and the boys were pleasant and responsive. The Holt, lived in again by George and Ruth together, became, as Mary O'Malley said, 'a very perfect expression of them both':

> Perhaps the most individual place of all was George's study – a long, low room on the first floor, with an abundance of books, an immense table presided over by a coloured stone group by Eric Gill, a cast of the Hypnos, and one or two arm-chairs of a mellow and agreeable shabbiness. The black plumes of some Scotch firs cut the sky at the level of the western window. George loved this room and this window. He was exceptionally sensitive to his surroundings always; beauty and ugliness had a kind of spiritual importance for him, beyond their external significance; and the actual material perfection of this house of theirs really contributed to his peace and strength and capacity. . . .
>
> On Sundays and 'halves' the house swarmed with boys; the work of getting to know them was immensely simplified by having a spacious house of his own to invite them to. And friends and colleagues and neighbours were always being brought in – or, more frequently, coming of their own motion. It was such a good house to drop in to! One of the two was always there, it seemed, and the other just coming; there was generally some other friend whom it was delightful to meet or meet again. There was always a welcome, and a meal, and a sense of freedom and well-being for mind and body in that house, with any amount of good talk – over the fire, or in the loggia, or strolling idly about the garden. . . .

But the old reasons for discontent still made it impossible for Mallory fully to accept life at a public school. It cannot be said of one so conscientious that he neglected his duties as a teacher, even though he gave increasing amounts of time to other concerns – the proper aims of education, the course of international affairs, mountaineering. Rather, it came to him that he was *sur la branche*. Sooner or later, he would have to break away and find a job that would allow him greater scope. He wondered how he might find time to write.

During the war he had started to write about education: he had begun the Book of Geoffrey and intended to follow the boy through his years at a public school; and in October 1917, after reading Alec Waugh's *The Loom of Youth* in hospital, he had planned a series of articles on the deficiencies of the public schools. In one passage, he imagined himself confronted by an accusing father:[1]

'I gave you a boy,' he seems to say, 'with the unspoilt beauties of boyish qualities. He wasn't exquisitely refined, nor was he a paragon of virtue, nor yet supremely talented. He was a decent little chap, truthful, honest, and persevering. He had a gay roguish way of fun, and his laughter was without malice or contempt. I hardly ever knew him short of a job. He was a creature of the open air, with an interest quick to be aroused. Books were not a great interest with him; but he knew how to consult them for information about birds or flowers, or whatever he was pursuing. In all a pleasant companion full of young curiosity, a healthy animal, a proper English boy. And to me how much more than that! For he had an open heart; open to me at least, and to his mother, so that we could easily know him. . . .

'And what has school done for my boy? It is a different tale I have to tell now. My son is a capable athlete; he can take hard knocks and give them; he won't funk and he knows it; he has any amount of what he would call "guts". I'm glad of that. And he has something that might pass at a pinch for manners – a method of light conversation, an assurance, an address. But of manners in the finer sense, the manners that "makyth man", he knows little enough. He may offer a glass of lemonade to a lady, and at best he may do it gracefully. But you are not to imagine that he puts others before self; he has never a serious thought about their feelings or their interests. He has no desire to look below the surface of men's minds, no delicacy of approach, no more than a scant degree of modesty. Superficial and self-satisfied, he is disastrously ill equipped for making the best of life.

'I cannot discover that he has acquired from any honest thinking the right to a single opinion; and yet he is more than superficially opinionated and easily contemptuous of any opposite view. He is no less mentally a coward than he is physically courageous, and as prejudiced as he is dependent. I find his whole scale of values petty and

[1] Pye, *George Leigh Mallory* (1927), pp. 99–101.

unenlightened; he judges by little forms and conventions without seeing to the heart of things; he will notice a man's tie and his socks without remarking that he is a liar; he will prefer him for being rich; and he will dub him eccentric if he is particularly in earnest. For literature, music, art, he cares nothing, and for Nature little more. He seems to have no interest beyond cricket and a motor bicycle, and no taste beyond the music hall vulgarities. It would be difficult to find anyone more readily bored.

'Nice things to say about one's own son! But I have tried to be just. Put him, you may say, in a responsible post and see how he will acquit himself. It would not perhaps be an ignoble performance; and that's so much to the good. But are you to take the credit? We can most of us rub along without making a mess of things; like others, I expect, he will be able to muddle through; you haven't destroyed that capacity. But his education was to give him so much more. Perhaps I am partly to blame. But from the first I was helpless. When I gave him to you, he was lost to me. I knew him no longer and couldn't know him. . . . His lips indeed spoke but his heart was closed from me and from his mother. We gave you youth with the bloom of childhood; you have rendered, not indeed Man, but youth again with Man's hard skin.'

In 1918 Mallory and Geoffrey Young, responding to a stimulus imparted by George Young, Geoffrey's elder brother, had begun to think about the school of the future. After talking at length with Ruth and with David Pye, Mallory drew up a statement which reveals at once his dissatisfaction with schools as they were and his hopes for schools as they might be. It is clear that, had he survived, he would have shared Geoffrey's active interest in the work of Kurt Hahn at Gordonstoun.

The first point was that 'School' and 'Home' must not be left in exclusive compartments. The parents of a young boy at school deserved, and should retain, responsibility for more than the arrangement of holiday fun. To succeed in efforts to foster clear thinking and spiritual awareness, parents and teachers would have to find ways of working together.

Second, boys at an established public school knew little of the kinds of work men have to do in the world and little of what they themselves might undertake and accomplish. Hardly any of them were acquainted with people of other sorts than their own; too many of them developed herd-feelings, and too few even attempted to cultivate individual tastes and aptitudes. The school of the future, situated on an estate with at least one farm, would provide experience of useful employment and teach 'the obligations of responsibility and the value of efficiency and disinterested effort'; moreover, by providing instruction in certain crafts, it would teach boys to discriminate between shoddy things and those designed well and made to last.

Third, public schools generally allowed boys to imagine a wide gap between 'Work' and 'Play', between 'Lessons' and 'Leisure'. This induced a belief that mental effort was the least enjoyable part of life and that free time was intended for mere slacking-off. In a school that filled the day with duties, in the usual way, a boy naturally thought of the duties as completed by successful recitation and examination; he was unlikely to undertake additional work on his own initiative. In the school of the future, there would be 'an atmosphere friendly to intellectual effort'. By requiring greater concentration in class and by cutting down the barrier between class time and free time, the school would be able to reduce the formal curriculum and still prepare boys for university entrance and even for scholarships. Classes would take boys to the edge of country where they would be expected to travel farther on their own.

Finally, games at public schools tended to become a system of compulsions, with excessive importance attached to it. No one with experience of games would deny their value 'for toughening of fibre, for alertness in emergency, and most of all for pure heroics'. Of course the school of the future would have games; but they would not be over emphasised, nor would they be allowed to take so much time. Some of the hours saved would be made available for other outdoor pursuits and for crafts.

Intellectually, as Maynard Keynes once remarked to Geoffrey Young, George Mallory lacked brilliance. He must have known that he could never expect to stand professionally, as an historian, beside his friends Trevelyan and Toynbee. His best hope in teaching, he believed, was just that he might help pupils to re-create something of the past, imaginatively but critically, and then to discern its connections with the present. Whatever other purposes a student of history held in view, he must contribute to the understanding of current political affairs and so assist in realisation of that better world for which, as Mallory persuaded himself, the war had been fought and won. The Peace Conference and the first sessions of the League of Nations encouraged such hopefulness for the future. This was a time for fresh effort to attain ideals. Mallory spoke in one of his lectures about the need for a new patriotism, larger, more civilised, and nobler than the old:

> If the individual man is conscious of himself as belonging to various groups, to the family, the trade, the class, and many others, why should his group consciousness stop with the state? Why should not an Englishman become conscious of Europe as a group and then of the whole world; become, in fact, a citizen of the world, so that patriotism is merged in cosmopolitanism?
>
> The question is one of psychological possibility. . . . I would go so far as to assert that there are already citizens of the world. . . . To accept a larger group is not to lose sight of the smaller one. On the contrary, we shall still love our country as citizens of the world; wish for her the noblest life, as we wish it for a friend; be pulsations in her tender conscience, stirring ions in her activities, drops of blood in her adventures.

Merely to read of political affairs was not enough. In 1920 Mallory spent part of the Christmas holiday in Ireland, determined to see for himself what was really happening under the Terror. Hamar Greenwood, who as Chief Secretary for Ireland defended reprisals against Irish acts of violence, evidently could not be trusted. Mallory held to a belief that he could find out something of the truth, in spite of discouraging reminders that everyone in Ireland would speak as a partisan, and in spite of awareness that his own sympathies already perceptibly favoured a people ready to fight for their independence. Some of his friends, he knew, counted him as already converted.

From the start, he was in touch with friends who had come to be profoundly concerned with the movement. One of them was Edith Stopford. Another was her aunt, Mrs. J. R. Green, widow of the historian; she had opened her house to the planners of the gun-running at Howth in July 1914, a protest against the illegal arming of Northern Ireland. Conor O'Brien had sailed his *Kelpie* in that enterprise; and Erskine Childers, author of *The Riddle of the Sands*, had sailed in *Asgard* with his wife. These, and Desmond Fitzgerald, who had been in prison with De Valera, contributed notably to the forming of Mallory's impressions. Fitzgerald, as Dail Director of Propaganda, wrote on the back of an identification photograph: 'Mr. G. Mallory is anxious to have first-hand information as to acts of oppression and terror. I shall be glad if he can be assisted.'[1]

---

[1] For this photograph I thank Lady Tweedsmuir and Mrs. John Carleton (Janet Adam Smith). On Lord Tweedsmuir's interest in mountaineering, see Janet Adam Smith, *John Buchan* (1965).

At first Ireland seemed almost normal: Dublin quiet on a damp Sunday morning; a few ruined farms near Limerick blending not inharmoniously in the *triste* landscape; unarmed soldiers mingling freely with the evening crowds in Cork, and a young girl walking alone by night, quite unafraid. But the Terror lurked everywhere, most threateningly in Dublin. At any hour a lorry full of soldiers, tin-hatted and armed with rifles, might dash past at breakneck speed; or a party of the Royal Irish Constabulary might appear from a side street and order citizens to line up with their hands held above their heads. Lunch in a restaurant was depressing because there was so little talk: 'I often felt there was but one subject to be talked about, and in public no one dared to talk about it.' The Castle was 'a place not only of blood and iron, of machine guns and barbed wire, and of bolts and bars, but also of secret and sinister chambers where strange things happen in darkness.'

In the circumstances, Mallory hid his letters before going out; he avoided the Black and Tans, kept his hands out of his pockets, knocked audibly enough but not imperiously on the doors of his friends, and gave up the habit of running because it might suggest an attempted escape. One night he was awakened at 1:30 by a visitor with a flashlight in one hand and a revolver in the other – 'Who are you? What's your name? Where were you born?'

He asked me finally, Was I a Protestant? I told him my father was a clergyman in the Church of England. And that settled it. My room was not searched. I blessed my English accent and lay awake a long while cogitating that irrelevant and impertinent question. Was I a Protestant? Was he living in Dublin? And hadn't he discovered yet that Protestants and Roman Catholics are equally Sinn Feiners?

I was glad in any case that no search was made, for my landlady's sake and perhaps for my own, too. I knew what a search might mean. I had been taken shortly after I came to Dublin to see a young lady's flat. The party who had visited it the night before had done their work thoroughly. What I saw was an illustration of chaos.

Having eyes and ears, Mallory simply could not treat with cold scepticism the reports of drunken behaviour by the Black and Tans, of dreadful visitations by night, of pillage and arson, of brutal beatings and random shootings. But to perceive that the Irish who protested were not all liars was only the first step toward understanding of their position. The next step was to see that they were striving for an ideal:

Nothing, perhaps, was more convincing to me than what I saw in a church's porch. The usual glass contained a number of black-edged cards put there with a pious purpose by the relations of the dead. Many of these called to mind Irishmen native in this country town who had been killed in action – men of the Inniskillings, the Munsters, the King's Irish, and the Irish Guards. Among these names was one I knew, that of 'A.B., brutally murdered at his residence on 27 March 1920' – by whom was not stated, but it was well understood. The fact was published in that hallowed place for the eyes of the devout, and with it this inscription:

> Thou art gone, noble soul, in the prime of life:
> Thou hast died for a righteous cause. . . .

There has been wrong on both sides; but national aspirations, a passionate idealism, are to be found only on one side. It is to this fact that Irishmen appeal when they exclaim, 'If only people in England knew! If only they would come and see!' They believe in the truth of their idealism. But how are they to project a message from this spirit to penetrate English apathy? They say to Englishmen, 'Come and see'; they believe that for Englishmen in general to see would be enough. And it is enough.

Meanwhile, the mountaineers had resumed their climbing. Geoffrey Young had written from Florence in January 1919: 'I am keen to revive all the hill activities at once and count on you, as almost the only survivor, to do the work of bringing in the young folk. We will do the social side, if you will set the climbing standard.' So there was a party at Pen-y-Pass again that Easter – twenty-eight, all told, including the Youngs, the Mallorys and Marjorie Turner, the Reades, Conor O'Brien and his sister Kitty, Claude Elliott, Harold Porter, David Pye, and Rupert Thompson. The weather was perfect; the climbing, particularly Geoffrey's, was extraordinary. The party spent Easter Day, as usual, on the buttresses of Tryfan; and Geoffrey made the 'new start' he had foretold in 1917, ascending the Milestone Ridge and the Gashed Crag – his first one-legged climbs:

> I have not lost the magic of long days;
> I live them, dream them still.
> Still am I master of the starry ways,
> And freeman of the hill.
> Shattered my glass, ere half the sands had run –
> I hold the heights, I hold the heights I won.

On Easter Monday, with Ruth, Claude Elliott, and David Pye, George invented a new traverse on the East Buttress of Lliwedd, from the Bowling Green to the East Gully – the Garter Traverse, so called because it lay 200 feet below the Girdle. 'This climb,' according to Harold Porter, who repeated it with Claude Elliott, 'is peculiarly typical of Mallory, and bears witness, perhaps more than any other of his discoveries in Britain, to his fertility in invention and his resourcefulness in action. The standard almost throughout is severe; and the first pitch, which is of unique character, is exceptionally severe.'[1] In the Climbers' Club book at Pen-y-Pass, Mallory himself described one move as 'sensational':

> It is necessary to grasp a small square bracket on the wall with both hands and make a clear swing. Once he has arrived and recovered his dignity, the climber finds a convenient leaf for his left hand, which renders his situation unexpectedly comfortable; and, by turning his body until he can use this with his right hand, he finds himself ready to start along the traverse. . . .

Ruth, though tired by the climb, responded to George's by no means unaffectionate proddings and finished like a veteran.

When July came, George returned to the Alps with Elliott and Porter. They crossed to Boulogne on July 27th and arrived at the Gare du Nord with seats booked on an evening train from the Gare de Lyon to Grenoble. But really, after so long an absence, they could not expect themselves to stay away from Mont Blanc and the Aiguilles; and they decided at the last moment to board the slightly earlier train for Chamonix. With a judicious *pourboire*, they secured a compartment to themselves for the whole night; and in the morning they saw the Alps –[2]

> I had not seen them now for seven years [George wrote]. Still, I had thought about them not a little; I had diligently read the *Alpine Journal*; I had reminded myself of their features by studying photographs. And yet their appearance as we were coming up towards St. Gervais was beyond belief, an appearance quite unconnected with any recollections, a startlingly fresh new vision, new as when I first saw the Alps, new so that I seemed never to have seen them before. . . .
> The whole of the Mont Blanc group was surprisingly white, and even on the west side of the valley great patches of snow were visible below the precipices. It was evidently not quite recent snow (there would have been nothing remarkable in that); the steep sides of the Aiguilles were not plastered, but ridges and ledges were everywhere

[1] 'Garter Traverse – Lliwedd', *A.J.*, 38 : 237–238 (Nov. 1926).
[2] From the unpublished introductory pages of Mallory's 'Our 1919 Journey', delivered before the A.C. on 4 May 1920 and revised for *A.J.*, 33 : 166–185 (Nov. 1920).

piled with it; great quantities had peeled off, and elsewhere the even couches were soft and dazzlingly white.

I found myself discussing these phenomena with a young man as we stood upon the platform of the electric train going up from St. Gervais. His rather delicate face was adorned by a reddish blond beard, always to me an attractive feature in a Frenchman; and we speedily fell into some manner of sympathy, as each of us was engaged in making out what he could through a glass whenever the train halted. I soon found out that he was very well informed about everything we saw. He was able to name every point which I had forgotten or never knew, and seemed to know of every ascent on this side, to the last gendarme, from the Charmoz to the Midi.

I had little doubt he had an ambitious programme and, though I had no intention of referring to my own performances, I began to question him about his. He made no difficulty about telling me. He climbed with two other Frenchmen, always without guides; and the story of his conquests came tremulously forth, his eyes shining with enthusiasm. It was not a long story; and it was a modest record, incredibly modest. I was amazed that so much mountain-lore as he evidently possessed should be expended on so little. 'Je ne suis pas fort,' he said simply in explanation. But the party, he confided, if they could get really fit, intended as a crowning exploit to ascend Mont Blanc this year from the Grands Mulets.

I have said that I intended not to speak about my own achievements or projects. I had indeed made some sort of resolve that I would not speak to foreigners about such things, because I usually find that I dislike myself when I do. . . . However, it seemed necessary to break my resolution; and I mentioned that I had twice been to the top of Mont Blanc. The Frenchman . . . questioned me eagerly and insisted upon hearing everything. I felt that I never had met so passionate a mountain-lover.

At Chamnoix the weather seemed unpromising: the valley was stuffy, the summits were obscured by low clouds blown up from the south, and the upper sky was hazy with fish-like clouds. Half-way up the path to Montanvert, the climbers fully expected a cloudburst, but felt only a few drops of rain; after their arrival, they could see nothing of the peaks until dusk, when the Grandes Jorasses, still partly veiled, appeared at the head of the glacier. In the Montanvert coffee room, hopeful that the weather would clear, the friends discussed possibilities for a first expedition – 'a nice little climb within easy reach'. Not the Moine (so much less interesting than the Verte), not the Géant (too far away), not the Grands Charmoz (too much snow for a first day). 'There remained, in fact, only one thing to be done – the Requin.' But instead of saying, 'We will do the Requin,' they concluded that it would be unreasonable to start a first day before 6:00 a.m. and said merely, 'We will go and look at the Requin.'

At 8:15 the next morning, having made their way up the glacier and passed the end of the arête of which the Dent du Requin forms a part, they decided to avoid the usual route to the summit, which would have required an arduous snow trudge up the Glacier du Plan, and to strike for the rocks of the south arête by way of a small tributary glacier. Here, too, however, the snow lay deep, half-way up the thigh. Both Mallory and Elliott suffered from mountain-sickness. It was not until 11:30 that they attained the rocks above, not until 12:45 that they stood on the south arête. When they started again at 1:15, Mallory thought that by 2:45 they might just reach the Epaule, from which the summit rocks are climbed, and by 4:00 the summit itself. But the route took them up one or two rather fatiguing chimneys and to the base of a conspicuous obstacle known as the Chapeau, or Cocked Hat. Their pace was not very rapid. At 3:45, when they reached the crest beyond the Chapeau, the only possible decision was to return. 'A failure,' yes; but at the same time 'a good day'.

On July 30th, after lunch, the three strolled towards the Plan des Aiguilles, hoping to inspect the Nantillons glacier; but the clouds came down. On the 31st, by a short-cut which eliminated much of a sweaty snow grind and gained time for the exploration of crevasses, they went up to the Col du Géant and the Rifugio Torino. 'A party of seven exuberant Italians hailed us cheerfully on arrival,' Porter wrote in his diary, 'and an amusing dialogue in French was held between them and George. *The Italians*: "Hurrah for the brave Americanoes! It was you and we who won the war." *George (pretending to be pleased)*: "Ah, you do us too much honour. The credit all belongs to you gallant Frenchmen!"'

Unfortunately, Elliott's knee had been so troublesome on the way up as to make it uncertain whether a big climb would be possible. On the perfect morning of August 1st, to test the knee and to see Mont Blanc, the party followed the ridge towards the Tour Ronde for two hours. The knee could not be trusted. Elliott had no choice but to go home and rest – 'a sickening blow to many hopes,' George wrote, 'and I hated it for Claude's sake: he had so set his heart upon the mountains!'

On August 2nd the two who remained set out to climb the

Aiguille des Grands Charmoz from the Glacier de Trélaporte. This face had been climbed twenty years before by A. B. Thorold with the guides Joseph Pollinger and Rudolf Lochmatter. In the *Guide de la Chaîne du Mont Blanc* (1914), summarising their report, Louis Kurz had mentioned falling stones and a very difficult chimney, 'haute de 6–7 mètres, qui constitue le point scabreux de l'escalade'. Was the route really so *pierreuse* and scabrous? The only way to find out, Mallory and Porter had agreed, was to go and see.

Mallory included a full acount of the expedition, 'for purely literary reasons,' in a paper for the Alpine Club.[1] 'It is possible,' he explained, 'to indicate the nature of an expedition quite briefly. But I confess I have not the art of making a story without some details, and to make a story seemed the best chance of interesting you.' This was the only post-war Alpine climb of which he left such a detailed record. That he should have been at pains to describe an expedition mainly on rocks was a little surprising:

> For the best that climbing can give us, variety is needed; but ice and snow seem to me to afford finer experiences than rocks. I should be inclined to accept as an expression of the first mountaineering instinct Shelley's simple words, 'I love snow and all the radiant forms of Frost.' I don't love an Alpine peak devoid of snow. . . . I envy no mountaineer so much as those who made the Brenva ascent when it was still comparatively safe. . . . But I don't deny the delights of the Charmoz, and I hope I am grateful for them.

'For sustained endeavour and dramatic moments,' he wrote to David Pye, 'the climb far excelled any rock climb I know and, I suspect, all but very few that I don't know.'

The day began inauspiciously. On the way from Montanvert to the Glacier de Trélaporte, Mallory lost his balance and tumbled, dashing the lantern against a rock and gashing the palm of his right hand. Then, instead of following easy ledges around the lower reaches of the Charmoz, he led onto difficult rocks. The Glacier de Trélaporte, when they reached it, set no serious problem but required some step-cutting. Above the bergschrund, heading for the conspicuous feature called the Tour Rouge, Mallory wasted three-quarters of an hour on impossibly steep rock walls before taking to relatively easy chimneys. These led to a bay at the level of the Tour Rouge but some distance to the right.

---

[1] 'Our 1919 Journey', *A.J.*, 33:166–185 (Nov. 1920).

It was now 8:30 a.m. Porter, who was carrying most of our burden, had been wonderfully patient behind an errant leader. But I was ill-satisfied. There had been no fizz about our performance, and while one may forgive hesitations and futilities when the obstacles are really formidable, he desires the preliminaries of an expedition such as this to go with a click.

From the bay they could see what lay above them. The central feature was a gully descending apparently from the Grands Charmoz. On their left, in the lower part, its wall was formed by the grim bare slabs of the Grépon; on their right, more helpfully, a rock rib led from a red wall some 300 feet above them right up to the first step above the nick between the Charmoz and the sharp Aiguille de la République. If they could get themselves onto the rib, the way would be clear; this had probably been the route taken in 1899. The gully, which already had an icy torrent in it, threatened to become a dangerous stone-chute; the red wall at the lower extremity of the rib looked altogether forbidding. But a traverse to the right made it possible to by-pass the wall. Mallory and Porter surmounted a pitch 'with snow on sloping ledges and an angle that permitted no liberties' and gained the crest of the rib at 10:30 a.m.

We paused only, and looked upwards; and I became aware that the whole face of things, for me at all events, had completely changed. I saw by Porter's expression that it had changed for him too. His smile had too much enjoyment to be grim, and was too serious for mere amusement. We looked up at the ferocious crags, and felt, I imagine, as a hunter feels when he gets sight of his tiger. I have in mind an optimistic hunter; for we were certainly elated. And yet we had not too much to be happy about. In four hours we had made perhaps 1500 feet from the bergschrund. We computed nearly as much again to the summit, and the great difficulties were all in front of us.

A few steps above us the buttress was notched, before rising again in an obstacle no less abrupt than the red wall which we had outflanked. We turned towards the gully and found a chimney. It was necessary to push up through a hole behind a chockstone – a tiring struggle, because the hole was iced and, while cutting out a way, much care had to be taken to avoid bringing down too large a flake. From the shallow cave above the chockstone direct progress was strictly barred. The left wall offered the only hope.

Luckily, it was possible for the second to give a shoulder, so that the leader could be thrust over the edge onto a sloping slab above. It was an unpleasant position standing there with no particular handhold, but for the encouragement of an excellent belay. A minute crack running vertically up the slab alone seemed to break its even surface. Luckily, the point of the axe could be inserted; by turning the shaft over to the left and keeping the point pressed in, it could be sufficiently secured; the left hand in this way did the required pulling, while the right fingers prevented a slip. Without an axe it would have been impossible to get up this slab, in height about twenty feet. The second dexterously availed himself of a stirrup-rope, which was just long enough to be within his grasp for the first struggle. We were still, as it were, in the middle of a pitch; but there was now a choice of alternative routes, of which the leader chose the worse. After ascending vertical flakes he had again to surmount a difficult slab when some distance above support. The second bore his burden up a chimney having a less malicious disposition. . . .

My next recollection after these salient events, which I see quite clearly engraved in my mind with the familiar characters of nervous tension, is of issuing from some sort of groove which we had followed without difficulty above the chimney last mentioned. We now found ourselves once again on the crest of our buttress, followed a ledge to the right, and saw above us on this side a deeply-cut chimney – or subsidiary gully, it might almost be called. Beyond the fact that we accepted what was offered with grateful hearts and some little show of enthusiasm, neither Porter nor myself could recall even a few hours later precisely what happened next.

We agreed that it was, like Prospero's island, a wholesome place, where the air breathed upon us sweetly; the rocks were steep and sound as one could wish to find them; the wedged axe was useful more than once, and strenuous but not desperate exertion was required. Buoyed by confidence in nature which had been so kind to us, happy, optimistic, we proceeded swiftly for about 200 feet. Even the final pitch, partially iced, a steep wall with very small holds – a difficulty we reckoned of the first order – detained us only for a few minutes; and when at 1:15 we gained a platform once more on the edge of the rib we were now proud of our progress. Here we halted for lunch.

The reflections engendered on this high perch were for the most part comforting; but two little doubts cast perceptible shadows. The sky was clouding over, and mist was gathering about the peaks. A sphinx, presumably one of the Charmoz summits, could be discerned, when we looked round the corner of the gully, coldly regarding us; but suddenly we could no longer see it. Neither of us much believed, after the past few days, in the malice of this omen. But even an innocent mist was undesirable if we were to find our way down by a route unknown to us.

The second doubt was perhaps more serious. Kurz's account of Pollinger's ascent makes mention of a six- to seven-metre chimney.

Why then was nothing said of the remarkable chimney we had just come up? Could '6–7' be a misprint for '60–70'? Such an explanation was far from satisfying us. Had Pollinger, in fact, ever been where we were? Kurz said not even so much as that this party had ascended a steep buttress; on the contrary, he spoke of a gully. The more one thought about it, the more clear it became that we had not followed the line of the first ascent. Whatever peace of mind may be drawn from the assurance that a man has been there before you could be ours no longer. What lay between us and our goal? And would it go? We judged that the distance could not now be great. We should soon know the issue. Such thoughts, if they gave ground for some anxiety, were chiefly exhilarating, entirely undepressing, and served, as did the sombre shadow of a cloud, to hasten our steps.

Immediately above us the rocks sloped back more gently than before. My pipe was scarcely well alight when we went on straight ahead. We had proceeded perhaps 150 feet when I knocked it sideways against a rock and out of my mouth; it slithered down snow, past Porter, apparently doomed; and then by some miraculous good fortune turned a somersault, took a header, and stopped. Porter, roused to sympathy by my cry of anguish, made no hesitation in unroping himself and quickly recovered my precious pipe. It was a good omen, but also a warning. The rocks were getting steeper – steeper than they had appeared from our luncheon place – and a little higher, I now saw, were probably impracticable.

We chose the obvious alternative, and mounted snow on our right into a gully continuing our previous line. The first pitch pulled us up. We had reckoned with rocks but not with ice, and I feared delay. It was necessary to set to work with the axe, chipping awkwardly with the left hand from a strained position. The issue hung on one small step cut in the frailest imaginable structure just clinging to the rock. From this it was necessary somehow to pull oneself over the awkward bulge above it. The obstacle was the most obstinate we had yet encountered – the sort where a man sticks and decides that he can't but, knowing he must, continues wriggling till he does.

We came forth finally from this second story of our great chimney or little gully to find a change of circumstances, showing that the end was near. The buttress had narrowed almost to a knife-edge, as a good buttress should, before the point of abutment. Its structure was becoming fantastic, and even was showing a dangerous tendency to indulge in superfluous ornament. Some curiously devised overhangs and angular projections in the first twenty feet above a narrow gap invited strange contortions in the climber; but we were too excited to contort ourselves for long; this obstacle was carried with a rush. . . . Separated from us by a square-cut gap was a gendarme about 100 feet high: it was no fantastic shape prancing upon the edge of space, but a solemn and utterly forbidding sentry with his back to the wall. We were faced by an obstacle unassailable.

On the right, vicious slabs swept down to the Aiguille de la République; by traversing across the head of them it might be possible to reach a farther wall apparently near the junction of the buttress with the arête. Porter thought this quite without hope; it could be the hope only of desperate men. It seemed to me just conceivable that a way might be found on that side, but the demand of nerve and strength would obviously be so great that I doubted whether we should be justified in launching the assault at so late a stage in our day's hard work. To the left, the situation appeared still more hopeless. The gully on that side had now opened into a bay; towards this the rocks fell away with appalling steepness, while the tower itself capped the precipice with an overhang. And beyond this, on the arête of the Charmoz, now so near, I noted a perpendicular wall some thirty feet high, which might be impassable should we gain the arête.

With all my optimism blown away like smoke, I climbed down into the gap, and proceeded to traverse carefully to the left side, towards the overhang. At least, I thought, I will look round the corner. My curiosity was gratified by a ray of hope. Here was a little bay perched above the precipice; it might be possible to get up the farther side of it. The entrance was difficult, but I managed to crawl under the overhang and land my knees onto a sloping slab. On the farther side I climbed in a corner up to a mantelshelf on my left. Above this was a short wall. It was evidently very difficult, and I couldn't tell whether it would go. I sent back a depressing account to Porter. My confidence was at a low ebb; but his reply showed that he possessed, or he assumed, the glorious gift of blind faith.

It was necessary in any case for him to move, for I should want more rope if I was to make the attempt. Happily, I was able to take up a position so as to press him inwards as he passed the overhang, and help his arrival onto the sloping slab, which the rucksack might otherwise have rendered extremely awkward; and by similar means I calculated we should be able to return. On the farther side of the recess was a patch of snow. Here Porter drove in his axe. It was not a sufficient protection, but it might serve, and it was the best available. If he had wavered at this point, I doubt if I could have tackled the pitch.

I mounted again in the right-angled corner and traversed out leftwards onto the mantelshelf. I was now almost directly above my second, and above me was a wall as nearly as possible perpendicular – a short obstacle, only some fifteen to twenty feet high, but I confess an alarming one. I was conscious during a few seconds' hesitation of confused reflections proceeding from the thought that, but a short time before, I had been in the mood to tackle such a pitch with a gesture of confident enjoyment, with the *élan* of a leader leading to victory.

Now it was different; the spirit was unwilling. Was the flesh any weaker for that, I wondered – or if more effort of will is required to start, is there less effort available to get up?

I looked down with a backward, uncomfortable glance, to see Porter in the most workmanlike fashion belaying the rope round his axe in which neither of us felt security. I positively disliked him for his imperturbability. Still, there he was, imperturbable, efficiently cheerful, a moral fact from which I saw no escape. I looked away from him, half in anger that he should combine so much genial amiability – more than usual – and so much veteran's righteousness round his damned belay; half in sorrow that any such fool could be found as to enjoy, apparently, our present situation; and at the same time, as I looked upward again, in some further strata of consciousness I was amusedly delighted that Porter was playing the game so well.

As to the difficulty of what followed I feel singularly incompetent to pronounce judgment. The steep little wall was climbed, safely, as it had to be; but the fingerholds seemed distressingly small and it was necessary to change feet on a minute foothold. Balance, no doubt, was chiefly required; perhaps it was not a particularly difficult pitch. Porter followed more easily than I had expected. However, my memory is left with the picture of a short intense effort of mind and body in a situation as exposed as I care for.

I had imagined once this wall was climbed that we should find a way up, one way or another, on this side of our arête; and I was disappointed, after ascending a few feet higher, to perceive that we could not proceed in that line. Porter, however, made a good lead up to the right, and by means of a slanting crack rejoined the arête. The great obstacle had been surmounted, but we withheld our cheers. Our hopes were not yet certainty. I had to take a shoulder to mount the next step in the arête, raced up fifty feet, crossed a gendarme, reached a farther point, and then shouted to Harold to follow. As he came up, stepping off his axe and by some ingenuity recovering it, I was seated on the final pinnacle....

We were now divided from the summit ridge of the Charmoz by a sharp snow arête interspersed by a few rocky obstacles. With feet dug in on the Montanvert side and arms over the crest, we worked quickly along the first of these, the perpendicular wall I had already remarked. It was easily surmounted, and our way was plain before us. The mountain no longer resisted; the day was ours.

They reached the northeast ridge at 3:45 p.m. and the summit half an hour later; then they descended by the Nantillons glacier and arrived at Montanvert in time for dinner. 'For persons hardly fit and certainly not yet hard,' Mallory wrote, 'it was a sufficiently strenuous day. But it was a proper expedition for two guideless climbers. They simply rubbed their noses against the rocks; and, if they could not have climbed these rocks safely, they would have retired.' A third man on the rope would have slowed them. The party of two had wasted at least an hour of the morning, but later had made good time. 'I don't think our pace was slow,' Mallory concluded; 'from the time we reached the bottom of the long chimney, and particularly after lunch, it was as fast as I have ever travelled on difficult rocks.'

Such exertions justified a day of idleness; moreover, the wind was rising, and the barometer falling. On August 4th, however, carrying provisions for three days, Mallory and Porter left Montanvert at 10:50 a.m. for the Plan de l'Aiguille; and in the afternoon they spent some hours studying a route proposed by Mallory on the Aiguille du Midi. Two parties had made incomplete ascents of the Midi from this side, by a great west-facing couloir that seams the northwest face. A line to the left of the couloir seemed preferable, starting in a smaller couloir and continuing up the rocks that form the true right bank of the larger one, to the steep snow slopes and the hanging glacier under the summit rocks. On the 5th Mallory and Porter put this route to the test; they started at 2:30 a.m. and reached the top at 12:15 p.m. 'There were difficulties in only two places,' according to Mallory, 'firstly, in crossing the bergschrund, which appeared possible at only one point. It was necessary to get up a crack in an ice wall. Secondly, where the final ice wall meets the rocks which were partially iced. This proved extremely difficult.' Seeing that the weather looked very bad, they descended in soft snow to the Plan glacier and returned to Montanvert.

After another slack day in Chamonix, for boot-mending and lunch at Couttet's, Mallory and Porter went up again on August 7th to the Rifugio Torino, planning a reconnaissance on the Brenva face of Mont Blanc. Two compatriots, A. C. Pigou and W. W. McLean, arrived a few minutes after them. Mallory considered the outlook quite unsettled, particularly for a strenuous day on the Brenva:

I was not happy about the prospects, and found myself awake at intervals during the night going over again in my mind the arguments for and against this expedition. Was it really a suitable expedition for a party of two? And for this party? And there constantly recurred the vision of a certain bleak edge of snow, or it might be ice, where we had seen powdered snow whisked in a fierce tourbillon such as might blow a party off the mountain. The wind was moaning during the night, and was still unquiet when we were called. . . .

A little later we were treading the steps up to the Col by lanternlight. We had hardly popped our noses above the rim when we were furiously assaulted by an unseen enemy, whose first act of violence was to blow out the candle. You may remember that there is a hut less glorious than the Rifugio Torino situated at the level of the Col. Its emptiness was slightly cheered at that early hour before the dawn, by two pipes peacefully smoked and a conversation dim, solemn, and fragmentary. The barbarian invasion, as it seemed, of Italy from the north did not cease; the hordes swept shuddering over the pass or fled screaming round the crags; and another project was born into the world.

This was to return to the Rifugio Torino and propose that the two parties – Mallory and Porter, Pigou and McLean – join forces, descend into Italy, and then go up to the Quintino Sella hut, above the junction of the Glacier du Mont Blanc with the Glacier du Miage. The wind would have a day to blow itself out before they made an attempt on the mountain from that quarter. Pigou and McLean agreed; and the four jogged down the steep path to Purtud and breakfasted there on omelettes and confitures so delicious that they were tempted to stay all day and overnight. 'The question was hotly debated,' according to McLean. 'We lacked passports; and the energetic guardians of the frontier threatened to visit Purtud. The prospect of arrest by the gendarmes and perhaps imprisonment at Courmayeur convinced us of the need to move on.'[1]

But it was far from easy on a hot summer's day to leave the green shade at Purtud, walk up the Val Veni, and then climb to the hut. The steep ascent was rendered all the more wearisome by a decision (Professor Pigou dissenting) to lug firewood from the bottom of the Miage glacier – four small logs tied together at the end of a spare rope, 'left sitting upon any convenient ledge and thereafter hauled up another stage, let down into a crevasse with a sickening swing, to be hoisted out on the farther side, and eventually pitched and pulled at the same time off the glacier altogether onto *terra firma*.' The four climbers and the four logs reached the Quintino Sella hut at 8:00 p.m.

After a night described by McLean as reminiscent of wartime hardships in France, the climbers set out at 5:15 a.m. on August 9th to traverse Mont Blanc. The route of ascent, first made by T. S.

[1] 'First Impressions of the Alps', *C.C.J.*, 14:63 (Dec. 1920).

Kennedy with Johann Fischer and Jean Antoine Carrel in 1872, led up an arête towards Point 4671, above the Bosses du Droma-daire, and so to the summit; the descent followed the normal route to the Grands Mulets (4:15 p.m.). 'Our descent was the worst part of our performance,' Mallory wrote to Geoffrey Young. 'How incompetent tired men can become, going down!' The youngest of the four slipped from a snow step on the Bossons glacier, but all reached Montanvert in safety at 11:00 p.m. Not a difficult expedition, Mallory thought –

But it has rarely, if ever, been my fortune to spend a more agreeable day on the Alps – a day more than agreeable, a satisfying day. It is not altogether easy to account for this feeling. In the ordinary way, I find a close correspondence between the intensity of the struggle and the keenness of enjoyment. In this case, the real struggle had taken place on the previous day; in so far as mountaineering qualities were required for this expedition, they were required chiefly for the ascent to the hut. Perhaps this fact was partially responsible for our enjoyment. The second day was a long, unchecked, and glorious reward for the first. . . . Another cause suggests itself as contributing to this day's enjoyment. The companionship of tried friends on the mountains is undoubtedly a blessing; but the converse is not true – that of untried friends need not always be a curse. . . .

There is a further delight which I connect with this last expedition of my climbing season. The tentative advances and temporary defeats, hesitations, and delays, linked together by a continuous persistence where the way is intricate and success is withheld for weary hours, or perhaps in the final decision – all that is a wonderful experience, and perhaps we like ourselves best for the efforts and endurance which the resistance of a great mountain demands. But easier successes have also their joys, and not the least of these is the mere rhythm of motion, the smooth, unchecked, harmonious advance of a party . . . that intimate combination between the members of a party which is itself not only the most important of means, but a sufficient end and a sufficient delight.

And, finally, is not an ascent of Mont Blanc under any circumstances supremely satisfying? Or is this merely a hymn of praise to my mistress? I confess I have never walked up to the summit from the Grands Mulets; but I should be far from despising such an enterprise. A great mountain is always greater than we know: it has mysteries, surprises, hidden purposes; it holds always something in store for us. One need not go far to learn that Mont Blanc is *capable de tout*. It has greatness beyond our guessing – genius, if you like – that indefinable something about a mountain to which we know but one response, the spirit of adventure.

The climbing season ended too soon, with Porter reluctantly declaring himself unfit to continue. Mallory half-heartedly sought another companion at Chamonix or Argentière, but found mostly A.C. members of older generations. On August 12th he and Porter lunched at Couttet's with R. W. Lloyd and had a good talk about the Charmoz with Joseph Pollinger, who confirmed that in 1899 he had stuck to the great couloir throughout. The next day, Mallory and Porter parted at Boulogne.

G.M. to Geoffrey Winthrop Young   *24 August 1919*

We were only out a fortnight and left perfect weather and perfect snow and the Verte inviting bold climbers. But it was a wonderful time. It was so thrilling, beyond anything I can keep in my head to imagine, merely to see the snow peaks again. And then I was so fit myself. I had so many doubts how I should feel, particularly about ice and snow, after seven years; and, my dear Geoffrey, I can say it to you, I was so much better than I had reason to expect.

In Geoffrey's mind, there was no doubt that George was now far better. 'His early idea of "leadership",' Geoffrey said, 'was to go "over the top" at the first rush. He lacked the detachment of an officer.' Now, after the war, he showed maturer judgment.

This came partly, no doubt, of being a married man. George had a few days by the sea with Ruth and the children before they all returned to the Holt; and in September George and Ruth went off together on a walking trip which helped to dispel remorseful twinges induced by the fortnight apart and to fix in mind the beauties of gentler country.

G.M. to David Pye   *3 October 1919*

R. and I had a wonderful week in the West Country, walking many miles in the fairest land of all. The Wye, the Monnow west of Monmouth, the Teme, and the Severn were our beat. R. went splendidly and walked thirty-one and twenty-four miles on two consecutive days. We just walked steadily on, lingering occasionally for a meal in a country inn or on a grassy bank commanding the view, or to eat red apples in an orchard, enjoying all the detail and the distance till some golden beauty seemed to have been distilled all about us. . . .

Ruth was expecting a third child in August 1920. Just before Easter, without her, George went up to Pen-y-Pass for a fortnight. On returning home, he completed 'Our 1919 Journey', for delivery before the Alpine Club on May 4th, and took up the burden he had accepted on being asked to edit the *Climbers' Club Journal.*

Fortunately, his friends produced manuscripts for him; and he put together what Geoffrey Young called 'the best number of *any* journal'. George himself reviewed Geoffrey's *Mountain Craft*, 'the most important work on mountaineering which has appeared in this generation'. Two excerpts will give some hint of the compatibility which the reviewer and G.W.Y. had enjoyed in climbing together:[1]

He cares supremely for personal relations in a party of climbers. No previous writer has so emphasised their importance. Here chiefly, he persuades us, lies the secret of success; and he examines them courageously in detail, in the details even of what we call manners. The standard laid down is one with which we are familiar, that of civilised men not competing, but co-operating. . . . We must obviate the least occasion for friction and do everything for harmony.

A section of this book is devoted to 'Pace', and it is perhaps the most valuable of all; the power and practice of pace by sustained rhythm (and not by a headlong rush) is the biggest factor of efficiency in a party, and there can have been no greater service to mountaineering than Mr. Young's advocacy of this thesis. . . . By 'pace' he means a synthetic movement actuated by a finer concentration, and advancing rhythmically, with a rhythm more definitely imposed and more compelling, so that we attain in our progress a more perfect touch, a more absorbing harmony with all that is about us. . . .

In June Ruth took Clare and Beridge to Trearddwr Bay, near Holyhead, where they joined the Longridge family; in July Eric Kennington, who was soon to go out and paint the Arab leaders for Lawrence's *Seven Pillars of Wisdom*, came down to the Holt for a week and made sketches for a large picture of Clare and Beridge in the garden. The third child was not due to arrive before the very end of August. It seemed not unreasonable, therefore, for George to take a month in the Alps with Herbert Reade, David Pye, and Claude Elliott: he would leave about July 24th and come home with time to spare.

In the event, this Alpine season of 1920 left a feeling of disappointment. The weather was unsettled, and the party was far from strong. H.V.R. at fifty was beginning to quote maxims and to fuss over details; David seemed never to be quite fit except on a mountain; Claude still could not fully trust his knee. The first part of the campaign, at the end of July, was based on the Gamba hut; young Othon Bron, later well known as a Courmayeur guide,

[1] *C.C.J.*, 14:108–109, 115–116 (Dec. 1920).

11. Charmoz from Montanvert

12. Ruth Mallory

came along as porter. 'George was convinced that there was a route up Mont Blanc straight from the Col du Fresnay,' Sir Claude Elliott writes, 'and we went up to the Gamba hut with provisions for five or six days. The weather, however, was vile; and all we succeeded in doing was to get to the Col du Fresnay via the east side of the Brouillard glacier and then come back to the Gamba over the top of the Innominata in rapidly worsening conditions.' On the way down, near the bottom of a slope, one of the party slipped and pulled the others from their steps; but only tempers and self-esteem suffered damage.

The Gamba was so cold that David was called upon to give instruction in Morris dancing, but the determined party stayed on until the lack of food and fuel drove them down to Courmayeur.

G.M. to Geoffrey and Eleanor Winthrop Young   *25 August 1920*

After this, everything in turn went wrong for us. We wasted time going to the Col du Géant, where it snowed, and failed to use the bad weather for getting up to Pré de Bar [at the head of the Val Ferret]. We then started on the alternate bad day for the Talèfre, and Claude's knee crocked. The next day was again too bad; but David, who had fallen out, was brought up to Pré de Bar; and on the following day we got the Talèfre – a rather obvious new route. H.V.R. managed to separate and get himself benighted at the end of the day and spent a very wet two hours of darkness before we found him. Two days later we traversed the Triolet from the Pré de Bar glacier to the Glacier de Triolet – a very pleasing expedition. But when we got down to Courmayeur, David fell out again and decided to give it up for the season.

H.V.R. and I then went off to Zermatt to pick up [George] Finch and [Guy] Forster; we traversed the Matterhorn (twenty-four hours from Courmayeur to summit) on the first day it was done from Breuil this year, and two days later went up the Rothorn from the Triftjoch. . . . Finch and Forster turned up on our slack day, and another day was wasted from our point of view. After this, the weather was hopeless.[1] We spent two nights at the Bétemps hut, meditating an extensive scheme on Monte Rosa; then crossed the Théodule and got to the Gamba once more (without H.V.R., who now dropped out), after a series of misadventures at nightfall next day.

This was Tuesday, and snow had fallen plentifully on Sunday. Mont Blanc was not at his best; and we decided to give him another day – which was in any case necessary before a midnight start. It was a

[1] Professor Finch recalls that G.M. grew very restless and wanted to move on to another district where conditions might be better.

quite perfect day, spent in blissful, sunlit idleness, except for a short reconnaissance by me. Finch had been gradually brought to adopt the expedition and was really keen about it, and I was absolutely confident we should get up next day: Eccles's couloir to upper Fresnay basin, and then by ribs west of Peuteret either direct to summit or joining Peuteret very high. And then in the evening there came those woolly clouds pushing up from the west. We ate our preparatory meal between 11:00 p.m. and midnight, but had scarcely finished when the thunder started. I need hardly say this was the end of my season. . . .

But from the point of view of *seeing* it was by far the most interesting season I have ever spent. Of course the whole world of the Gamba was magnificent, but so was all one saw from that other end of the chain, particularly from the Talèfre. And the head of the Val Ferret is one of the most beautiful scenes in the Alps, I'm sure.

George reached home on the morning of August 21st, half an hour after his son John, 'a thumping great bruiser of a boy,' who made his appearance ten days early. 'We're highly delighted,' George wrote, 'and Ruth is as bright and well as possible.'

CHAPTER 7

Everest 1921

Five months later arose the question of Everest. For almost two years, the talk of an expedition to the highest mountain in the world had been growing livelier and more purposeful. On 10 March 1919, at a meeting of the Royal Geographical Society, Major J. B. Noel had described his secret journey in 1913 into Tibet. 'Now that the poles have been reached,' he said, 'it is generally felt that the next and equally important task is the exploration and mapping of Mount Everest.'[1] His audience included members of the Alpine Club as well as of the R.G.S. Captain Farrar, as President of the A.C., promptly announced his readiness to nominate two or three young mountaineers for an Everest expedition. Sir Francis Younghusband, a former President, who remembered talking of Everest in 1893 with a young fellow-officer named C. G. Bruce, said that he hoped something really serious would come of the meeting. Here was a task that must be accomplished, and he would be sorry to see it left to men of another nation.

Younghusband was not given to speaking so without taking action. Since Nepal had been closed to travellers, permission for an expedition would have to be obtained from the Tibetans. In June 1920, as the new President of the R.G.S., Younghusband led a deputation to the Secretary of State for India, who placed no obstacle in the way of negotiations with the governments of India and Tibet. Lieutenant-Colonel C. K. Howard-Bury, of the 60th Rifles, then undertook a mission to India; he enlisted the sympathy of the Viceroy and the Commander-in-Chief, and went on to Sikkim to see Charles Bell, the political officer for Tibetan affairs. Bell discussed the project at Lhasa with his friend the Dalai Lama; and word reached London, at the end of the year, that permission to enter Tibet had been granted.

In January 1921 the R.G.S. and the A.C. jointly established the

[1] 'A Journey to Tashirak in Southern Tibet, and the Eastern Approaches to Mount Everest', *G.J.*, 53:289 (May 1919).

Mount Everest Committee, with Younghusband as chairman. The three members for the A.C. were Captain Farrar; Professor J. Norman Collie, the new President, who had gone to Nanga Parbat with Bruce and A. F. Mummery; and C. F. Meade, who in 1913 had made a camp at 23,420 feet on Kamet. The Secretaries of the Committee were Sydney Spencer for the A.C. and A. R. Hinks for the R.G.S. On January 24th the Committee formally appointed Howard-Bury as Chief of the Expedition and Harold Raeburn, a 56-year-old Scot who had gone to Kangchenjunga in 1920, as leader of the climbing party. The first young mountaineer nominated by Farrar was George Mallory. 'It looks as though Everest would really be tried this summer,' Farrar wrote to him on January 22nd. 'Party would leave early April and get back in October. Any aspirations?'

At first Mallory suspected, as he told his sister Avie, that this might be 'a merely fantastic performance'. Moreover, the moment was not one in which Ruth could fairly be expected to lend any sort of encouragement: John was just five months old, and Clare and Beridge and the nurse were all down sick. George thought of saying No. And yet he knew that he wanted a change; he had already decided to leave Charterhouse after the summer and find a job of larger scope. Then Geoffrey Young came down to Godalming, talked with George and Ruth together, and in twenty minutes persuaded them that Everest was an opportunity not to be missed: it would be an extraordinary adventure; and it would be something for George to be known by, in his future work as an educator or a writer. Ruth gave her support, and George agreed to go. On February 9th, with his mind made up, he lunched with Younghusband, Farrar, and Raeburn. Younghusband observed that Mallory accepted the formal invitation to join the expedition 'without visible emotion'.[1]

It appeared that the four-man climbing party would include a second veteran, the remarkable Dr. A. M. Kellas, who had made seven journeys to the Himalaya, and a second young man, George Finch. Major H. T. Morshead, an experienced Himalayan traveller whose brothers Mallory had known at Winchester, and Major O. E. Wheeler, a Canadian, would accompany the expedition as surveyors; and A. F. R. Wollaston, who had explored the mountains of Africa and of New Guinea, would come as medical officer and naturalist.

[1] *The Epic of Mount Everest* (1926), p. 28.

G.M. to Geoffrey Winthrop Young   *21 February 1921*

I expect I shall have no cause to regret your persuasion in the cause of Mount Everest. At present, I'm highly elated at the prospect, and so is Ruth – thank you for that. My view about the party is chiefly that it is inadequate in numbers: there is no margin. Raeburn says he doesn't expect to get higher than about 24,000 to 25,000; Dr. Kellas presumably will get no further; so that the final part is left to Finch and me, and the outside chance that Wheeler or Morshead will take to climbing and make a success of it. Perhaps, after all, I shall be the weakest of the lot; but at present I feel more doubtful of Finch's health.

Evidently the enthusiasm of the planners, above all of Captain Farrar, had induced a notion that the party might well complete the reconnaissance of the mountain and make a bid for the summit. Taking this notion into account, Mallory began to worry about equipment. With only a month left before sailing, Raeburn had still not taken hold.

G.M. to Geoffrey Winthrop Young   *9 March 1921*

Finch and I have had to put on pressure through Farrar, and I hope it will all come right; but such a vital matter as tents has not been properly thought out, and no proper provision for cold at great heights came within Raeburn's scheme of things. I have moments of complete pessimism as to our chances of getting up – or of getting back with toes on our feet. . . .

You were evidently right as to the press campaign, and I'm much amused by letters I get from respectable friends who are easily wrought on by journalists. But Younghusband amuses and delights me more than anything – grim old apostle of beauty and adventure! The Everest expedition has become a sort of religious pilgrimage in his eyes. I expect I shall end by sitting at his feet, hearing tales of Lhasa and Chitral.

In mid-March the climbers underwent medical examinations in London. Mallory passed comfortably. 'This man,' the doctors reported, 'is in every respect fit': height, 5 feet 11 inches; weight, 11 stone 5 pounds; 'movements of all joints full and free.'[1] Finch, however, at this deplorably late moment, was declared unfit; he could not go. The outlook for the climbing party now seemed very dim, and the first efforts to find a substitute did nothing to relieve Mallory's anxiety.

[1] Reports in the files of the Mount Everest Foundation: H. Graeme Anderson, M.D., 17 March 1921; F. E. Larkins, M.D., 18 March 1921.

I consider we ought to have another man who should be chosen not so much for his expert skill but simply for his power of endurance. . . . You will understand that I must look after myself in this matter. I'm a married man, and I can't go into it bald-headed.

Fortunately, Mallory heard that Guy Bullock had come home on leave from a consular post. He had already suggested Bullock's name to Farrar; he believed that his fellow-member of the Ice Club would be right for the job – 'a tough sort of fellow who never lost his head and would stand any amount of knocking about'. Mallory wrote thus to Younghusband on March 31st; Graham Irving sent a supporting letter to Collie; the Committee acted promptly; the Foreign Secretary, Lord Curzon, granted an extension of Bullock's leave. The climbing party's prospects, saved at the last possible moment, seemed now to depend on Morshead: if he could be relieved from some of his surveying, he would pretty certainly prove himself a strong and congenial companion on the mountain.

Morshead and Wheeler were already in India; so was Dr. A. M. Heron, appointed to the expedition by the Indian Geological Survey. Kellas had gone off, on his own, to the mountains of Sikkim. Raeburn had left England in March; Howard-Bury, Wollaston, and Bullock sailed from Marseilles. On April 8th, with a load of equipment, Mallory set out alone. The voyage on the *Sardinia* was worse than he had anticipated: nights uncomfortable for sleeping, days unproductive of good talk. He found a spot in the bows where he would be left to himself.

The Lord knows what I shall find to do hereafter or where it will be done. I can't think I have sufficient talent to make a life-work of writing, though plenty of themes suggest themselves as wanting to be written about. Perhaps I shall get a job at a provincial university. I decided before leaving Charterhouse that, if I were to teach, I would prefer to teach adults – unless indeed I were to be enthroned one day as a God Almighty Headmaster. Ruth is bravely content to be comparatively poor for a time, but I must make some money one of these days.

He read Strachey's *Queen Victoria*, a lot of *Martin Chuzzlewit*, and a little of Santayana; he made a stab at finishing his Book of Geoffrey, started a journal, wrote detailed instructions for Ruth on work to be done in the garden at home. When he saw or heard anything interesting or amusing, he felt the distance from her; when he saw anything beautiful, he missed her most acutely.

The *Sardinia* reached Calcutta on the evening of May 9th. Mallory spent the next day completing arrangements for transport of the equipment and then set out northward to Siliguri, where he took the mountain railway to Darjeeling. On arrival, he was put up, with Wollaston, in the guest house of Government House. Everything, he reported, went with a click. All but Dr. Kellas had arrived, and on the 11th the Governor of Bengal gave a grand dinner party for the expedition: printed guest list, two A.D.C.'s, a small host of native servants in red coats with gold and silver braid, and a band playing. Dr. Kellas walked into the middle of it, and Mallory took to him immediately.

George to Ruth   *17 May 1921*

Kellas I love already. He is beyond description Scotch and uncouth in his speech – altogether uncouth. He arrived at the great dinner party ten minutes after we had sat down, and very dishevelled, having walked in from Grom, a little place four miles away. His appearance would form an admirable model to the stage for a farcical representation of an alchemist. He is very slight in build, short, thin, stooping, and narrow-chested; his head ... made grotesque by veritable gig-lamps of spectacles and a long pointed moustache. He is an absolutely devoted and disinterested person.

On May 13th Morshead, with a surveying party, left for the Teesta valley. The others, in two groups, each accompanied by twenty coolies and fifty government mules, planned to cross southeastern Sikkim and enter Tibet by the Jelep La (14,390 feet); follow the Lhasa road up the Chumbi valley to Yatung (9800 feet) and Phari (14,300 feet); cross the Tang La (15,200 feet) and turn westward north of Tuna; and so, by way of Kampa Dzong and Tinki Dzong, to reach Tingri Dzong, which seemed a likely starting-point for reconnaissance, some forty miles north-west of Everest. The native explorer Hari Ram ('m.H.') had visited Tingri in 1871–72 and again in 1885.[1]

Howard-Bury, Wollaston, Wheeler, and Mallory set out from Darjeeling on May 18th, with monsoon clouds blowing up from the south; Raeburn, Kellas, Bullock, and Heron started a day later. Questions of compatibility came up almost at once. Mallory

[1] H. T. Morshead, 'Report on the Operations of the Mt. Everest Survey Detachment, 1921', *Records of the Survey of India*, 16:114–115 (1922). For Hari Ram's Tibetan journeys, see *Records of the Survey of India*, 8:116–132, 383–400 (1915).

had known Bullock for years and liked Kellas on sight; he already hoped to count Morshead and Wollaston among his friends. But he saw Howard-Bury as a military man with some of the traits of a Tory landlord –

George to Ruth   *Gnatong, 24 May 1921*

I felt I should never be at ease with him, and indeed in a sense I never shall be. He is not a tolerant person. He is well-informed and opinionated and doesn't at all like anyone else to know things he doesn't know. For the sake of peace, I am being very careful not to broach certain subjects of conversation; there are realms which are barred to our entrance together. However, we are rubbing along quite well now. He knows a great deal about flowers and is very keen about them, and is often pleasant and sometimes amusing at meals.

And I saw and still see Raeburn as a great difficulty. . . . He is evidently touchy about his position as leader of the Alpine party and wants to be treated with proper respect. And he is dreadfully dictatorial about matters of fact, and often wrong. . . . Luckily, I had a friendly little walk with Raeburn before we left Darjeeling and rather played up to his desire to give advice, so we get on very nicely. He has some very nice qualities; he has a good deal of fatherliness and kindliness. But his total lack of *calm* and of sense of humour at the same time is most unfortunate.

Very bad weather made it impossible to see much of Sikkim, and strenuous marches on paths slippery with mud left the government mules fit only to be sent back to Darjeeling. It was decided to hire Tibetan animals along the trade route.

George to Ruth   *Kampa Dzong, 5 June 1921*

To get into Tibet from Sikkim we had to cross a high pass, the Jelep La (14,390). As we came up from 2500 feet in three days, this was likely to be rather a mountain-sick affair, compared with ordinary Alpine standards. Most of the party rode ponies, which apparently didn't feel the height; no more did the coolies, cooks, saises, and all the riffraff, with one or two exceptions. But I made this an occasion for testing my wind, and found it quite as much as I wanted, and was tired and headachy on the descent (down to 9000 feet) – which is contrary to all my Alpine experience, though Bullock says it corresponds with his.

We went down to the Chumbi valley and afterwards followed it up to the tableland. It was a remarkable change of scenery from the moist and semitropical Sikkim to a much drier climate and a vegetation much more like Europe, with pine and birch trees very prominent. The Chumbi valley in fact was not at all unlike many valleys in the Alps –

only I doubt whether any Alpine valley can display such a variety of orchises, primulas, fritillaries, anemones, ranunculus, or such a mass of strawberry flower, to say nothing of rhododendrons, which cover the hillsides. It was not otherwise a great change from Sikkim to Tibet. . . .

The great change was coming up to the plains . . . in a few hours after waking in a small mountain valley among flowers and trees, where everything seemed near and friendly, to debauch into a great grey arid basin among rolling hills where the eye was carried an incredible distance and saw at the end of the prospect a steep snow mountain towering up alone – a country where everything was unfriendly and far. And then Phari, after ten miles' dusty walking in the glare of the plain itself. . . . Phari seemed to prove that we had come to a new world altogether ruder than the mountain valleys. . . . It is the most incredibly dirty warren that can be imagined. . . .

So far we had been on the high road, so to speak. In turning west-wards to Kampa Dzong, we must leave the road to Lhasa. . . . Nothing, I suppose, will ever be more dreary than the first stage from Phari: twenty-one miles, mostly across an absolutely flat desert of gravel. The two fortunate circumstances were that the cruel wind was at our backs and that there was a snow mountain to be looked at. It is no use pretending that mountains are always beautiful. Chomolhari (about 24,000 feet), rising abruptly out of the plain to more than 9000 feet above us, was certainly a very tremendous sight, astounding and magnificent; but in broad daylight, however much one may be interested by its prodigious cliffs, one is not charmed – one remains cold and rather horrified. But in the evening light this country can be beautiful, snow mountains and all: the harshness becomes subdued; shadows soften the hillsides; there is a blending of lines and folds until the last light, so that one comes to bless the absolute bareness, feeling that here is a pure beauty of form, a kind of ultimate harmony.

Our great enemy, of course, is wind. On the best days it is absolutely calm in the early morning, chilly at first and as the sun gets up quite hot. (The sun is always *scorching* and threatens to take one's skin off.) Any time between 10:00 and 12:00, the wind gets up – a dry, dusty, unceas-ing wind, with all the unpleasantness of an east wind at home. Towards evening it becomes very cold, and we have frost at nights. . . . The real problem for comfort now is to get a tent pitched so as to have some shelter when the day's destination is reached.

I suppose no one who could judge us fairly as a party would give much for our chances of getting up Mount Everest. . . . Dr. Kellas arrived at Phari suffering from enteritis and, though he is somewhat better now, has been carried from there on some form of litter. Wheeler has constantly been suffering more or less from indigestion and has been sufficiently bad these past two days to make it a real difficulty to come on. Raeburn seems frail and has suffered two falls from his mule, which haven't helped him to enjoy this kind of life. All have been more or less upset inside at different times. However, Heron (the geologist), Howard-Bury, and myself are all very fit, and Bullock and Wollaston seem likely to survive. We've all been better since we opened our stores at Phari, but we're still cursed by the same abominable cooks.

Not even Wollaston knew before June 3rd that, during the two months before the expedition assembled at Darjeeling, Dr. Kellas, climbing in severe conditions, with inadequate nourishment, had lost a stone's weight. He died of exhaustion on June 5th, near Kampa Dzong. Mallory felt deeply distressed; he wrote at once to Ruth, hoping to allay her anxiety, and soon after to a few close friends.

G.M. to David Pye   *Tinki Dzong, 9 June 1921*

At Phari it was a matter of doubt till the last moment whether he would come on. He was not urged to stop, partly no doubt because no one realised his weak state of health, partly that Wollaston was needed with the party, which was far from fit as a whole. Still, it would have been possible for one of us to stay behind and take him back if necessary the last two stages to Yatung, where he would have been by no means well off but 6000 feet lower.

He decided in the morning to come with us, and a chair was rigged for the twenty-mile stage. At the last moment his courage failed, and he said he wanted to stay. But by that time all the troop, the cooks with their cooking pots, and everyone's kit, were spread across the plain; and to change plan was so difficult that Kellas was persuaded to come on. Once we had started on this trek, there could be no turning back before Kampa Dzong, whence it would be comparatively easy, if he should not recover, to get him down into Sikkim. And so it came about that each day he said he was unable to ride, and something – a more or less uncomfortable hammock – was arranged for his conveyance. He was carried by his own head coolie and bearer and several Tibetans hired for the purpose; and generally speaking, after seeing him off, no one of us accompanied him; and he arrived in camp two hours or so after the rest of us.

Can you imagine anything less like a mountaineering party? It was an arrangement which made me very unhappy and which appals me now in the light of what has happened – he died without one of us anywhere near him. And yet it was a difficult position. The old gentleman (such he seemed) was obliged to retire a number of times en route and could not bear to be seen in this distress, and so insisted that everyone should be in front of him. Well, once one is in front, one doesn't linger much in dusty places on the windswept plain; and after our first anxieties none of us lingered much for Kellas. After all, there was nothing to be done for him if one did stay to see him, and he didn't want it. . . . I know that I was deterred particularly on that last day from staying behind by the feeling that I should be pushing into some-one else's business.

'It was an extraordinarily affecting little ceremony, burying Kellas on a stony hillside', Mallory wrote to Geoffrey Young. 'I shan't easily forget the four boys, his own trained mountain men, children of nature, seated in wonder on a great stone near the grave while Bury read out the passage from I Corinthians.'

Before the expedition left Kampa Dzong, Wollaston decided that Raeburn was unfit to go on; he set out with him for Sikkim, where medical care would be available. So the climbing party had been cut to two, neither of them experienced in the Himalaya – two members of the old Ice Club, with hardly more than ordinary gear, moving closer and closer to unmapped territory.

On June 13th these two came to a great plain between Gyangkar Nangpa and Shiling, near the point where the Bhong Chu, flowing from the west, bends southward into the valley of the Arun; and from a hill they had their first real sight of Everest.

George to Ruth   *15, 20, and 22 June 1921*

As we rode out into this sandy plain to take stock of our surround-ings and make out the map, such as it is, I felt somehow a traveller. It was not only that no European had ever been here before us, but we were penetrating a secret: we were looking behind the great barrier running north and south which had been as a screen in front of us ever since we turned our eyes westwards from Kampa Dzong. From the most distant viewpoint, it is true, Makalu and Everest had peeped over the top; but for some days now, since the morning of our first day's march from Kampa Dzong, even the ultimate tops of these great mountains had been invisible. What were we to see now? Were they really to be revealed to us in their grandeur?

We knew them to [be] somewhere at the end of the Arun valley as we looked down it. There was nothing to be seen there at present but a bank of cloud. And it seemed likely in any case that Everest might be hidden by some of the high ridges coming down from the west from our barrier range. We sat out there in the plain and consulted and ate a little and then resolved to make the best of our opportunity, though it seemed a poor hope for that day, by ascending a little peak. . . . We left our ponies to graze on some grass at the bottom, and after about an hour's steep going up, sat down to examine the country through our glasses. If only they could penetrate the bank of clouds that still lay thickly down to the south as we looked along the valley!

Suddenly our eyes caught glint of snow through the clouds; and gradually, very gradually, in the course of two hours or so, visions of great mountainsides and glaciers and ridges, now here, now there, forms invisible for the most part to the naked eye or indistinguishable from the clouds themselves, appeared through the floating rifts and had meaning for us – one whole clear meaning pieced from these fragments, for we had seen a whole mountain range, little by little, the lesser to the greater until, incredibly higher in the sky than imagination had ventured to dream, the top of Everest itself appeared.

We knew it to be Everest. It is always unsafe to say of a mountain that it is too high to be any other, but besides recognition we had certain mathematical calculations to convince us. And we saw not only the summit but, by this series of partial glimpses, the whole of the east face, no less than four groups of peaks which form its northward continuations, immense and quite unknown peaks, perhaps 1500 feet lower than Everest itself and very nearly connected with it to the southeast, and finally two most notable cols to left and right, dividing the great mountain from its neighbours.

It was a gradually clearing view. The dark clouds were brightly lit, but still a great band lay across the face of Everest, when we turned at last to go down and catch up our train of coolies and donkeys, which we had observed crossing the plain to the west. The wind was blowing the sand as we followed up the party, and all the landscape to leeward was like a wriggling nightmare of watered silk. We found them on a little green bank rising from the dry plain, where by some miracle is a spring of water. Our friends were shuddering in their tents; but the wind dropped towards sunset, and they came out. We walked 200 yards or so to a little eminence, and there to the south was Everest absolutely clear and glorious. . . .

Everest had become something more than a fantastic vision. . . . The problem of its great ridges and glaciers began to take shape and to haunt the mind, presenting itself at odd moments and leading to definite plans. Where can one go for another view, to unveil a little more of the great mystery?

Mallory and Bullock left the main party, to carry out an independent reconnaissance for two days, and reached Tingri Dzong on June 20th. There was every reason to move on quickly: the available quarters were in a very dirty house, an old Chinese post; and a break in the weather induced anxious speculation about the monsoon.

Eager to get away from Tingri, Mallory and Bullock planned

a fortnight's exploration of the northwest side of Everest; they would take sixteen or eighteen coolies, set a base camp between 17,000 and 18,000 feet, and carry a high camp to perhaps 20,000 feet. They started southward on June 23rd, and two days later entered the Rongbuk valley, which leads straight up to the mountain. Near the Rongbuk monastery, in a fairly sheltered spot with a beautiful spring, at about 16,500 feet, they fixed their base. Everest loomed just a little east of south, sixteen miles away.

'Suffice to say,' Mallory wrote on the 25th, 'that it has the most stupendous ridges and appalling precipices that I have ever seen, and that all the talk of easy snow slope is a myth.' The long, narrow Rongbuk glacier came down from the south, its eastern wall formed by a ridge culminating in Changtse, the first peak north of Everest. Between Changtse and the north ridge of Everest lay the North Col, presumably visible from the head of the glacier. Between Everest and Lhotse, the first peak to the south, lay the South Col; and below it, apparently, a great bay or cwm dropped westward, bounded on the north by a ridge descending from Everest to a low pass and on the south by a ridge dominated by Lhotse and Nuptse. Mallory promptly focussed attention on the 'two most notable cols'. The problem was to find out how to reach them. It soon became quite clear that the Rongbuk glacier in fact descended from a cwm under the North Col; it took longer to get a proper look at the mysterious cwm under the South Col. The fortnight spun out to a month.

Mallory and Bullock made their first mountaineering excursion from the base camp on June 27th:

George to Ruth   *Base Camp, 28 June 1921*

Started at 3:15 a.m. with five coolies; one and a half hours to the terminal moraine of the [Rongbuk] glacier; 5:45, crossed a torrent with difficulty; then across a flat basin to the end of the glacier, which is covered with stones and made of enormous hummocks; bore across to the true left bank of the glacier and worked up a dry stream bed. Breakfast at 7:00 a.m. near a great stone, just as the sun hit us. An hour's fast walking brought us to a corner where a glacier [West Rongbuk] comes in from the west. We worked round this corner and up onto a shelf on the mountainside whence we could see round it. . . .

We then crossed the glacier to investigate the other bank. It has a section of pure white ice in the middle, which is nothing but a jumble of surprising pinnacles, many of them over fifty feet high. It took us three hours (2:15 p.m.) working to the far side of these, and I had to cut many steps – very amusing work and very good training for the coolies, but very tiring for me. Then an hour's halt. After this we made our way to a shelf above the right bank where we discovered an excellent camping ground. It was a very long and tiring descent. We had to go back onto the glacier to get round a torrent which luckily runs under it, and then down a long vale of stones. We got in at 8 : 15 p.m. . . .

I found it pretty hot on the glacier; there is no doubt the sun tends to take the heart out of one, but not unbearably so. I must confess to a degree of tiredness after the glacier work which I have never quite reached in the Alps, but in all I was very pleased with myself from a physical point of view. . . .

My darling, this is a thrilling business altogether. I can't tell you how it possesses me, and what a prospect it is. And the beauty of it all!

On June 29th Mallory and Bullock led their party to the breakfast place of the 27th and, pushing on along a shelf above a clean stream, came to a little lake near which they pitched their first advanced camp. They spent the next day in finding an easy way across the West Rongbuk glacier. Bullock seemed tired, and it was arranged that he should rest on July 1st while Mallory reconnoitred in the direction of the cwm under the North Col.

George to Ruth   *1st Advanced Camp, 6 July 1921*

This proved a very interesting expedition. After four hours' going, we took to the snow-covered glacier and there plodded for three hours (1 : 15 p.m.). The coolies went very well, and I was feeling strong myself. I had seen a good deal and got an idea of the distance (not so great as I had expected), but the weather came on very thick, and it was too late in the bad snow to proceed to the col [Lho La] under the northwest arête. As it was, we weren't back till 6:15; and I was very tired – not less so the coolies.

It is a remarkable fact about mountaineering here, so far as our experience goes, that the descent is always very tiring. It is only possible to keep oneself going by remembering to puff like a steam-engine. Of course there was little descent about this expedition: we had only risen 1600 feet – which gives you an idea how flatly the glacier goes into the cwm. It was a long walk, mostly over big stones.

G.M. to J. P. Farrar   *1st Advanced Camp, 2 July 1921*

You will be wanting to know something of the mountain, and in one respect it is very easily told. It's a colossal rock peak plastered with snow, with faces as steep as I have ever seen. . . .

This [Rongbuk] glacier runs itself up into a cwm, like the Charge of the Light Brigade, up under a 10,000-foot precipice and, as I saw it yesterday, round to the left towards something like the Col du Lion on the Tiefenmatten side. The slopes of the first peak [Changtse] on the north ridge beyond the col are impossibly steep, except perhaps near the col – I could not make that out through the mist. The west side of the cwm is formed by a huge buttress [northwest arête] coming down from a snowy shoulder to a low, broad col [Lho La] where the glacier presumably sweeps round into the W.N.W. bay [Western Cwm], into which we have not penetrated. . . .

It's difficult to believe the face we see continually is nearly 10,000 feet, but it may well be 9000, and it is completely unassailable. The W.N.W. face is impossible near the top; and the same, roughly speaking, though with less certainty, must apply to the northeast and southeast faces – all this from a number of distant views.

There remain the arêtes. The west [Lhotse-Nuptse] ends in very steeps rocks – we have seen no more. The northwest could be ascended to the snowy shoulder I mentioned if we met it in the Alps – a crampon job, I should say. Above this, a long stretch of snow ridge leads to a steep pitch of rocks; and there is a further but shorter steep pitch where one of the vertical bands meets the ridge; but in both places the rocks appear broken by gullies, and I don't think them impossible. The actual summit is rock at a moderately easy angle.

The north arête does not come down from the summit, but from the east arête, which is comparatively flat and snowy above the point. I think it might go if one could reach the col between it and the first peak to the north. It is a sort of rock rib with a steep drop to the east and slope to the west, flat enough higher up for what looks like a permanent snow slope, the only one on the whole of this prodigious face except what lies under the band near the top. The E.N.E. arête comes up to a very nasty corner where it meets the north arête, and I've little hopes of it.

The S.S.E. arête leads to another huge mountain (guessed at one and a half miles away from Everest and about 1500 feet lower), a black rocky crest [Lhotse]. The two peaks are divided by a snow col [South Col] from which the ascent of Everest would be easy, but it is almost certainly inaccessible. The rocky peak has great rock precipices falling northeast; and the east face of Everest, the only snow face we have seen, has hanging glaciers that look impossibly steep.

Well, that is about all we know of the mountain from the point of view of attack. . . . All the faces on the north are frightfully steep, so I doubt there being an accessible col on this side near Everest, even should the west arête be a line of attack.

You'll understand from this that we have a formidable job. I've hardly the dimmest hope of reaching the top, but of course we shall proceed as though we meant to get there.

Having rested on July 2nd, Mallory and Bullock tried on the

next day to reach a high point between the Rongbuk and West
Rongbuk glaciers. With a party of coolies, they climbed steep
snow and ice to an altitude reckoned by aneroid reading as about
21,000 feet. Mallory, though heartened on finding that he could
cut steps quite happily at this altitude, decided that further
advance would be unsafe for the coolies and called for a retreat
to camp. The 4th, another slack day, was marked by the visit of
Howard-Bury and Heron, who brought with them 'a fine leg
of goa – very much better meat than the skin and bone which
passes for mutton in these parts'. Well fed, Mallory and Bullock
set out on the 5th to reach their high point by another route,
ascending directly from the camp:

George to Ruth   *6 July 1921*

An early start at 4:15 a.m., straight up the stony slopes above our
camp. After about an hour's going, I took some photos of Everest and
some of his neighbours, all looking magnificent in the early sun. It was
about 2500 feet to the crest of our ridge: B. and coolies rather tired at
this point; forty minutes' halt and some food. Roped up for snow towards 8:00. A long upwards traverse to a snow col, where we halted,
9:30 to 10:10.

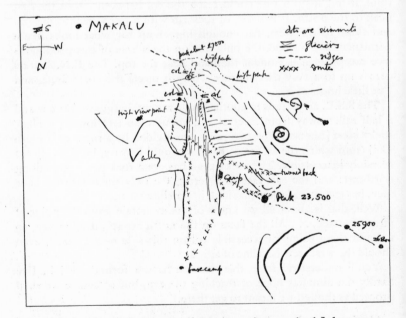

Mallory's Sketch-Map of the Northern Approach, 6 July 1921

THE NORTHERN APPROACH TO EVEREST, 1921
13. Everest and Lingtren Peaks at Head of Rongbuk Valley
14. Everest and South Peak over the Snow Pass leading towards
Western Cwm

ROUTES NOT TAKEN, 1921

15. (*Left*) Khombu Glacier below Western Cwm

16. North Col from Rongbuk Glacier

From this point we had to follow a long snow ridge and then rock and snow. Two coolies dropped out here, and the other three after an hour and a half more. B. and I plugged on, climbing now and then little steep bits of slaty rock, treading carefully along snow crests, occasionally cutting a few steps in ice to reach the arête again after a short traverse. Our interest was partly in what we saw, partly in the sheer struggle of getting on. We moved very slowly, keeping up muscular energy and overcoming lassitude by breathing fast and deep. It was a colossal labour.

We reached the top at 2:45. The aneroid, which reads about 400 feet low, registered 23,500, so that it must be, we think, the second highest peak which has been climbed. Longstaff climbed one 23,600 feet. . . . After a week at our camp I consider this a good performance – a rise of 5500 feet in the day. I have no doubt when we get better acclimatised and start from a higher camp we shall be able to go – well, a great deal higher.

The peak, which Mallory and Bullock hoped to name for Dr. Kellas, figures in later accounts of the region as Ri-ring (22,520 feet). Though remarkable enough, the climb had been surpassed by several others.[1]

The problem of access to the cols had not been solved. From the head of the Rongbuk glacier the approach to the North Col had looked impossibly steep. Perhaps there was a more promising approach from the east. 'We have,' Mallory wrote, 'to explore the other side, where a deep valley exists.' At the same time, the South Col seemed almost certainly unapproachable from the east, but just possibly attainable from the Western Cwm. Somehow, whether by crossing the pass sighted on the 1st, under the north-west arête, or by following the West Rongbuk glacier to its head, Mallory and Bullock had to find their way to the Western Cwm. It seemed possible that the West Rongbuk glacier descended from the Western Cwm and then swept round to the north. There might be a good spot for a new camp beside the West Rongbuk glacier, not far from the 'island peak', Lingtrennup.

Bad weather delayed the reconnaissance; but on July 9th a second advanced camp was established 'around the corner', on the north side of the West Rongbuk glacier, at about 19,000 feet. The first days there were depressing. The special high-altitude Primus stoves would not work; the nights were cold, and efforts to start the day's work before 4:15 a.m. were unwelcome. On

[1] See A. R. Hinks, 'The Mount Everest Maps and Photographs', *A.J.*, 34:231 (May 1922), and Kenneth Mason, 'High Climbs in the Himalaya prior to the Everest Expedition', *Records of the Survey of India*, 16:107–108 (1922).

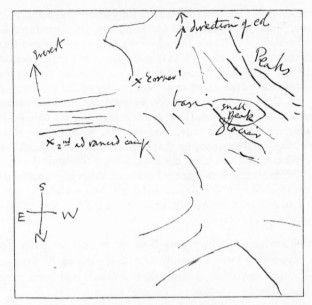

Mallory's Sketch-Map of the Route followed on 13 July 1921

the 12th, the first fine day after the bad spell, Mallory and Bullock made a vain attempt to reach the Western Cwm by the glacier west of their camp – much step-cutting, and clouds obscuring the view. Their only consolation was that the coolies had some very good practice. Mallory wrote to a Pen-y-Pass friend:

G.M. to Rupert Thompson   *12 July 1921*

I sometimes think of this expedition as a fraud from beginning to end, invented by the wild enthusiasm of one man, Younghusband; puffed up by the would-be wisdom of certain pundits in the A.C.; and imposed upon the youthful ardour of your humble servant.... The prospect of ascent in any direction is almost nil, and our present job is to rub our noses against the impossible in such a way as to persuade mankind that some noble heroism has failed once again. And the heroism at present consists in enduring the discomforts of a camp at 19,000 feet in company of a band of whose native tongue I can scarcely understand a syllable, in urging these good folk to rise before daylight, and by the same token urging oneself, in the most usually vain hope that by the time we have got somewhere something may still remain unhidden by the clouds.

What is rhetoric but the exclamation of a man unable to describe his sensations? Believe about one quarter of this mood; and supply the others, which are beyond me to describe, from your sympathy. . . . I plan to start at dawn with all the possible and musterable energy to get right up under the western slopes of the mountain. We are in this spot for that purpose; and 250 feet of rope is ready to slide down on the side of a great ice pinnacle on the far side of the glacier, so that we shall lose no time tomorrow as we lost it today; and the rucksack is packed with tomorrow's provisions; the compass and glasses and aneroid are to hand, waiting for the start; and – I must to bed soon with the alarm watch under my pillow, and not without bed-socks (it's a bed-sock altitude) – a frowsty plan, but then it saves time in getting to sleep. The snow? It's a passing shower, we hope, we hope. The peaks will be clear and glorious in the morning. We shall continue to do no small part of hoping.

July 13th was indeed fine. Mallory and Bullock left camp at 4:20 a.m. and crossed the West Rongbuk glacier to a corner at the northwestern foot of Lingtren, planning to go southward up the glacier between Lingtren and Lingtrennup, in the hope that it would lead them to the Western Cwm. By 7:00 a.m. they had passed the corner and seen that a branch of the glacier, on their left, came down from the fastnesses of Lingtren – a *cul de sac*. Following the main glacier, therefore, they climbed about 1500 feet and at 9:30 a.m. reached the narrow col between Lingtren and a high peak to the west, later known as Pumori:

George to Ruth   *17 July 1921*

The weather was very thick, with much snow falling; and we saw nothing except a general impression of steepness on either side and below us. But we had exploded the theory of an easy entrance into the mysterious cwm from this side; our col, we imagined, must cross a west ridge of Everest into Nepal. It was a great disappointment to see nothing, as we had been early enough for anything. Still, we felt we were a step further.

After a day of rest, Mallory and Bullock started at 6:00 a.m. on the 15th to explore the glacier to the west. While Bullock went off on snow shoes toward the Nup La at the head of the West Rongbuk glacier, on the Nepalese frontier, Mallory stayed with his camera on the moraine near Lingtrennup. 'The shoulders of two great mountains, one south and one west of Everest, appeared,' he wrote; 'and I raced over the glacier to get better views of them, as they belong in some way to our mysterious cwm – a race with the clouds which were coming up.' He returned to Lingtrennup on the 16th:

George Mallory

I started early (2:30) with two coolies and got up the 'small peak' by
5:30. It was a clear dawn, and the mountains were indescribably
wonderful – and the best of it was I now saw over our col of the 13th
into the cwm. It is an amazing cirque. The great rocky peak south
of Everest is joined by [a] serrated ridge to the broken top of another
huge crinkled mountain to the west. The west-facing slopes of Everest
are a series of fierce rock ribs, and all the other sides of the cwm which
I saw are fearsomely steep. Everest itself blocked out all sun, and the
cwm remained a cold dark hollow behind the brightly lit snows. . . .
Our next plan is to force a way over our col and down into the cwm.

To carry out this plan, Mallory and Bullock moved on July 18th
to a light camp on the south side of the West Rongbuk glacier,
between Lingtren and Lingtrennup. 'I greatly enjoyed our highest
camp,' George wrote to Ruth, 'because the mountain views were
as beautiful as any I have ever seen. At night, before we turned in,
the moonlit scene was half-veiled in cloud; and in the early
morning the moon was still up, and the peaks clearer. One mountain [Pumori] in particular, on the far side of the snow-covered
glacier, was singularly lovely. I call it for the present Mount
Clare, and I hope the name will stick.'

At 3:00 a.m. on July 19th, Mallory and Bullock set out on snow
shoes for the col between Lingtren and Pumori. Mallory wrote in
his diary:[1]

An exciting walk. I so much feared the cloud would spoil all. It was
just light enough to get on without lanterns after the moon went down.
At dawn almost everything was covered, but not by heavy clouds. Like
guilty creatures of darkness surprised by the light, they went scattering
away as we came up, and the whole scene opened out. The north ridge
of Everest was clear and bright even before sunrise. We reached the
col at 5:00 a.m., a fantastically beautiful scene; and we looked across
into the West Cwm at last, terribly cold and forbidding under the
shadow of Everest. It was nearly an hour after sunrise before the sun
hit the West Peak.

But another disappointment: it is a big drop, about 1500 feet down
to the glacier, and a hopeless precipice. I was hoping to get away to the
left and traverse into the cwm – that, too, quite hopeless. However,
we have seen this western glacier and are not sorry we have not to go
up it. It is terribly steep and broken. In any case, work on this side
could only be carried out from a base in Nepal, so we have done with the

---

[1] Quoted by him in 'The Northern Approaches', *Mount Everest: The Reconnaissance,
1921* (1922), pp. 214–215.

western side. It was not a very likely chance that the gap between
Everest and the South Peak could be reached from the west. From
what we have seen now, I do not much fancy it would be possible, even
could one get up the glacier.

Mallory and Bullock descended on the 19th to their first
advanced camp and on the 20th to their base. The rain and snow
were hard enough to endure; something else hit even harder,
distracting attention from plans to explore east of the Rongbuk
glacier:

George to Ruth   *22 July 1921*

I have had a bitter blow. All the photos taken up here with the
quarter-plate – practically all I have taken – have gone wrong. Apparently I put the plates in the wrong way round. I know nothing
about plates and followed instructions given me by Heron. I have taken
enormous trouble over these photos: many of them were taken at
sunrise from places where neither I nor anyone else may go again –
for instance, those on our ascent of Mount Kellas. However, I'm
determined to replace them as far as possible. . . . It will mean two days
spent in the most tiresome fashion, when I thought all our work in
those parts was done.

Eight inches of snow fell at the base camp that night, but by
noon on the 23rd the weather had cleared. Mallory raced up about
3000 feet, caught some beautiful views of the mountain, and at
dark rejoined Bullock in a camp below their second advanced
camp. In the morning their alarm failed to go off; but by 4:00 a.m.
Bullock had started for the cwm under the North Col, and
Mallory yet once more for Lingtrennup.

George to Ruth   *28 July 1921*

About half-way up the peak I had a clear view for about thirty
seconds of Mount Clare; and there I stayed, or thereabouts (we moved
up a bit further), from 6:45 to 1:15 – patiently I can't say, but with
indescribable excitement as I watched the movements of the clouds and
speculated when if ever I should obtain a clear view of Everest and the
great West Cwm.

On the evening of the 24th Mallory and Bullock returned to the
base camp. A heavy snowfall dispelled all thought of finding a way
to the expedition's new base camp at Kharta by crossing the
mountains to the east – and so may well have delayed the discovery
that the East Rongbuk glacier, descending from the east side of
the North Col, could be reached from the main Rongbuk by a

narrow gap. On July 25th Mallory and Bullock descended to Chobuk, north of Rongbuk, and there met Howard-Bury, who had come from Tingri. Wheeler arrived later on the same day; he had made an extensive photographic survey to the west and now intended to go up the Rongbuk valley. Mallory thought it rather unfortunate that Wheeler could not have been up there with the climbing party.

As Wheeler began his Rongbuk survey, which found the easy route to the East Rongbuk glacier, Howard-Bury led Mallory and Bullock eastward by the Doya La (17,000 feet) to the Arun valley.

George to Ruth   *Kharta, 28 July 1921*

I have been half the time in ecstasy. My first thought on coming down to Chobuk was that the world was green again. A month had made all the difference to the appearance of the hillsides. . . . And ever as we have come down lower, and nearer to the Arun valley, the appearance of greenness has steadily increased. We have crossed two passes on the way, and we have slept near two clear bubbling streams; and all that we have seen of snow mountains has been of interest, but none of that counts with me. To see things grow again as though they liked growing, enjoying rain and sun – that has been the real joy. . . .

I collected in a beautiful ramble a lovely bunch of wild flowers. The commonest were a pink geranium and a yellow potentilla and a little flower that looked for all the world like a violet but turned out from its leaf to be something quite different; and there was grass of Parnassus, which I really love, and in places a carpet of a little button flower, a brilliant pink, which I think must belong to the garlic tribe. But most of all I was delighted to find kingcups, a delicate variety rather smaller than ours at home, but somehow especially reminding me of you – you wrote of wading deeply through them in the first letter I had from you in Rome.

Much though Mallory enjoyed the pause for rest at Kharta, he soon immersed himself in plans for the next phase of the reconnaissance: search for a route to the North Col from the east. A big glacial stream ran down from the west and joined the Arun just below the camp. The obvious first move would be to follow this stream westward up the Kharta valley. Again Mallory and Bullock would go together; for Morshead and Wollaston, who had been exploring the country west of Everest, had not yet arrived at Kharta.

On August 2nd Mallory and Bullock left the base camp, and at the end of a short march they reached a valley junction. Local guides said that Chomolungma (as they called Everest) stood five days' march up the valley to the left. Though disconcerted to see that this valley had only a small clear stream, Mallory and Bullock accepted the information; and on the second day they ascended 4000 feet to the Langma La, delighting in the flowers and the little lakes, and then went down to a grassy shelf where yaks were grazing. Who could say where they were? Their course should have been westward; it had in fact borne considerably south of west. 'The mystery was partly solved when we learned from our local guide that there were two Chomolungmas. The other, we guessed, must be Makalu, which is twelve miles south-west of Everest; we explained that we wanted to go to the one which was to the right.'

On the third day, which was cloudy and rainy, they came to a glacier descending below tremendous cliffs and rightly guessed that they were under Makalu. Their choice at the junction had taken them away from the Kharta into the roughly parallel Kama valley, further south. The question, then, was whether they could find a way around the end of Everest's east ridge to the valley running up to the North Col. On the fourth day a thinner veil of cloud parted occasionally, disclosing the huge cirque of impossible cliffs from Makalu to Everest. Mallory and Bullock could see well enough that no way to a valley beyond the east ridge would be easy, but they longed to know more; and on August 6th they carried an advanced camp to 17,700 feet. Snow fell from about 4:00 p.m., but at 2:30 a.m. on the 7th the sky was cloudless and starry.

George to Ruth   *9 August 1921*

We walked for about three-quarters of an hour by candlelight up a moraine. Even before the first glimmer of dawn, the white mountains were somehow touched to life by a faint blue light – a light that changed, as the day grew, to a rich yellow on Everest and then a bright grey blue before it blazed all golden when the sun hit it, while Makalu, even more beautiful, gave us the redder shades, the flush of pink and purple shadows. But I'm altogether beaten for words. The whole range of peaks from Makalu to Everest far exceeds any mountain scenery that ever I saw before. . . .

And then we plugged on over the [Kangshung] glacier, well covered with fresh snow, till we took off our snow shoes and for the first time the party (four coolies) found themselves on steep rocks – not a very formidable precipice, but enough to give us all some pleasure. The rocks took [us] to a pass [Karpo La] which was our first objective. Below us on the far side was a big glacier [Kharta glacier], but we couldn't yet see certainly whether it led to the North Col of our desire.

After a hurried breakfast, they pushed on toward Kartse (21,390 feet) and, looking to west and north from a steep snow shoulder, concluded that a ridge intervened between the upper Kharta glacier and the North Col. George's letter continues:

We now wanted to see over a high ridge to the col itself, and the only way seemed to climb our peak. The next section was exceedingly steep. B. thought it would prove impossible, and it was stiff work; I had a longish bit of cutting in good snow. We then reached a flat plateau, put on snow shoes, and hurried across to the far edge. The party then lay down and slept in various postures while I took photographs and examined the north peak through my glass. It was clearly visible down to the level of the col, but no more than that – so that, though the view was in many ways wonderful, the one thing we really wanted to see was still hidden. Eventually I asked for volunteers to come on to the top, and two coolies offered to come with me. It was only a matter of 500 feet, but the snow was very deep and lying at a terribly steep angle. One coolie refused to come on after a time; the other struggled on with me. . . .

And then suddenly we were on the summit: a beautiful little cone, steep on all sides, entirely snow-clad – in all respects a lovely summit. And as the wind blew rifts in the snow I had glimpses of what I wanted to see, glimpses only, but enough to suggest a high snow cwm under this northeast face of Everest, finding its outlet somehow to the north. And it is this outlet that we have now to find – the way in and the way up. We are going back to the valley junction, the glacier stream we left, with the idea that at the head of one of its branches we shall find the glacier we want.

Mallory and Bullock recrossed the Langma La on August 10th, turned westward at the valley junction, and established a new mountain base camp in the Kharta valley at about 16,200 feet. For the first time, Mallory felt really unwell; he had been feverish on the night of the 7th and subsequently developed glandular swellings. The illness lasted almost a week, curtailing activity and even putting him to bed for a couple of days. On the 13th, therefore, Bullock went up without him to explore the right branch of the upper Kharta valley; he sent back a chit saying that this branch ended discouragingly in a col between two high peaks, identifiable as Khartaphu (23,800 feet) and Khartichangri (23,420 feet).

Morshead arrived in camp, bringing medicine from Wollaston; and Mallory promptly recovered. On the 14th, with Morshead, he explored the left branch of the upper Kharta valley – and found it much more promising. The three moved their camp to 18,800 feet, up the valley to the left, and on the 16th climbed a 20,500-foot peak from which they sighted a distant snow col in direct line with the North Col. From a still higher camp, at nearly 20,000 feet, they set out on the 18th to reach the snow col and see over it.

George to Ruth   *22 August 1921*

When we started at 3:00 a.m., our hope was to reach our snow col while the snow was still hard, in four or five hours from the camp. It was a dim hope, because we knew fresh snow had fallen, but it is always difficult to estimate how much. After a few steps on the glacier, we found it necessary to put on our snow shoes – blessed snow shoes in that they save one sinking in more than a few inches, but a dismal weight to carry about on one's feet on a long march. . . .

We reached the col at 12:30 p.m. Apart from a couple of hours (or rather less) on snow-covered rocks when we were getting round above the icefall, this time was all spent in the heavy grind on soft snow. It is no use pretending that this was an agreeable way of passing time. Once we had regained the glacier from the rocks and eaten breakfast at about 8:15 a.m., we were enveloped for the most part in thin mist which obscured the view and made one world of snow and sky – a scorching mist, if you can imagine such a thing, more burning than bright sunshine and indescribably breathless. One seemed literally at times to be walking in a white furnace. Morshead, who knows the hottest heat of the plains in India, said that he had never felt any heat so intolerable as this. It was only possible to keep plodding on by a tremendous and continually conscious effort of the lungs; and up the steep final slopes I found it necessary to stop and breathe as hard as I could for a short space in order to gain sufficient energy to push up a few more steps. . . .

The clouds of course hid the peaks when we got there, but in the most important sense the expedition was a success: we saw what we came to see. There, sure enough, was the suspected glacier running north from a cwm under the northeast face of Everest. How we wished it had been possible to follow it down and find out the secret of its exit! There we were baffled. But the head of this glacier was only a little way below us, perhaps 700 feet at most; and across it lay our way, across easy snow up into the other side of the cwm, where the approach to the North Col, the long-wished-for goal, could not be difficult nor even long. And so, whatever may happen to the glacier whose exit we have yet to find, we have found our way to the great mountain. In such conditions as we found it, it cannot of course be used; but there it is, revealed for our use when the weather clears and the snow hardens.

As we came down the long, weary way, my thoughts were full of this prospect and this success. I don't know when I have allowed myself so much enjoyment from a personal achievement. . . . Some such thoughts were certainly required during the hours that followed, to stimulate the mind. It was the most dismal of processions. Poor Morshead had been 'cooked' going up to the col; and, when at 5:15 p.m. we at last got off the glacier, he was apparently in a state of collapse. The coolies had all left our high camp, leaving three tents standing, it is true, but cold and unprovided. We pursued our course to the base – a long, long trudge. When daylight failed us, we missed our way and were compelled to make an arduous ascent up a steep, rough hillside. A faint misty moonlight made it possible to step from boulder to boulder, but poor tired Morshead was compelled to rest at frequent intervals. Without him, we should have been home sufficiently late, probably before 10:00 p.m.; as it was, we went sleepily stumbling along till 2:00 a.m. . . .

Well, my dear, that's the history of a day and also of a climax. . . . It is now only a question of waiting for the weather and organising our push to the summit. They say the monsoon should break at the end of this month and the fine spell should set in with September. I hope it may. . . . Good night, and God bless you a thousand times, and Clare and Beridge and John.

Returning from the snow col, later known as Windy Gap or Lhakpa La, the party reached the base at Kharta on August 20th.

For ten days, the members of the expedition caught up on photographic work and laid plans, enjoying pleasant weather, hardly wetter than an English summer, but feeling somewhat confined in crowded quarters and unsettled by much coming and going. Howard-Bury and Wollaston left for a trip southward; Wheeler arrived, having completed his Rongbuk survey.

Wheeler had already sent a surprising preliminary report on the course and the exit of the glacier seen from Windy Gap on the 18th: this was the East Rongbuk glacier, and the glacier stream turned west and came down through a narrow valley opening on the east side of the main Rongbuk glacier. This report stimulated inevitable discussion. Given that Wheeler's solution of the mystery was correct, then which way to the North Col would in fact be easier, to ascend the East Rongbuk from the terminus to the head, or to strike for the head across Windy Gap? For the moment, the latter alternative had to be preferred. The plan was to move to a mountain base camp at 17,300 feet, to reoccupy the advanced camp at 20,000 feet, and to put further advanced camps on Windy Gap (22,200 feet) and under the North Col (21,500 feet).

Mallory and Bullock went up to the mountain base camp on August 31st. It seemed very cold, and the weather looked threatening – thin, wet clouds and drifting snow. The only activity in prospect was the stocking of the 20,000-foot camp. Mallory felt not altogether fit. Not unnaturally, personal irritations had been rubbed by now to the point of soreness.

George to Ruth   *1 September 1921*

Frankly, I was quite glad Bury was away. I can't get over my dislike of him and have a sense of *gêne* when he is present, which he too feels, even though we talk quite cheerfully. And now I've had trouble with him about stores – a most miserable petty business, so miserable I really can't bring myself to explain it. But his attitude amounted to an accusation of greed on my part in taking more than I ought up here for the use of the higher camps; and meanwhile B. and I are providing meat and tea for the coolies out of our own money, because we know they must be fed up and encouraged in this way if we are to get them up the mountain; and Bury will allow nothing outside their base rations. . . .

I have established somehow, I hope, a fresh relation with Bullock. We weren't getting on quite happily. We had rather drifted into that common superficial attitude between two people who live alone together – competitive and slightly quarrelsome, each looking out to see that he doesn't get done down in some small way by the other. I have been thinking B. too lazy about many small things that have to be done (indeed he certainly was, at one time), as a result of which I have sometimes tried to arrange that he shall be left to do them; and he has developed the idea that I habitually try and shift the dirty work onto him; and so we have both been forgetting Christian decency and even eyeing the food to see that the other doesn't take too much – horrible confession! But a passage has happened between us to put it all right, or so I hope; and we've been talking together today, much more friendly and cheerful than usual.

The weather stayed bad for more than a fortnight. On September 6th Howard-Bury and Wollaston came up, bringing Raeburn, who looked extraordinarily old and grizzled. Mallory and Howard-Bury amicably talked out the problem of stores and on the 8th, with Bullock, enjoyed 'a most agreeable little scramble along a rock ridge near by'.

Letters arrived on the 9th, sent from England in July but delayed by floods in Tibet. From Ruth came 'six weeks' love in envelopes';

from David Pye, a report that he had seen Ruth and Avie one Sunday at the Holt; from G.W.Y., an exhortation:

Geoffrey Winthrop Young to G.M.   *20 July 1921*

The result is nothing compared to the rightness of the attempt. Keep it 'right', then; and let no desire for result spoil the effort by overstretching the safe limits within which it must move. . . . The summit may, in any particular case, lie outside the course. . . . Good fortune! and the 'resolution to return', even against ambition!

G.M. to Geoffrey Winthrop Young   *9 September 1921*

The excitement of the reconnaissance is all over. It *was* exciting, and we have found a good way to approach the mountain. That last push to a snow col which we had to see over was the biggest effort I have ever made on a mountain. The whole thing is on my shoulders – I can say this to you. Bullock follows well and is safe; but you know what it means on a long, exhausting effort to lead all the time, and snow shoes in deep snow on a steep slope are no small added burden. Height tells, too, but I think rather less than people imagine. I can still do 1500 feet an hour undistressed (and also unladen), at least up to 20,000 as I found before breakfast this morning; and the other day, up to our col about 23,000, we were doing what would have taken the wind of any party in the Alps. . . .

Lord, how I wish you were here to talk it all over. It has been rather a strain, Geoffrey, altogether – both ways. I was unfortunate in having an attack of tonsillitis just before we finished our reconnaissance, and I feel somehow I'm not so strong as I was – less reserve, somehow. And then relations with Bury have not been easy. They're re-established pretty happily now, I believe. . . . I begin to feel that sort of malaise one has before putting a great matter, as it seems, to the touch. Geoffrey, at what point am I going to stop? It's going to be a fearfully difficult decision; there's an incalculable element about other men's physical condition, and all the more so under these strange conditions. I almost hope I shall be the first to give out!

On September 11th Mallory and Bullock carried the last stores to the 20,000-foot camp, on a stony ledge 500 feet above the Kharta glacier. Mallory read himself to sleep, slept soundly for nine hours, and woke to see – 'well, of course the roof of my tent bulging ominously and a white world outside'. Soft grey monsoon clouds were drifting up the valley, and no high peak stood clear. Climbing was quite out of the question. Yet Mallory could not bring himself to descend; he sat on a rock, musing, writing a little, watching the changes of light, taking a few photographs, letting the morning drift away.

At last a mood of common sense returned; I ordered the whole party to pack up and go down. We were still pulling down tents and covering stores when the clouds came up with a rush and [the] sizzle of hard driving snow was about us again. B. put up his pink umbrella, which he invariably carries, picturesquely, on the march; I donned my shepherd's overall (you remember the garment made of wing-fabric, now oiled and a dirty yellow colour from a variety of undesirable contacts, because the oil has never quite dried out); and we sped down the hillside, facing wind and snow, and sped on in one unbroken rhythm of motion down the long valley, dancing over the stones half-snow-covered and leaping the grey waters of many streams, as it seemed (though I suppose they were all the conjoined waters from two glaciers at the valley head, winding and separating and meeting again), and so at length to the humpy grass in the flat hollow where the big tents are pitched.

And no more snow mountains have I seen except a distant glimpse at sunrise, and no more boulders in the big stream bed since then – nothing but the other tents, green and yellow and pale and gloomy black from our tent door, and the hummocky turf in the hollow or the snow that covers it by night and melts in the morning, and the clouds that drift by continually, clinging to the hillsides: that, and the occasional rocks in a near gully where a delicate saxifrage is blooming, pale cream with spots of gold, and the strange bearded faces and teeth of my companions. . . .

The month is too late already for the great adventure. We shall have to face great cold, I've no doubt; and the longer the delay, the colder it will be. But the fine weather will come at last. My chance, the chance of a lifetime, I suppose, will be sadly shrunk by then; and all my hopes and plans for seeing something of India on the way back will be blown to wherever the monsoon blows. But the interest remains for me; and I feel that, when we make tracks for Darjeeling, the moment our great assault has failed (or in the thousandth chance succeeded), I shan't leave these scenes without regret. I would willingly spend a few weeks longer here, if only for the sake of seeing Everest and Makalu and the excitement of new points of view. I would like to undertake a few other ascents, less ambitious but perhaps more delightful. And it will be a loss not to see again that strangely beautiful valley over the hills, and the green meadows dominated by the two greatest mountains, and not to linger there, as I had vaguely hoped, sniffing the autumn and collecting hopeful seeds.

Of the pull the other way I needn't tell you. . . .

For the first time since Kampa Dzong, all the members of the expedition were together in one place. Morshead and Wheeler arrived at the mountain base camp on September 11th, ready now to give up surveying for a while and join the mountaineers; Heron, the geologist, 'as cheerful and good-natured as ever,' arrived on the 14th for a brief visit. There was plenty of good talk at mealtimes. Then the weather cleared – 'We just woke and found it different.'

On September 17th Mallory, Howard-Bury, and Morshead started at 2:00 a.m. under a full moon for a snow peak (21,300 feet) on the ridge to the south, overlooking the Kama valley. At sunrise they could see from Everest to Kangchenjunga, a hundred miles away. 'Such a scene,' Howard-Bury wrote, 'has seldom been the privilege of man to see, and once seen leaves for ever a memory that the passing of time can never efface.'[1] But neither Mallory nor Morshead had gone well on the ascent. Above 20,000 feet the snow, powdery under a thin crust, was impossible without snow shoes. George admitted in a letter to Ruth that his hopes now fell to zero.

Two days later, however, he moved up to the 20,000-foot camp with Bullock, Morshead, and Wheeler. On the following day, with Morshead, he led a party of coolies carrying fourteen loads to Windy Gap for the second advanced camp. The last 700 feet required an unforgettable effort:[2]

Morshead and I looked down as we were approaching the pass: we were all stragglers, ones and twos in the tracks all the way down that final slope, and lower still a lone figure huddled up in the snow. I don't know how they managed to struggle up with their loads in that powdery stuff; but somehow the loads reached the pass, eleven out of fourteen. It was about the gamest thing I've ever seen. . . .

Meanwhile, Howard-Bury, Wollaston, and Raeburn had come up to 20,000 feet; and at 4:00 a.m. on September 22nd six Europeans (all except Raeburn) and a party of coolies started for the camp on Windy Gap. On the way they saw tracks described by the coolies as those of Metohkangmi, 'the abominable snow man' – better acclimatised, perhaps, than the Europeans or even the coolies themselves.

I got up last (except Wollaston), very tired; I wasn't fit that day. And there were the rest sitting under the rim, the best shelter that could be found, and shuddering in the dry smother of snow blown up by

---

[1] From the uncorrected first proof (13 January 1922) of 'The Mount Everest Expedition', *G.J.*, 59:97 (February 1922).

[2] This, and the next three quoted passages, are from a letter to Geoffrey Winthrop Young, dated 11 November 1921.

every gust. There was a suggestion of going down to encamp on the other side, which I resisted. Then the tents were pitched, and each crawled into his hole. In a few minutes all was still. We were at close quarters, seven tents, I think, in the little shallow snow basin; but hardly a remark passed from one to another. No cooking, no hand stirred for a thought of comfort; only rest, not sweet but death-like, as though the spirit of the party had died within it.

That night, at 22,350 feet, the temperature dropped to zero.

Yet Mallory, Bullock, and Wheeler pushed on. While the others returned to 20,000 feet, these three, with ten coolies and three days' supplies, descended 1500 feet of snow to the East Rongbuk glacier, crossed it, and made their third advanced camp at about 21,500 feet on a tributary glacier flowing down from between Everest and the North Peak. There they spent the night of the 23rd:

It might have been an endless stretch of snow about us, it was so flat and the world was so big; but at the same time the great cliffs on three sides of us were a felt presence. And down there we were at the bottom of something: the wind found us out; there was never a more determined and bitter enemy.

On September 24th Mallory, Bullock, and Wheeler, with three coolies, started at 7:00 a.m. and struggled up the great snow wall to the North Col:

Nothing very remarkable remains in my mind about the ascent to the North Col, except perhaps Wheeler's black beard coming up behind me. I seem to know too well the form and angle of a particular snow slope; I must have looked up a great number of times as we traversed it. . . .

At 11:30 a.m., as they approached their goal, they became 'aware of the devil, dancing in a sudden tourbillon of snow'. The minutes at 23,000 feet brought success and frustration:[1]

A sudden gust of violent wind made a miniature cyclone of blown snow which caught us in its vortex just below the crest; and we halted, before exposing ourselves to the full blast, under the shelter of an ice wall. We looked up at the flat edge ascending at no very steep angle – easy rocks and snow all the way to the northeast crest. . . . No obstacle appeared, or none so formidable that a competent party would not easily surmount it or go round it. If one harboured a doubt about this way before, it was impossible to keep it any longer.

[1] From a letter to Sir Francis Younghusband, dated 13 October 1921 and now in the files of the Mount Everest Foundation.

And yet it was impossible to look long without a shudder. From top to bottom this ridge was exposed to the full fury of a gale from the northwest. . . . Under these circumstances the proper course for us was too clear. However, we decided to test the strength of the wind; and the three sahibs walked on 200 yards or so to the col itself. It was not a wind to blow one off the mountain; and, by inclining the head at an angle away from it, it was possible to breathe even in the stronger gusts. But it was strong enough to leave no shadow of doubt in any of our minds. . . . I question whether anyone could have survived in it more than an hour or so.

The party descended and spent a second night at the last camp. Wheeler found that he had lost all sensation in both legs below the knees; he was in the first stage of frostbite. Mallory rubbed his legs for more than an hour, until sensation was fully restored. 'Only you who have been at those great altitudes,' Wollaston commented, 'can realise the immense labour involved in this effort.'[1] The final effort was to recross Windy Gap:[2]

On the return journey we reached Windy Gap in what seemed like a blizzard, though it was really only blown snow once again. The men stood gasping, unable to go on at the very moment of reaching it; and I tugged in vain. Then they tried to shelter under the rim on the site of our camp. As they stood with their backs to the winds, I drew their attention to a number of loads left there by the other party. Suddenly with one will we dragged them to the edge, hurled them down the slope, and stood there laughing like children as we watched them roll and roll, 600 or 700 feet down.

Mallory reached Kharta on September 27th.

George to Ruth   *29 September 1921*

This is a mere line at the earliest moment, in the midst of packing and arrangements, to tell you that all is well; that is to say, that I am well in spite of all efforts and disappointment. It is a disappointment, there is no getting over it, that the end should seem so much tamer than I hoped. But it wasn't tame in reality; it was no joke getting to the North Col. I doubt if any big mountain venture has ever been made with a smaller margin of strength. . . . I had plenty of reserve personally and could have carried on another 2000 feet anyway, with ease, had the conditions been favourable.

As it is, we have established the way to the summit for anyone who

[1] From the first two pages (unpublished) of Wollaston's paper on 'The Natural History of South Western Tibet', read at the meeting of the R.G.S. on 20 February 1922.
[2] G.M. to Geoffrey Winthrop Young, 11 November 1921.

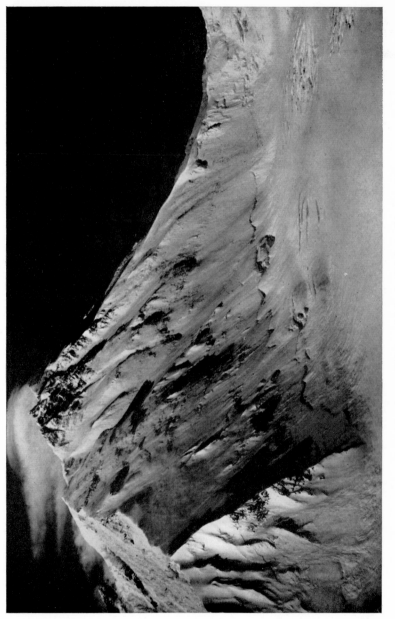

17. Northeast Ridge and North Col from Lhakpa La

18. North Face of Everest

cares to try the highest adventure; and I don't much regret having failed to beat a record, as we could have done easily had fortune favoured us.

Now homewards with all speed.

G.M. to his sister Avie   *Approaching Marseilles, 10 November 1921*

They've had thoughts of organising an expedition for next year; but I've said it's no use going out except early in the spring, to climb before the monsoon. They can't possibly organise another show so soon, particularly as I've also said that it's barely worth while trying again, and anyway not without eight first-rate climbers. They can't get eight, certainly not soon, perhaps not even the year after. Hinks (Hon. Sec.) already wants to know whether I'll go again. When they press for an answer, I shall tell them they can get the other seven first. How they'll pore over the A.C. list and write round for opinions about the various candidates! I wouldn't go again next year, as the saying is, for all the gold in Arabia.

G.M. to David Pye   *11 November 1921*

Never mind Everest and its unfriendly glories. I'm tired of travelling and travellers, far countries and uncouth people, trains and ships and shimmering mausoleums, foreign ports, dark-skinned faces, and a garish sun. What I want to see is faces I know, and my own sweet home; afterwards, the solemn facades in Pall Mall, and perhaps Bloomsbury in a fog; and then an English river, cattle grazing in western meadows. . . .

I've been writing solidly for ten days since leaving Bombay – a report for the A.C., vastly long and, I fear, not a little indiscreet. . . . When I think of that wonderful Everest Committee and all the solemn divergences of opinion that must have passed between their nodding heads, the scrutiny of photographs and discussion of letters, with grave doubts coughed up in phlegmy throats as to whether the party are really 'on the right track', and all the anxious wisdom devoted to spoon-feeding the Glaxo-loving public – lord, when I think of it, something bubbles up inside me. The effervescence is sternly repressed, of course. I settle down to pondered judgments; and then – a bubble outs and bursts.

G.M. to Geoffrey Winthrop Young   *11 November 1921*

I think it was disappointment more than anything else that prevented me from writing before: the terrible difference between my visions of myself with a few determined spirits setting forth from our perched camp on that high pass, crawling up at least to a much higher point where the summit itself would seem almost within reach, and coming down tired but not dispirited, satisfied rather, just with the effort; all that, and on the other hand the reality as we found it – the blown snow endlessly swept over the grey slopes, just the grim prospect, no respite, and no hope.

Well, that mood has passed long ago; and now, after writing my report for the A.C., I'm conscious of the only feeling that's left: Thank God it was like that, with no temptation to go on. We came back without accident, not even a frostbitten toe. It seems now a question not as to what might have happened higher, but what would have happened with unfailing certainty. It was a pitiful party at the last, not fit to be on a mountainside anywhere.

Geoffrey Winthrop Young to G.M.   *15 November 1921*

This is to welcome you into quiet waters, in a very sincere spirit of relief, pride, and congratulation. You write, in the natural reaction after a touch with superhuman circumstance, of 'failure'. You will find this end of the world is only using the word *success* – success unexpected, tremendously deserved, and beyond what we hoped. . . .

I can assure you that the colossal effort of lifting an entirely unsuitable party, at the first attempt, on a single pair of shoulders, not only onto the right line but well up it, against hopeless conditions, forms an episode by itself in the history of mountain exploration, and will only be the more appreciated the more time goes on.

CHAPTER 8

Everest 1922

As Mallory neared Marseilles, where he was to meet Ruth for a short holiday 'wander from one charming town to another in southern France', a letter for him started on its way from the Travellers' Club:

Sir Francis Younghusband to G.M.   *9 November 1921*

You seem all to be of opinion that May and June will be better months than September, so we are organising an expedition to start from Darjeeling on March 21st next year. We could not wait until 1923 because we cannot afford to lose the opportunity which the present friendliness of the Tibetans affords. . . . Also, the public interest in the Expedition is now so extraordinarily keen we could not allow it to cool. So we are very much hoping you will be able to go out again next year.

This prompt invitation proved irresistible, after all. Mallory had just three months in England between expeditions, and precious little of that time to spend with his family or on thoughts of a future career. Everest kept him busy. On December 20th, in the Queen's Hall, Howard-Bury and Mallory described the Reconnaissance at a joint meeting of the A.C. and the R.G.S.; and in the next ten weeks Mallory filled nearly thirty lecture engagements. Somehow, he managed also to finish his manuscript for *Mount Everest: The Reconnaissance, 1921* and to give attention occasionally to the Mount Everest Committee's preparations for 1922.

The leader of the new expedition was Brigadier-General the Hon. C. G. Bruce. For thirty years the General had served with Gurkha regiments, treating his men as if they were his young brothers, making uproarious jokes in their own language, and delighting them by his feats of strength. They affectionately called him 'The Bear'. In the old days, near the Khyber, he had carried his orderly up a hill every day, for fitness' sake; and once, wrestling, he had thrown three opponents simultaneously. Few men had tuch extensive knowledge of the Himalaya. Bruce had gone with Martin Conway to the Karakoram in 1892, with Mummery and Collie to Nanga Parbat in 1895, with Tom Longstaff and Mumm to Trisul in 1907; he had talked of Everest with Younghusband in 1893, and had even laid plans to go there in 1907 and 1910. At the age of fifty-six he could no longer expect to go high; but as Bruce Sahib to some, as Old Bruiser or Charlie to others, the General was the best leader imaginable.

As second-in-command, the Committee appointed Lieutenant-Colonel E. L. Strutt, who had climbed regularly in the Alps for more than thirty years, winter and summer. At forty-eight, he would direct activities at the mountain base camp. Some acquaintances thought of Strutt as the stiff soldier-diplomat who had rescued the Austrian imperial family from a revolutionary mob and acted as High Commissioner at Danzig. Close friends knew quite well that Strutt had old-fashioned and insistently aristocratic tastes, that he spoke his intolerances freely, and that he could wither a shortcomer with contempt or blast him with maledictions; but they greatly valued him as a loyal comrade and a good talker.

Tom Longstaff, at forty-seven, made a spirited third among the elders. His travels had changed the map of the Himalaya. In 1905 he had explored the region of Nanda Devi; in 1907, climbed Trisul (23,360 feet), the highest summit attained before 1930; in 1909, visited the Karakoram and discovered Teram Kangri. During the war he had served as assistant commandant of the Gilgit Scouts. Trained as a doctor at St. Thomas's, he was appointed medical officer to the expedition. In this capacity, having never engaged in active practice, he had the aid and support of a physician and a surgeon selected for the climbing party.

In the early stages of planning, the climbers numbered six. Two of them, Mallory and Finch, had been chosen in 1921. Finch, now passed as medically fit, took leave from his post in chemistry at the Imperial College of Science and Technology and again applied his mind to the Everest problem.

Major E. F. Norton, already in India, where he served before and after the war, had a high reputation as an officer and a sportsman. Climbing came to him naturally: as a grandson of Mr. Justice Wills, he had stayed in boyhood at the Eagle's Nest, the family chalet near Sixt, and learned in Haute Savoie the skills of the mountaineer and the chamois-hunter. Like Mallory, he was connected with the Powells of Piccard's Rough: his mother's half-brother had married one of Ruth Mallory's aunts. Norton was very tall and erect; methodical, decisive, even-tempered, gracious in manner.

T. H. Somervell, a climber of stockier build and apparently limitless durability, had completed in 1921 a remarkable season in the Alps – nearly thirty peaks, in four different districts. A Kendal man, he had gone from Rugby to Caius College, Cambridge, and thence to University College Hospital for training in surgery. After service as a captain in the R.A.M.C., he had begun to practise in London. He possessed the painter's gift of seeing, the music-lover's gift of hearing, and (as Younghusband said) 'a great and a stout and a warm heart'.

A. W. Wakefield, also from Kendal, had proceeded from Trinity College, Cambridge, to the London Hospital; he had then spent some years as medical officer with the Grenfell mission in Labrador, but returned to England on the outbreak of war. Some ten years older than the other high climbers, he had begun serious mountaineering in 1904; he had climbed with the Abraham brothers in Skye, Wales, and the Lake District. 'He is a gem,' Geoffrey Young assured Mallory. 'In all respects.'

C. G. Crawford had entered the Indian Civil Service in 1914, two years after leaving Cambridge, and during the war had served with a Gurkha regiment in Mesopotamia. He had to his credit seven seasons in the Alps, two in Kashmir, and an expedition to Kangchenjunga with Raeburn. As Strutt testified ten years later, he had 'great powers'.

Attached to the expedition as transport officers were Captain Geoffrey Bruce, of the 6th Gurkhas, a young cousin of the General; and Captain John Morris, of the 3rd Gurkhas. Both had served in the Afghan War of 1919 and in Waziristan; neither had had experience of mountaineering. J. B. Noel, whose address to the R.G.S. in 1919 had stirred Younghusband to action, was appointed photographer and cinematographer.

Beginning in mid-January, the equipment committee (Farrar and Meade) distributed a series of 'Suggestions for Climbing Party'. The first note on Clothing works as a reminder that in 1922 special Himalayan gear did not exist. 'Probably coat and knickers of ordinary climbing weight,' the note reads, 'but the coat made very loose to allow of wearing two or three sweaters and a leather windproof waistcoat coming at least to the fork, are most suitable, linings, if any, to be *all wool*.' Later, a windproof smock and Finch's balloon-cloth coat quilted with eiderdown were made available for inspection at the A.C. Four kinds of footgear were recommended: ski boots ('highly advisable to use as *few nails as possible* to avoid conduction'); unnailed felt boots, with lambskin legs to the knee; high moccasins, ordered from Canada at Wake-field's suggestion; and finneskoes, ordered from Norway on the advice of C. W. Rubenson, who had climbed to 23,900 feet on Kabru in 1907. All footgear would be made to take three pairs of heavy socks. Crampons would be of light duralumin.

Quite the most consequential new move was the decision to provide high climbers with oxygen. Professor Georges Dreyer, F.R.S., the Oxford pathologist who had worked with the R.A.F. during the war, stated his opinion persuasively: 'I do not think you will get up without, but if you do succeed you may not get down again.' A subcommittee (Farrar, Finch, Somervell, and P. J. H. Unna) took up the problem of oxygen equipment; and the Air Ministry and Messrs. Siebe Gorman produced an apparatus consisting of four Swedish steel cylinders, a breathing mask (or pipe mouthpiece, for use in case of claustrophobia), and a Bergans carrying-frame. Loaded with four full cylinders, the apparatus weighed thirty-three pounds; and the four cylinders would supply oxygen to a climber above the North Col for about seven hours. On emptying a cylinder, the climber could discard it and thus lighten this load by five pounds. Ten sets, with extra cylinders, were ordered for the expedition, and one for demonstration.

The decision to try oxygen was practically inevitable, but it created new problems and stirred heated discussion. Would the benefits offset the effort required to carry the load? Would the apparatus stand up under hard use, and what would happen if it failed at high altitude? How could reserve supplies be provided above the North Col, where the oxygen would be used? Given a strong corps of porters, might it be possible to lay a line of caches at high camps and then to send a party of climbers up 6000 feet from the Col in one great rush? Some hold-outs questioned whether the use of oxygen was admissible under any circumstances: would it be in keeping with the spirit of the enterprise, or would it turn the whole effort into something different?

All agreed, of course, that breathing on Everest was formidably difficult. Climbers, flyers, and physiologists working in pressure chambers had quite sufficient evidence that shortage of oxygen forced men to breathe repeatedly at every exertion, cut their will to carry on, and sometimes made them react slowly or behave strangely. Remembering Mallory's own report of breathlessness on the ascent to the North Col, Unna raised the question, 'Where Mallory blows what chance is there for others?' But as a solution of the problem Mallory persistently favoured acclimatisation over oxygenation. At Oxford on January 31st, Sir Walter Raleigh mentioned to him the physiologists' opinion that oxygen would be needed. 'I told Sir Walter,' Mallory recalled, 'that the physiologists might explode themselves in their diabolical chamber, but we would do what we could to explode their damnable heresy. . . .'

Mallory sailed on the *Caledonia* at the beginning of March. Again he kept to himself sometimes, particularly in the very early mornings, when he would ascend from his stuffy cabin and sit alone in the fresh breeze on deck, clad only in shorts and a khaki silk shirt Ruth had given him. He was reading *The Economic Consequences of the Peace* and Virginia Woolf's *Night and Day*, and he felt the need for moments of 'seasoned silence', as he called it.

But this voyage was by no means so lonely as the first, for now several members of the expedition were travelling together – 'a happy, smiling company with plenty of easy conversation.' Somervell and Wakefield turned out for deck tennis; Noel told good yarns of his wanderings in far places; Strutt recounted an incident for which Curzon had tried to get him court-martialled (Mallory concluded that Strutt must be a good man); Finch ran an extremely interesting oxygen class. Mallory disliked the thought of having to breathe through a rubber tube; but after long discussions of oxygen and of the apparatus, which seemed simple enough, he wrote, 'I have very good hopes it will serve us well enough and *without physiological dangers* from a camp at 25,000 feet.'

The party landed at Bombay and endured a hot, dusty journey across India. As they approached Darjeeling by rail-motor from Siliguri, the General himself happened to come down the road by car; he 'made great cheer at seeing us'. Mallory stayed with the Morsheads and rejoiced on hearing that his stalwart friend would be coming again to the mountain. The thirteen Europeans were to be accompanied by a Tibetan interpreter, five Gurkhas of Geoffrey Bruce's regiment, forty Sherpa porters selected by the General from an assemblage of 150, an assortment of cooks and orderlies, and probably a large gang of Tibetans hired en route to assist in the carrying. There would be more than 300 baggage animals and ponies. Quantities of stores had already started on the way to Phari; more than two tons of luggage had come with the passengers on the *Caledonia*. Obviously this expedition was to be run on the grand scale.

For the march to Phari, the expedition divided into groups. Mallory left Darjeeling with the first, under the General, on March 26th. A cold was plaguing him; and repetition within a twelvemonth of the miles through Sikkim, not yet at its green best, seemed rather tedious; but the company continued to be most enjoyable. The General, as leader, was 'absolutely splendid'.

George to Ruth   *Gnatong, 1 April 1922*

Everyone is cheerful and happy, particularly General Bruce, who is making heroic exertions to get rid of his tummy. He walked nearly the whole way up yesterday, a rise of 5500 feet. It was rather exhilarating to feel the high keen air again and to sleep above 12,000 feet; and, except for some cold and a cough lingering about, I feel fit enough. . . .

George to Ruth   *Phari, 7 April 1922*

Norton is one of the best – extraordinarily keen and active and full of interest, and gentle and charming withal. He is to be my stable companion, I understand; and I don't doubt I shall like him in that capacity as well as anyone. But I would have said the same of Somervell or young Bruce, while Morshead is naturally more my friend than anyone – so you may judge how happy I find myself in my companions.

North of Phari, where the groups came together and re-formed, the main body of the expedition took a short route which eliminated two stages on the way to Kampa Dzong, but required longer marches. The first, in cold and snow, went on too long.

George to Ruth   *Kampa Dzong, 12 April 1922*

When at last we halted, late in the afternoon, most of the men were a long way behind, and the few who had arrived up to the time were more or less demoralised. It was as much as we could do [to] get the tents up and provide some shelter for those who had been knocked out by cold and fatigue. An uncomfortable affair, even for the sahibs. . . .

But imagine the animals! Before going to bed, I walked over to have a look at them. The snow was no longer falling, and the moon was breaking through the clouds; and there they were, standing in untidy rows, with the snow lying on their backs, a picture of misery. The mule-men were squatting round me in a circle behind some sort of shelter, but with no tent to cover them, apparently cheerful and contented. A

little later, from the warm snugness of my sleeping bag, I heard the
low jangling of animals' bells and presently saw through the tent-door
another detachment of our transport, some bullocks which had started
late, following another of these amazing figures, who slouched along
in his Tibetan garment hitched up round the waist and red Tibetan
boots, as though he would have been content to go on all night.

After a second long march on April 9th, the party rested for a
day near Tatsang; and Mallory lay out much of the morning, just
not too cold, reading Balzac's *Curé de Tours*. 'I found myself
pondering on the remark, "Chez les gens toujours en présence
l'amour et la haine croissent toujours." I haven't got the words
exactly right, but what a motto to take along with an expedition
like this!' Under heavy doses of talk about oxygen and lab
practices, he feared that he might develop a 'Finch complex'. The
other problems were the low temperatures, the dust, and the
stultifying routine.

George to Ruth   *Tinki Dzong, 18 April 1922*

The journey hither passed happily enough in warmer weather. . . .
Longstaff was unwell yesterday – an internal chill, I suppose. He is
alarmingly frail, but looks better today. I find myself liking Longstaff
very much. He hasn't the physique for the job, and carries it through on
his tremendous spirit. No one is more splendidly full of humour, so
gay and talkative.

The difficulty I have been finding altogether is simply to make enough
of this sort of life. . . . The repetition of aesthetic experiences is not very
stimulating; the march in the sun and the wind in the camp have a
somnolent effect; and one is apt to feel too much of an animal, to take
rather than to give, to accept so much more than one invents.

George to Ruth   *Shekar Dzong, 26 April 1922*

It is happening very much as it happened before. One starts in the
crisp sunny air, generally about 7:30 a.m. or 8:00 at the latest. . . . As
a rule, one walks for a good stretch at the start. Perhaps half a dozen
join up in some sandy spot for tiffin (cheese and biscuits and chocolate)
and later flog our tired animals along the last weary miles into camp.
Our enormous mess tent has usually preceded us and is waiting at the
end of our day's march to provide a welcome shelter when we come
in. . . .

A usual and by now a welcome sound in each new place is Strutt's
voice, cursing Tibet – this march for being more dreary and repulsive
even than the one before, and this village for being more filthy than any
other. Not that Strutt is precisely a grouser; but he likes to ease his
feelings with maledictions and, I hope, feels better for it. . . .

I suppose in the last analysis it is not a time of active interest with me.
I keep sufficiently interested, one way or another, to keep my head above
water; but I function in a sort of undertone. Life seems more of an
endurance and a waiting than an active doing of things that seem worth
while.

Morris recalls that Mallory showed extraordinary absent-minded-
ness in Tibet. He would leave things scattered about on the floor
of his tent, and the Sherpa assigned as his personal servant could
not understand that he wanted them to be kept. 'After the first
few days,' Morris writes, 'we took it in turns to see that none of
his kit was left behind.'[1]

The 'one little adventure on the way' was an attempt with
Somervell to climb Sangkar Ri (20,490 feet), 7000 feet higher
than the camp at Gyangkar Nangpa and at a considerable distance.
Finch and Wakefield decided to come along; and the party walked
up toward the mountain for about five hours, with porters
bearing light tents for the night. At sunset they looked out across
the flat basin to the east:

George to Ruth   *Shekar Dzong, 26 April 1922*

It does seem a big world, seen like that, the same type of country
stretching on almost for ever; and it was wonderfully beautiful at that
moment. We proceeded for nearly two hours in the dark, with the usual
difficulties of keeping the coolies going. The four sahibs shared a
Whymper tent, lying head to tail across it. Unfortunately, a wind
sprang up, and from the wrong direction, towards the door of our tent
and I was sleeping in the door. It was a bitter cold night.

We got off soon after 4:00 a.m. next morning. ... Somervell and
I had a good climb. We followed up a rock ridge and had a great struggle
with a gendarme; but after climbing it, it was so late that we had to
turn back, though only about 500 feet from the summit. We got back
to a col below the climbing very tired and headachy at one o'clock and
to Gyangkar at 4:30. Somervell went very well ... a thoughtful, sensible
person and quite perfectly modest. ...

'We were neither of us well acclimatised at the time,' Somervell
wrote; 'moreover I had had a severe attack of dysentery, and
frequent halts and slow progress were necessary for me. Mallory
could, I think, have got to the top without me, but instead he
chose the safety of a party of two. In his place I should continually
have said to my companion, "Come along now, don't be slow,"
and so on, but Mallory was absolutely patient, and while one

[1] John Morris, *Hired to Kill* (1960), p. 144.

could see his eagerness to get on one could see far more clearly his infinite consideration for his slower companion.'¹

Instead of going on to Tingri, the expedition turned southward from Shekar Dzong, proceeded by the Pang La and the Dzakar Chu to Chobuk, and arrived on April 30th at the Rongbuk monastery. The old Lama of Rongbuk received appreciatively the General's inspired explanation that the Englishmen had come on a sort of pilgrimage. He blessed the porters and uttered a warning: 'The country is a very cold one; only those who come for religious purposes can live here – it is difficult for the others. Moreover the deity of the place is a very terrible one, so please take care of yourselves as much as possible.'²

The plan had been to drive yaks as far as possible up the true right bank of the Rongbuk glacier and to fix the base camp near the outlet of the East Rongbuk, three stages from the North Col. This plan failed, owing to the defection of Tibetans hired en route. The base camp was established just below the foot of the main Rongbuk glacier; and three camps, not two, had to be located on the East Rongbuk. A reconnaissance party (Strutt, Longstaff, Norton, and Morshead) set out on May 4th to find the best line and to choose the three sites. Meanwhile, Mallory and Somervell, in the belief that a long mountain day would do them more good than a slack day in camp, climbed a 21,850-foot peak west of the Rongbuk. Mallory scraped one hand and bruised a big toe; he gratefully accepted a little whisky in his tea after the return to camp. But both men had seemed to be getting acclimatised.

On May 9th Strutt's party came down with a report: Camp I would be at 17,800 feet, three hours from the base camp; Camp II, four hours on, at 19,800 feet; Camp III, four hours from Camp II, on good moraine at 21,000 feet, about an hour from the slopes leading up to the North Col. It would be some days before a party could be trained and supplied for a climb with oxygen from the North Col. The ascent to the Col and the first attempt to go higher therefore had to be undertaken by a party not carrying oxygen. Mallory wrote on May 10th: 'The General's new plan is for Somervell and me to go straight through to No. 3 camp (the one below the North Col) and at once cut steps up to the Col, establish

¹ T. H. Somervell, 'George Leigh Mallory', *Journal of the Fell and Rock Climbing Club*, 6:385–386 (1924).
² The Lama's words, as recorded in his journal, are quoted with thanks to E. O. Shebbeare by W. H. Murray in Appendix I of *The Story of Everest* (1953).

a camp there two days later, and then get as high up the mountain as we can – a tremendous undertaking at this stage.'

Mallory and Somervell, with a band of coolies, left the base camp on the 10th and reached Camp III without difficulty on the 12th. Two coolies and a cook stayed with them; the rest descended to fetch more loads from Camp I.

George to Ruth   *Camp III, 15 May 1922*

Our first object of course was to establish a route to the North Col. This we did with no delay on the 13th. It was an interesting day. The problem was to get up without cutting an immense number of steps in hard ice. All the lower part of last year's route was blue glittering ice; and, besides the fearful labour of making a staircase there, that way would not have been satisfactory for coolies. . . . We chose a route to the left . . . and very fortunately were able to go on snow almost the whole way. It seemed very hard work, with a lot of chipping and kicking of steps. One coolie came with us (the other was sick); we took some ice pegs and 400 feet of rope and fixed two lengths, each of 200 feet, in the worst places. And the coolie carried a Mummery tent, which of course remains *in situ* – the first tent to reach the North Col.

It was about midday when we reached the snow shelves below the edge, all quite sufficiently tired. The wind was blowing up the snow occasionally, though not so badly as last year, and was cold enough. The great broken cubes of ice above us were wonderfully impressive. After a little halt, Somervell and I proceeded to work along the shelf to our left, with the intention of reaching the lowest point of the Col and looking over the other side, just as Bullock, Wheeler, [and] I did last September; and for the same reason we roped together – we were afraid of the wind. We had not gone far before we found our way blocked by a crevasse just too wide to jump. The main edge joining Everest to the North Peak was on the other side of this gap, not more than ten feet wide. However, a way appeared to the left; and we went on in the confidence that in such broken country we should be able to get through. But a few moments later we were up against an obstacle not to be climbed without a ladder, and there was no alternative. Can you imagine how it felt when it dawned upon us that we had come all this way to find in the end a broken link? Of course it was unbelievable. . . .

Anyway, we must make certain now, if we used every minute of daylight; and, with the prospect of a longer job than we had bargained for, we munched a few sweet biscuits and some mint cake on the shelf where we had left the coolie. Immediately above us the ice cliffs were clearly impassable. But there was evidence of some sort of a gap where a steep ice slope came down from the North Peak. We proceeded along the continuation of our shelf in that direction, turned the flank of an ice gendarme, and were able to work up not steep ice but steep snow to the ridge and look out over the westward view.

The whole broken mass of snow ridge between the North Peak and Everest was still to be traversed. . . . In fact, we had to leap two crevasses, just not too wide, in the first fifty yards. But we soon found easy going and reached a minor snow summit. The view to the west was opening out at every step, and here we sat down to look at it. . . . For a time we completely forgot our quest. And then, shortly after going on again, we saw a clear way ahead – so that we can get to Everest by way of the North Col. . . .

The only trouble is the labour of getting up to the pass; and that will seem small a second time, with the steps all prepared. As it was, we were back in camp about 5:30 p.m., each with a bad height-headache and too tired to eat a pukka meal. . . . But isn't it a venture?

By the standards of Mallory and Somervell, there was not much to do at Camp III during the next few days – sleep, eat, and keep the camp in order. Activity ended early in the day: sun down soon after three o'clock in the afternoon, and 15° of frost in the tent by five. For a less congenial pair, this existence at 21,000 feet might have become desperately trying; but Mallory and Somervell managed very well indeed. 'I have *The Spirit of Man*, a volume of Shakespeare, and a pack of cards,' George wrote, 'so there is no real difficulty about passing the time agreeably.' They played picquet, or read aloud to each other, or just talked about poetry or the condition of the world. 'I forget the details of George Mallory's views on most of the many subjects we discussed,' Somervell has said, 'but in general he took always the big and liberal view. . . . He hated anything that savoured of hypocrisy or humbug, but cherished all that is really good and sound.'[1]

The passing days were not quite indistinguishable. On May 14th the two men crossed the wide snow basin to the Rapiu La and looked into the Kama valley and away to the peaks of Sikkim. Makalu stood clear, to the southeast. The monsoon, George thought, was far away. On the 15th Strutt, Norton, Morshead, and Crawford came up to the camp with a large convoy of porters. Strutt was to take charge of the camp; Norton and Morshead were to join Mallory and Somervell for the high climb. Eight porters stayed at the camp; the rest of the convoy, having discharged their loads, went down with Crawford as their escort. On the 16th the climbers returned to the Rapiu La and looked

[1] *After Everest* (2nd ed., 1938), pp. 61–62.

down on 'a sea of clouds boiling up from the southeast' – the weather had unmistakably changed for the worse, and the question of time had become urgent. The camp on the North Col would have to be expanded and stocked without delay.

On the 17th, therefore, the five climbers, with the ten available porters carrying about thirty pounds each, established Camp IV on a terrace close to the North Col. They descended to Camp III and rested on the 18th, intending that Mallory, Somervell, Norton, and Morshead should sleep at Camp IV on the 19th and, climbing without oxygen equipment, make camp the following afternoon at about 25,000 feet – higher than anyone had ever gone before. And then?

George to Ruth   *Camp III, [18] May 1922*

I write to you on the eve of our departure for the highest we can reach, just because I shall feel happier, in case of difficulties, to think that I have sent you a message of love. The difficulties will be such as we know, in all human probability; our endurance and will to go on taking precautions are less known factors. But with such good people as these I feel sure that we shall all be anxious to help each other. . . . Well, it's all on the knees of the gods, and they are bare cold knees. We shan't get to the top; if we reach the shoulder at 27,400, it will be better than anyone here expects.

Dearest one, you must know that the spur to do my best is you and you again. In moments of depression or lack of confidence or overwhelming fatigue, I want more than anything to prove worthy of you. All my love to you. Many kisses to Clare and Beridge and John.

The attempt began on May 19th, a fine and sunny day. Mallory, Somervell, Norton, and Morshead, with nine porters, started at 8:45 a.m. and in four hours reached Camp IV. Mallory and Norton put up five tents for the party, while Somervell and Morshead fixed a rope to secure the route between the terrace and the North Col itself. Mallory's dispatch to *The Times* gives the earliest account of the ensuing three days:

Domestic activities occupied the afternoon; and, when the sun left us at 4:30 p.m., we turned in for the night, all well fed and comfortable enough and proud in the possession of six thermos flasks filled with water for the morning meal. Our prospects seemed extraordinarily promising. It was our intention to carry on next morning only four loads: two of the smallest tents, two double sleeping-sacks, food for one and a half days, our cooking pots, and two thermos flasks. For this purpose, we had nine coolies, now well housed by threes in Mummery tents, so that we should have two coolies for each load and even so a margin of one. Everything had been managed so happily and satisfactorily that one could hardly doubt these men would be able to establish our camp a great deal higher up the mountain next day.

At 5:00 a.m. on the 20th Mallory got up and tried to rouse the party for a prompt start. The porters showed no sign of life; they had sealed themselves in their tents by tying the flaps, and all nine were suffering from mountain-sickness. They felt better on emerging from the tents, but only five were fit enough to climb. Another contretemps delayed breakfast. It was no problem to make tea with water from the thermos flasks; but two tins of spaghetti, 'instead of being gently nursed during the night against the warmer parts of the human body, had been left in the cold snow.' Thawing them took time.

We had hoped that in the two hours from 6:00 a.m. to 8:00 a.m. before the sun has power and mountain lassitude makes itself felt, we should gain 1500 feet above the North Col, and that afterwards, proceeding slowly and halting often, we might reach a height of 26,000 feet. In the event we started an hour late, at 7:00 a.m., and quickly made our way to the North Col. From here a broad ridge of snow ascends at a gentle but increasing angle. It was clear that, sooner or later, steps would have to be chipped in its hard surface. We were able to avoid this labour at first by following an edge of stones on the west side. Major Morshead, who, if good cheer can be taken as a sign of fitness, seemed the strongest of the party, went first; and we proceeded at a satisfactory pace. It was a fine early morning. Perhaps after all we should camp at 26,000.

Presently we became aware that it was not a perfect day: the sun had no real warmth, and a cold breeze sprang up from the west. I found myself kicking my toes against the rocks whenever we paused, and finally put on my spare warm clothes, a Shetland woollie and a silk shirt. The coolies were evidently feeling the cold as we went higher. Our edge of stones ended abruptly; and it became clear that, if we were to establish our camp, we must race for shelter to the east side of the ridge. It is always hard work cutting steps at high altitudes. The proper way with hard snow is to give one blow with the axe and then stamp the foot into the hole that has been made. But the blow requires a man's full strength, and he must kick hard into the hole. In the Himalaya an amateur will probably prefer to make three chips of a feebler sort. In any case, 300 feet of such work, particularly if it is hurried, is extremely exhausting. We were glad to rest in shelter at last, about midday, under the lee of some rocks at about 25,000 feet.

There was no question of camping much higher. The important

matter was to send the coolies down before they were frostbitten, and before the weather changed for the worse. Under other conditions it would have been necessary for some of us to accompany them on their descent; at present we could safely send them alone. There was no visible camping place where we were. We traversed round on the sheltered side, vaguely hoping that one would appear. Eventually the coolies, with Somervell, professed to have found the right place. On the steep mountainside they proceeded to build a wall and so eventually construct a comparatively flat place for one Mummery tent. Norton and I, in feeble imitation of their efforts, proceeded to select another place; but somehow our walls wouldn't work. One site after another was a failure, until eventually we found a steep slab which at all events was a secure piece of ground, and here ultimately pitched our tent in such a way that the slab was half our floor.

No more uncomfortable arrangement could have been devised, for the inevitable result must be to push one man down upon the other as they lay, and squeeze them tight together, so as to increase to agony the pain of sharp rocks forming the other parts of the floor. There, at all events, were the two little tents, perched fifty yards apart in some sort of fashion for security on the rocks, containing each a double sleeping-sack for a night's warmth in that cold place, and soon to contain the hopes of a day's mountaineering unlike all others from the mere fact that we should start from a point on the earth's surface higher than any reached before.

Perhaps none of us yet realised how much we had suffered already from cold. Norton had an ear three times the normal size, which soon proved a considerable inconvenience when we came to share a sleeping-sack. Three of my fingers were touched by frost. Luckily, the effects of frostbite are not very serious in their early stages. Far more serious was Morshead's condition. Too late in the day he had put on a sledging suit to protect him against the wind. He arrived in camp in a chilled condition and was evidently unwell. A further disaster had been the loss of Norton's rucksack, which slipped from his knee during a halt and must now lie somewhere near the head of the Rongbuk glacier. It contained some warm things for the night; however, we still had enough among us.

Mallory had an uncomfortable night and thought at times of Mr. Salteena, in *The Young Visiters*, 'rolling over in his costly bed'. He felt anxious about the weather. Mercifully, the west wind had dropped; but the stars, though visible, were never clear. Snow fell before dawn, and a fine hail soon after. Thick clouds gathered to the east.

About 6:30 a.m., with rather better signs, we extricated ourselves

19. Mallory and Norton approaching 26,800 feet

20. The Way on to the Summit, 21 May 1922

from our sleeping-sacks and set about the business of preparing a meal. Only one thermos had turned up the night before, so the preparations were both cold and long. Another ill-fated rucksack containing provisions slipped from its perch and by some miracle, after bounding down a hundred feet or more, stopped on a little ledge. Morshead, with heroic exertions, recovered it.

At about 8:00 a.m. the party was ready to start. There had been no discussion as to whether under these circumstances we ought to go on. The snow that had fallen would obviously be an impediment, and more might be expected to fall. But it was a monsoon type of weather; and this sort, with all its advantages to the mountaineer, does not as a rule mean mischief. At high altitudes the snow falls finely and is never driven hard by the wind. So far as getting up was concerned, therefore, we had little fear on this count. None of us, I suppose, after a long, headachy night, felt at his best. For my part, I hoped that the mere effort of deep breathing in the first few steps of the ascent would string me up to the required efforts, and that we should all be better once we started. It was a disappointment at the very moment of setting out to hear bad news from Morshead. 'I think I won't come with you,' he said. 'I am quite sure I shall only keep you back.' About such a question only one man can be judge. The three of us therefore went on without him.

The details of our climbing during the next few hours are not such as merit exact description. The conditions, of course, were unfavourable. Fresh snow covered the ledges, concealed loose stones, and was everywhere an obstruction; but the general nature of the ground was not difficult. . . . We stepped up from ledge to ledge, and the ledges were uniformly tilted to our disadvantage. Plainly, the rock was stratified and sedimentary and, from all we could see, must have the same general nature up to the summit itself, varied only by recognisable bands of lighter quartzite. It was a disappointment that the angle was not sufficiently steep to require a more strenuous use of the arms, for the arms help one up and seem to relieve the monotony of the balanced footwork.

It was a matter of slowly pushing up, first regaining our ridge by slanting to the west and then up the ridge itself directly towards the great tower which caps the northeast shoulder; and ultimately our power to push up depended on the capacity of our lungs. Lungs governed our speed and made our pace a miserable crawl, from the point of view of an Alpine climber; and lungs made us pause to admire the view a great deal more often than is correct in the best circles. But our lungs were remarkably alike; we went well together. Personally, I contrived some looseness of the muscles which made it easier to draw a deep breath.

We had for a long time good hopes of reaching the northeast

shoulder; but the long descent had to be borne in mind, and the retard-
ing circumstance of fresh snow. It was agreed that we should turn back
not much later than two o'clock. At 2:15 we reached, as it were, a head
of rocks still 600 or 700 feet below the northeast ridge of the mountain
and commanding a clear view from here to the summit. The pace of
the party had become extremely slow. There was obvious risk in going
much farther; and, greatly as we desired to gain the shoulder (there is
no doubt we were physically capable of getting there), the only
wisdom was now in retreat. The aneroid registered 26,800 feet.

We turned to go down with sufficient strength, we believed, for the
long task before us. Away to the west the ground appeared less rocky
and more snow-covered. It was an obvious plan to make use of the
snow slopes hereabouts for our descent. We were very quickly dis-
illusioned. The snow slopes turned out to be a series of slabs lying
treacherously under their fresh white mask. We were obliged to get
back to our ridge and follow down the tracks of our ascent. About
4:00 p.m. Morshead welcomed us back to our camp of the previous
night (25,000 feet approx.). Gathering up our few belongings, while
leaving the tents and sleeping-sacks, etc., we proceeded to traverse
back along the ledge which we had followed the previous day. It was
difficult to realise that the fresh snow had made of this a dangerous
passage. A nasty slip occurred, and three men were held by a rope
belayed over the head of an ice-axe.[1]

The party proceeded with great caution after this incident, and it soon
became evident that we should be racing against darkness. When we
regained the great snow ridge, no trace of our upward steps appeared.
The cutting of steps had now to be repeated; and the grim, slow
process was observed about 6:00 p.m. by Strutt below in Camp III.
Nor were our difficulties ended after this passage.... Morshead,
though he had been climbing in the pluckiest fashion, with tremendous
efforts of breathing, had now come to the end of his tether. At best,
he could proceed but a few steps at a time. Fortunately, it was easy going
all the way down to the North Col as we watched the diminishing light.
Norton supported Morshead on his shoulder while I found the easiest
way down and Somervell brought up the rear. Sinister grey clouds
away to the west, and some flickering lightning, after the sun had set
over one of the most amazing of mountain views, seemed full of malice.
What sort of a wind should we find on the Col after dark, when our
difficulties were due to begin again?

By good fortune or good providence, when the moment arrived and
the dimly starlit crevasses confronted us, Somervell produced a lantern
from his rucksack; and so calm was the air that even a Japanese match,
after a dozen trials or so, was found to light the candle. We groped a

[1] See p. 196, below.

little to find our way, but no one had fallen through the surface before we reached the edge of a little cliff. Here it was necessary to jump about twelve feet down into the snow – a sufficiently alarming prospect at that hour. But the leap was safely accomplished. One fixed rope, if we could find it, would take us down to our terrace – the terrace where we had seen our five tents still neatly pitched in a row, awaiting our arrival. The rope was buried in snow, and the last of our candle burnt out. We groped for some time along the edge of the precipice and then began to go down at a steep slope, in some doubt as to whether this were the way. Suddenly someone hooked up the rope from under the snow. We knew then that we could reach our tents.

Ten minutes later a cry was raised in the camp that the most essential thing of all was missing. The porters had gone down to Camp III the previous day; apparently they had taken with them our cooking pots – and so the drink that we had yearned for all the long day was to be denied us at this late hour. It was now 11:30 p.m., and we were all ready for bed, but one act suggested itself to the fertile imagination of Norton. He opened a tin of jam and a tin of milk, and mixed these in a mug with snow. I followed his example. The result he thought delicious; to me it seemed disgusting, but at least it could be swallowed. ... Were anyone's toes frostbitten? It would be little short of a miracle had they escaped. But a kind fate had calmed the air, and it seemed the same kind fate had kept our feet warm. With a little rubbing of them, we turned in to our sleeping-sacks and slept the sleep of tired men.

Snow had covered the tracks and the fixed ropes below Camp IV, and the descent to Camp III on May 22nd demanded still more hard work:

The effort of cutting steps through the snow under a strong sun, four hour's work where we might have expected one, and with thirst still unslaked, was almost unbearable. At the bottom of the slopes we met Finch and G. Bruce, carrying oxygen cylinders on their backs, and Wakefield; they had set out as a relief party as soon as the weather became sufficiently clear. Among them were two thermos flasks of hot tea. They kept none for themselves. But it was not till we got down to a running stream just above Camp III that we drank our fill, and then it was that Morshead said, 'It was thirst that did me in, and nothing else.'

Finch had given instruction in ice craft to Geoffrey Bruce and a Gurkha N.C.O., Lance-Corporal Tejbir, both novices at mountaineering; and these three had come to Camp III as the oxygen party, prepared for a second attempt on the mountain. On May 24th, with twelve porters, they moved up to Camp IV.

Meanwhile, the participants in the first attempt retired to the base camp.

George to Ruth   *Base Camp, 26 May 1922*

The frostbites are nothing to worry about. Of four fingers touched on the right hand, only the third gives trouble. Even that one has no harm below the top joint; and, though I imagine it will be sore for a long time, I think there is no danger of losing any part of it. Poor Morshead is in a very different case – we can't know yet what the damage will be.

I suppose it was stupid or careless of us to be caught like this. It is easy enough to keep one's hands warm with clumsy gloves so long as one is doing nothing in particular with them. But you may imagine what happened: as soon as it came to cutting, I took the lead over from Morshead and went all out to get the job done as quickly as possible, for fear the coolies would be done in by the cold and refuse to come on; and then of course I thought no more about my fingers. . . .

It was a big strain altogether. Personally, I wrecked myself with that cutting and, when we were pitching tents, had hardly the strength to lift a stone; and the trouble is that one doesn't recover. The night at 25,000 was miserable, and I didn't expect to go on. Somervell was really our reserve man all through and was particularly useful in cooking at the high camp. Norton went first on the final day, chiefly because I judged he would go his best in that place; he was very nearly done at the end and was climbing very slowly. But we could all have gone farther; we turned to allow time for the descent, and we allowed none too much. On a fine morning we should have started two hours earlier and reached the northeast shoulder.

Coming down, I led all the way, except where we had to cut steps. Norton and I shared the cutting, as I judged I should be quicker than the others. I felt pretty strong on the descent. The slip was nearly a bad business. I hadn't realised then how shaky Morshead was and had cut rather poor steps; but there was good holding for the pick. Norton and Somervell must have been caught napping. I hadn't the rope belayed round my axe, as I was on the point of cutting a step, but, hearing something wrong behind, drove in my pick and belayed and was ready in plenty of time when the strain came. Morshead must have made a very fine effort coming down the steps of the snow slope, and he appeared to tread quite safely; but the moment we were on easier ground he collapsed. I didn't much like the idea of being out after dark above 23,000 feet, and it was a very trying and anxious time. We were well out of that! . . .

All the rest very pleased with our performance. As a first attack, I feel satisfied with it, too; but the trouble is that three of us appear to be out of it now. . . . I should have liked to make one more try, from a camp at 26,000 feet; and nothing but this finger would prevent my going up again in a few days' time. Perhaps my prevailing thought about the whole adventure is that we were a *perfectly* happy party – not a word of anything but what was friendly and helpful among the five of us (Strutt included) at Camp III. Altogether, anxiety apart, I have tremendously enjoyed it. . . .

We are waiting for news of Finch and G. Bruce, who is with him. I think they will certainly break our record – they have had very good weather – but I don't expect them to have reached the top at the first attempt. All depends upon whether they succeed in dumping cylinders ahead of them. I shan't feel in the least jealous of any success they may have. The whole venture of getting up with oxygen is so different from ours that the two hardly enter into competition.

On May 25th the oxygen party had made camp on the crest of the ridge at about 25,500 feet, and the porters had descended safely. Finch and his two companions endured full twenty-four hours in the camp, immobilised by a violent blizzard. When it blew away, late in the afternoon, porters sent by Noel from Camp IV brought up thermos flasks of hot beef-tea and tea; they had to start down again at once, with darkness coming on. On the 27th, after a second restless night, Tejbir managed to climb only about 500 feet before returning alone to the tent; but Finch and Bruce, carrying forty pounds apiece, reached 27,235 feet, a new record. At that point, Bruce's oxygen apparatus stopped working. Promptly and skilfully, Finch repaired it; and the two descended 6000 feet to Camp III, picking up Tejbir on the way. On May 29th they reached the base camp. Mallory could not understand why they had made a new high camp, instead of moving the old one; and he expressed concern when he heard that unescorted porters had climbed to the high camp late in the day. Unquestionably, however, the second attempt had been, as he said, a very stout effort.

The problem was that these first two attempts had made it nearly impossible to rally fit climbers for a third. Only Somervell had come down to the base camp undamaged and unfatigued. Morshead was suffering great pain; even with two grains of opium, he could not sleep. 'Although outwardly and in company he was always cheerful,' Somervell wrote, 'yet he used to get away by himself as often as he could and cry like a child.'[1] Norton's feet,

[1] *After Everest* (2nd ed., 1938), p. 68.

as well as his ear, had been frostbitten; and his heart had been strained. Mallory's heart, too, misbehaved worryingly, with a 'thrill' more serious than the worst of his nipped fingers. Bruce had frostbitten feet; and Finch, though he might recover in a few days' time, seemed exceedingly tired. For Wakefield and Crawford, slow acclimatisers, the North Col had been set as the limit. Longstaff strongly expressed the opinion that the expedition had done enough and should go home.

But on May 31st Wakefield examined Mallory and declared his heart quite sound: at the risk of no more than a finger, he could go up again. General Bruce, swayed more by the pressing instructions of the Mount Everest Committee than by his own misgivings and the protests of Strutt and Longstaff, assented to the planning of a third attempt. Three climbers would participate – Mallory, Somervell, and Finch. More than a dozen porters were still fit for high carrying. Wakefield and Crawford would provide support.

George to Ruth   *1 June 1922*

No doubt you will have mixed feelings about another venture, but you will feel chiefly as I do that it would have been unbearable for me to be left out. . . . The finger is far from well, and I risk getting a worse frostbite by going up again, but the game is worth a finger, and I shall take every conceivable care. . . . The weather gets steadily more unpromising and as likely as not will settle our affair. It seems much windier than last year. I fear getting caught on that ridge in a bad gale. . . . Finch seems to have an altogether different standard of caring for the coolies from mine. I'm determined we will run no risks with their lives during this next venture. . . .

I have escaped from the camp to write this letter. Somehow these past three or four days it has seemed to be a less serene, rather a discontented place. Poor Morshead suffers from his fingers constantly . . . and bears it wonderfully well, but he is not a cheerful figure. Norton is even more depressed. Strutt is more than usually full of curses. Crawford and Wakefield, who were last down from the mountain, are not very pleased with the prospect of going up again so soon. Longstaff is still far from well, with indigestion and sleeplessness, and at present is in one of his moods of bustling activity, when he becomes tiresome, interfering, and self-important. The General, who has been tied to the camp almost the whole time by a sore foot, shows a better temper than anyone. . . .

I shall think of you very often at the higher camps, and the thought of you will be present in the most important decisions. Dear love, believe that I will never forget the beautiful way you have behaved about this adventure.

G.M. to David Pye   *1 June 1922*

The mountain has taken his toll among us; but lord, how much worse it might have been! No coolies frostbitten, to speak of – almost a miracle when one considers that a party were sent up from the North Col at 4:00 p.m. to Finch's high camp and got in again at 11:00 p.m.!

David, it's an infernal mountain, cold and treacherous. Frankly, the game is not good enough: the risks of getting caught are too great; the margin of strength when men are at great heights is too small. Perhaps it's mere folly to go up again. But how can I be out of the hunt? And then, given the right weather, there's quite a good chance of reaching the top, at all events with oxygen. We've learnt something, too; and I have good hopes of preserving toes and fingers, though almost infinite care is required. . . .

It was a pretty killing affair. Norton as well as Morshead is clean out of it now; Morshead will lose a toe besides six fingertips. Poor man, I'm awfully sorry about it; but he won't be incapacitated in any way. It sounds more like war than sport – and perhaps it is.

G.M. to his sister Avie   *2 June 1922*

People talk about hard and easy lives, but I think it is largely a matter of temperament. Conscience and a sense of duty are hard masters. Perhaps one ought to be just a little happy-go-lucky, in order to have the whip hand of circumstance and the better to perform the social obligation of spreading gaiety. . . .

I have it in mind for the future that I should rather like a job as lecturer in English literature at a provincial university in some live place. I wonder if Harry knows any of the staff at Manchester. Probably not, but if he does he might mention my name. I could be ready for next term, but of course it's fifty to one against there being a vacancy.

– Precisely the odds, as Mallory and Bullock had agreed in 1921, against a given party on Everest in a given year.

The 1922 expedition ended in disaster. Blaming himself and sorely oppressed, Mallory described for Ruth and for his closest mountaineering friends the avalanche in which seven porters lost their lives:

George to Ruth   *Base Camp, 9 June 1922*

I will answer what I imagine to have been your first thought: it *was* a wonderful escape for me, and we may indeed be thankful for that together. . . . It's difficult to get it all straight in my mind. The consequences of my mistake are so terrible; it seems almost impossible to believe that it has happened for ever and that I can do nothing to make good. There is no obligation I have so much wanted to honour as that of taking care of these men. They are children where mountain dangers are concerned, and they do so much for us; and now through my fault seven of them have been killed. . . .

When we started from the base camp on June 3rd, the clouds were thickening, and it was evident that very soon the monsoon would be upon us. . . . I walked up half despondently with Finch to No. I Camp. He was clearly quite unfit and could barely reach the camp. Next morning he went back to the base, leaving Somervell and me for the high climbing, with Wakefield and Crawford to back us up.

During the night of the 3rd snow fell heavily and continued on the 4th. We spent a cold day in the poor shelter at Camp I, a little hut with walls about three feet six inches high, built of the stones that lay about there and roofed with the outer fly of a Whymper tent. The white snow dust blew in through the chinks; and one wondered naturally, 'Isn't it mere foolishness to be attempting Everest now that the snow has come?' It was clear that, if we were to give up the attempt at once, no one would have a word to say against our decision. But it seemed to me too early to turn back, and too easy – we should not be satisfied afterwards. It would not be unreasonable to expect a spell of fair weather after the first snow. . . . And if we were to fail, how much better, I thought, to be turned back by a definite danger or difficulty on the mountain itself.

On the 5th, with too much cloud still hanging about the glacier, we went up in one long march to Camp III – a wet walk in the melting snow and with some snow falling. At the camp not less than a foot of snow covered everything. The tents, which had been struck but not packed up, contained a mixture of ice, snow, and water. . . . There was no question of doing anything on the 6th. The best we asked for was a warm day's rest. We had a clear day of brilliant sunshine, the warmest by far that any of us remembered at Camp III. The snow solidified with amazing rapidity; the rocks began to appear about our camp; and, though the side of Everest facing us looked cold and white, we had the satisfaction of observing during the greater part of the day a cloud of snow blown from the North Ridge. It would not be long at that rate before it was fit to climb.

The heavy snow of the 4th and 5th affected our plans in two ways. As we should have to expect heavier work high up, we should have hardly a chance of reaching the top without oxygen; and, in spite of Finch's absence with his expert knowledge, we decided to carry up ten cylinders with the two apparatus[es] used by Finch and G. Bruce to our old camp, established on the first attempt, at 25,000 feet. So far we should go without oxygen. . . . Our chief anxiety was to provide for the safety of the porters. We hoped the conditions might be good enough to send them down by themselves to the North Col; and it was arranged that Crawford should meet them at the foot of the ridge, to conduct them properly roped over the crevasses to Camp IV. There they would remain until we came back from the higher camp, and all would go down together.... With these plans we thought we might move up from Camp IV on the fourth day of fine weather, should the weather hold, and still bring down the party safely, whatever the monsoon might do. A change of weather was to be feared, sooner or later; but we were confident we could descend the north ridge from our high camp in bad weather, if necessary; and three of us (or, if Wakefield came up, four) would then be available to shepherd the coolies down from the North Col.

But the North Col had first to be reached. With the new snow to contend with, we should have hard work; perhaps it would take us more than one day. The steep final slope might be dangerous; we should perhaps find it prudent to leave our loads below it and come up easily enough in our frozen tracks another day.

We set out from Camp III, Somervell, Crawford, and I, with fourteen porters, at 8:00 a.m. on the 7th. A party including four of the strongest porters was selected to lead the way over the glacier. They did splendid work trudging the snow with loads on their backs; but it took us two hours to the foot of the great snow wall; and it was 10:15 a.m. when Somervell, I, one porter, and Crawford, roped in that order, began the ascent. We found no trace at first of our previous tracks and were soon crossing a steep ice slope covered with snow. It was remarkable that the snow adhered so well to this slope, where we had found bare ice, that we were able to get up without cutting steps. In this harmless place we had tested the snow and were more than satisfied.

Higher up, the angle eases off; and we had formerly walked up at comparatively gentle angles in the old snow until it was necessary to cross the final steep slope below Camp IV. Now we had to contend with snow up to our knees. Crawford relieved Somervell, and then I took a turn. About 1:30 p.m. I halted, and the porters following in three parties came up with us. Somervell, who was the least tired among us, now went ahead, continuing in our old line and still on gentle slopes about 200 feet below some blocks of fallen ice which mark the final traverse to the left over steeper ground.

I was following up in the steps, last on our rope of four, when at 1:50 I heard a noise not unlike an explosion of untamped gunpowder. I had never before been near an avalanche of snow, but I knew the meaning of that noise as though I were accustomed to hear it every day. In a moment I observed the snow's surface broken only a few yards away to the right and instinctively moved in that direction. And then I was moving downward.

Somehow I managed to turn out from the slope so as to avoid being

George cMallory

pushed headlong and backwards down it. For the briefest moment my chances seemed good, as I went quietly sliding down with the snow. Then the rope at my waist tightened and held me back. A wave of snow came over me. I supposed that the matter was settled. However, I thrust out my arms to keep them above the snow and at the same time tried to raise my back, with the result that, when after a few seconds the motion stopped, I felt little pressure from the snow and found myself on the surface.

The rope was still tight about my waist, and I imagined that the porter tied on next me must be deeply buried; but he quickly emerged near me, no worse off than myself. Somervell and Crawford, too, were quite close to me and soon extricated themselves. Apparently their experiences were much the same as mine. And where were the porters? we asked. Looking down over the broken snow, we saw one group some distance below us. Presumably the rest must be buried somewhere between us and them. No sign of them appeared, and those we saw turned out to be the group who had been immediately behind us. Somehow they must have been caught in a more rapid stream and carried down a hundred feet further than us. They pointed below them: the others were down there.

It became only too plain as we hurried down that the men we saw were standing only a little way above a formidable drop. The others had been carried over. We found the ice cliff to be from forty to sixty feet high. The crevasse below it was filled up with the avalanche snow, and there [were] signs enough to show us that the two missing parties of four and five were buried under it. From the first we entertained little hope of saving them. The fall alone must have killed the majority, and such proved to be the case as we dug out the bodies. Two men were rescued alive and were subsequently found to have sustained no severe injuries. The remaining seven lost their lives.

There is the narrative – the bare facts. . . . You may read between the lines how anxious I was about this venture. S. and I knew enough about Mount Everest not to treat so formidable a mountain contemptuously. But it was not a desperate game, I thought, with the plans we made. Perhaps with the habit of dealing with certain kinds of danger one becomes accustomed to measuring some that are best left unmeasured and untried. But in the end I come back to my ignorance: one generalises from too few observations, and what a lifetime it requires to know *all* about it! I suppose if we had known a little more about conditions of snow here we should not have tried these slopes – and, not knowing, we supposed too much from the only experience we had. The three of us were deceived; there wasn't an inkling of danger among us.

G.M. to Sir Francis Younghusband 　　　　　　　　*11 June 1922*

I'm very much to blame for this terrible accident, and I'm very sorry.

202

I want you to believe that it was not the result of any spirit of reckless-ness or any carelessness of coolies' lives.

If I had known more about snow conditions here, the accident would not have happened, and so one may say that it was due to ignorance. . . . I am particularly sorry for the loss of these men. They had done remarkably well.

The seven victims were left buried in the snow, as their comrades wished; and the expedition withdrew from the mountain. One group (Strutt, Longstaff, Finch, and Morshead) had already left for Darjeeling; Norton and Geoffrey Bruce had gone over to Kharta. By mid-June the others had finished their work at the Rongbuk base and likewise set out for Kharta, to rest for a while below the tree line. They spent the last days of the month in the Kama valley, camped at Sakyeteng on a little knoll beside a mountain torrent, with juniper forests around them and beds of irises in the clearings.

Somervell and Crawford planned to spend a fortnight climbing in the upper Lhonak valley of Sikkim. Mallory made the journey with them, by way of Kampa Dzong and the Nago La, and then went on alone, southward through Sikkim, to Darjeeling. He sailed for home on August 5th, burdened by thoughts of the accident.

General Bruce to A. R. Hinks   *4 July 1922*

I am very sorry for Mallory, as he genuinely took great interest in all the porters and was generally very upset.

E. L. Strutt to G.M.   *2 August 1922*

I am awfully sorry for you, and I know well how much you are feeling this disaster. You ask me for comments – well, I will not criticise from a distance. When Longstaff, Finch, and I read Charlie's account in the paper, going up to London from Dover, I remarked, 'We never saw an avalanche on the mountain, and Mallory therefore concluded that the snow evaporated instead of sliding.'. . .

I will add, if you will allow me, that after the great fall of fresh snow, seventeen persons on the North Col was fifteen too many, even after *two* days' perfect weather. Don't think that these are criticisms; the man on the spot must be the sole judge, and he gets the reward or pays the penalty. I am only too thankful that only a partial punishment was exacted.

As to the British Public, the middle classes, shop-keepers, gillies, etc., who alone show a real interest in the expedition, these rather welcome the accident (dead bodies always appeal to them) and think us real 'eroes in consequence. . . . I suppose you will all be coming home soon, when I much hope to see you.

T. G. Longstaff to A. F. R. Wollaston   *19 August 1922*

The reason that meeting was edgy was because we all three felt that 'the Committee' . . . had consistently treated Bruce meanly: had not appreciated his difficulties: had quite unnecessarily and most ungenerously urged him to repeated attacks on the peak and hence had landed us in an accident which made us all feel horribly humiliated. . . . To attempt such a passage in the Himalaya after new snow is idiotic. What the hell did they think they could do *on Everest* in such conditions, even if they did get up to the North Col?

Geoffrey Winthrop Young to G.M.   *18 August 1922*

Put *entirely* out of your mind that anyone has ever thought of placing any responsibility for the accident on you or the mountaineers. . . . You see, we *knew*; we were impressed throughout by the enormous percentage of 'chance' in such climbing. If in the Alps we admitted it existed, in such an attempt it loomed indefinably great. There was no surprise when at last it took this form – only, I think, a great relief that it spared our friends. . . . Remember that to us, at a distance, you were all equally under that shadow of huge, dangerous 'chance'. Only to you, in contact with the real forms it took, was it possible to distinguish between degrees of responsibility, between what was evitable or inevitable in its threat. Hence, to no one but yourself would it ever occur for an instant to attempt to assign responsibility, even to question any particular decision. . . .

As for your own view of your own responsibility. There is nothing more terrible than the actual contact with these mountain deaths. . . . I remember saying, in agony, to his mother, after Donald's death, 'How you must hate us all!' – and realising that she did not even understand me.[1] The nearness of a great shock or grief *distorts*; it distorts even our own sense of our part in it. The proud man's instinct is to dispute that chance could have produced all those grim effects; the very magnitude of the pain he suffers forces him to bite on the aching tooth, to blame himself with a larger share in the responsibility for it than is rightly his to claim. . . .

In this case I have no doubt. You made all the allowance for the safety of your party that your experience suggested. . . . The immense percentage of 'chance', or we may call it of the 'unknown', present still in this hitherto unattempted region of mountaineering, turned for once against you. Well? What then? You took your full share, a leading share, in the risk. In the war we had to do worse: we had to *order* men into danger at times when we could not share it. And surely we learned

[1] See p. 62, above.

then that to take on ourselves afterwards the responsibility for their deaths, to debate with ourselves the 'might-have-beens', was the road to madness. . . .

It has been a great and very gallant attempt, and has accomplished far more than I for one ever expected.

Sir Francis Younghusband to G.M.   *23 August 1922*

However much you may blame yourself, I certainly am not one to blame you, for I have done precisely the same thing myself in the Himalaya, and only the purest luck can have saved me and my party from disaster. . . . But anyhow we do recognise that you performed a magnificent feat in beating all previous records by such a big amount as 2200 feet – and that in itself made the expedition worthwhile.

Some months later, as Mallory sat composing his chapters for the 1922 expedition book, he concluded that even a good A.C. man like himself might sometimes wobble in his sympathy for attempts on Everest, 'for half the charm of climbing mountains is born in visions preceding this experience – visions of what is mysterious, remote, inaccessible': [1]

It is true that I did what I could to reach the summit, but now as I look back and see all those wonderful preparations, the great array of boxes collected at Phari Dzong and filling up the courtyard of the bungalow, the train of animals and coolies carrying our baggage across Tibet, the thirteen selected Europeans so snugly wrapt in their woollen waistcoats and Jaeger pants, their armour of wind-proof materials, their splendid overcoats, the furred finneskoes or felt-sided boots or fleece-lined moccasins devised to keep warm their feet, and the sixty strong porters with them delighting in underwear from England and leathern jerkins and puttees from Kashmir; and then, unforgettable scene, the scatter of our stores at the Base Camp, the innumerable neatly-made wooden boxes concealing the rows and rows of tins – of Harris's sausages, Hunter's hams, Heinz's spaghetti, herrings soi-disant fresh, sardines, sliced bacon, peas, beans, and a whole forgotten host besides, sauce-bottles for the mess tables, and the rare bottles more precious than these, the gay tins of sweet biscuits, Ginger Nuts and Rich Mixed, and all the carefully chosen delicacies; and besides all these for our sustenance or pleasure, the fuel supply, uncovered in the centre of the camp, green and blue two-gallon cans of paraffin and petrol, and an impressive heap of yak-dung; and the climbing equipment – the gay little tents with crimson flies or yellow, pitched here only to be seen and admired, the bundles of soft sleeping-bags, soft as eiderdown quilt can be, the ferocious crampons and other devices, steel-pointed and

[1] *The Assault on Mount Everest, 1922* (1923), pp. 123–124.

terrible, for boots' armament, the business-like coils of rope, the little army of steel cylinders containing oxygen under high pressure, and, not least, the war-like sets of apparatus for using the life-giving gas; and lastly, when I call to mind the whole begoggled crowd moving with slow determination over the snow and up the mountain slopes and with such remarkable persistence bearing up the formidable loads, when after the lapse of months I envisage the whole prodigious evidences of this vast intention, how can I help rejoicing in the yet undimmed splendour, the undiminished glory, the unconquered supremacy of Mount Everest?

CHAPTER 9

America and Cambridge, 1923

For six weeks after his return home in August 1922, Mallory
managed to keep free of public engagements. Then he was
caught up once more in the business of Everest. The joint
meeting of the A.C. and the R.G.S. came on October 16th, and
the first public lecture in London on October 20th. These
occasioned a little flare-up over oxygen. Mallory had included in
the draft of his lecture some unmistakably adverse remarks;
indiscretions, as he said, would bubble out. Finch thought it
'very naughty of George'; and Farrar, on reading the manuscript,
urged restraint.

Mallory spent a great deal of time away from home that winter.
Needing the money, he undertook a heavy burden of lecture
engagements and kept on the move from mid-October to mid-
December – up to Aberdeen, down to Brighton and Torquay,
across to Dublin, and so on: schools, geographical societies,
climbing groups. In January he sailed on the *Olympic* for a three-
month tour in America.

His first impressions of New York were unhappy. On landing,
he was chilled by 20° of frost and a wind that made him think of
Tibet; he was met by the lecture manager, informed that few
engagements had materialised, carried off to the tenth floor of
the Waldorf-Astoria, rehearsed in what he should say for the press,
and interviewed by four newspaper reporters and a young press
agent for the hotel:

George to Ruth　　　　　　　　　　　　　*New York, 19 January 1923*
The young man wanted me to say that the great mountaineers of
the expedition were all men of scientific training, or that mental training had more to do with the matter than physique. Can you imagine
anything more childish? But I expect that is just what Americans are –
boyish.

New York itself often gives the impression of a splendid gesture
against a background of emptiness. Each individual skyscraper is

making its own gesture, rather than being part of a whole street; and, as you see their immense silhouettes against the sky, they are all playing a part in a grotesque world of toy giants. . . . At night the streets are amazing and I think wonderfully gay and jolly – again in a quite unreal world. . . .

Mallory enjoyed seeing a cousin in New York, and he had been given guest privileges at two clubs; but for more than a week, working on his lecture and on his chapters for the 1922 Everest book, he was much alone. His initial distaste for New York never quite left him.

He faced his first American audiences in Washington, where he lectured twice, afternoon and evening, on January 26th. Towards midnight, in bed, he wrote:

George to Ruth   *Washington, 26 January 1923*

I've been busy, busy, busy ever since I wrote, firstly finishing my chapters . . . and then with the lecture, much more work than you would suppose, cutting out one scrap and another, making a new beginning and a new end, incorporating Somervell's slides and about ten showing the reconnaissance, and, most important of all, winnowing it all over to get the expression better for an American audience.

And in the end this afternoon they were the most unresponsive crowd I ever talked to – never a clap when I meant them to applaud and almost never a laugh. They weren't comfortable with me. I don't know why. But they *were* held, just. And afterwards much handshaking and kind words, as though it had been a *grand succès*. I believe they were just like the Torquay audience, only kinder.

And this evening it came right off, from the first word to the last. I did what I liked with them; they took all my points; it was technically better than any lecture I've ever given, either year, and had any amount of spontaneity, too. There: if it doesn't 'take' now – well, I can do no more. . . .

For a while, prospects for the tour improved. Philadelphia entertained Mallory very hospitably and turned out in crowds to hear him, a thousand for one lecture and more than two thousand for another – 'I had barely a moment to myself, but the people were pleasant and I enjoyed it'. Even New York seemed less intolerable when he returned. He dined with his cousin and her husband, the Wathens; dropped in at the University Club to read the weekly *Guardian* and browse among new books; went to see *Hamlet* and found a Marlowe Society friend, Reginald Pole, playing the Ghost; and read Boswell's letters to Temple, in manuscript, at the Morgan Library. The Librarian, Belle Dacosta Greene, took him to an amusing luncheon party – 'the richest little crowd I've been in, and the food was good!' Four doctors gave him lunch at a pleasant club and then bore him off to the Presbyterian Hospital, where they concluded, after a thorough examination, that he had twice the normal lung capacity.

On January 31st about forty members of the American Alpine Club gathered for dinner at the Hotel Pennsylvania. Mallory sat between the Reverend Harry Pierce Nichols, who was then President, and a lady 'who had climbed a peak in Alaska and endured a temperature of – 60°!!' The occasion seemed to call for a serious talk on Everest problems. 'There was not much fun or fizz in it,' Mallory reported, 'but it went well enough. After that, we sat on round the table while I was bombarded with questions. Altogether a very pleasant, homely party.' At the end, however, having had nothing but water to drink, Mallory felt very dry. A new friend, Henry Schwab, proposed a visit to his club and there conjured up, for George and another guest, the makings of Tom Collinses that kept the three men talking until after one o'clock.

A public lecture in New York had been scheduled for Sunday, February 4th, at the Broadhurst Theatre in West Forty-fourth Street. If the New York audience responded well, and the New York papers came out with good notices, there might be more engagements in other cities. The evening began badly, with the theatre only half full and an incompetent operator running the slides:

George to Ruth   *9 February 1923*

However, I had friends in the audience, amongst them *all* the members of the American Alpine Club who had been present at the dinner they gave me, so I didn't worry. I got them all right at the start; and they proved quite a pleasant, appreciative audience. They really went away *fizzing*, and I had reports of nice things said as they were going out. . . . Afterwards, the Wathens, Mrs. Cobden Sanderson, Friskin (Cissie's musical friend),[1] Pole, and an actress friend of his came on to a hotel near by and ate ices. . . . I must tell you that Pole, who has a highly critical knowledge of the stage, said he hadn't a single hint to give me and he didn't see how it could be better. . . .

But the whole importance of this lecture was to have a good press;

[1] James Friskin, pianist and composer, was teaching at the Institute of Musical Art, which became the Juilliard School of Music. Like the Turners, he was a friend of Mrs. Craies and her daughter Cissie.

and, when I read the papers at breakfast, there was almost nothing. The *New York Times* (the most important) had a large heading and one-third of a column, but the whole thing was turned into anti-Prohibition propaganda.

Later in the day, the *Tribune* appeared with praise for Mallory's 'unaffected manner of speech which made him immediately a friend of his audience': 'He described the perils of the climb in simple language, and kept his personal part in the expedition very much in the background.' The second-in-command at the lecture agency sent out for a hundred copies.

The next engagement took Mallory to Montreal, where he enjoyed an unusually good audience and a happy stay with the family of Basil Williams, professor of history at McGill and an old friend of Arthur Clutton Brock. George felt warmed by the thought that Mrs. Williams had been to the Holt and met Ruth; and, when a Toronto lecture fell through, he gladly spent the week end at Ste. Marguerite in the Laurentians, learning to ski under the tutelage of young John Williams. 'I really began to learn something about it,' he wrote to Ruth, 'and had some glorious runs downhill. The clear days of a Canadian winter are very delightful, but it *is* cold.'

Discouraging news awaited him in New York: public interest, according to the lecture agent, had not materialised; the tour simply was not working out. The lecture in New York had lost money; the one in Montreal had made only $48. The agent would neither risk taking a large hall himself nor permit a lowering of the lecturer's fee. Few of the schools and societies Mallory would have liked to visit could afford to pay him $250. After a month in the States, he had just three definite engagements ahead of him; he thought that possibly, with the help of friends, he might pick up as many as half a dozen more. 'It's distressing,' he confessed to Ruth, 'but it can't be helped'.

He moved to a hotel less prestigious than the Waldorf; and for the next ten days, though he diligently attended to correspondence that might help the tour, he occupied himself largely with other interests – his manuscript for the 1922 Everest book, the Boswell letters in the Morgan Library, music at the Metropolitan Opera House and the Aeolian Hall, a week end on Long Island with the Schwabs, an occasional tea, frequent dinner parties. Separation from Ruth seemed harder to bear in New York than in Tibet, and a liverish spell made him feel somewhat less than eager to go about; but he went anyhow, determined to miss no chance for better understanding of the country and the people. 'The difficulty,' he wrote, 'always is to know what set one has to do with.' In the set that dined him, the conspicuous deficiency was in conversational powers: too many women put on a show of intelligence, but collapsed at any threat of really serious talk; too few men knew or cared what was happening in the Ruhr or in Turkey.

Boston seemed less strange. The old houses reminded him of Dublin; hospitable Bostonians welcomed him and conversed in a manner to which he was accustomed; and the Appalachian Mountain Club provided an audience which he described as resembling the Rucksack Club and the Pinnacle Club put together. At Cambridge he spoke to an audience as responsive as any he could remember – 80% Harvard undergraduates: 'They received me very well and were evidently thrilled and amused.' The best of it all was staying in Chestnut Hill with the Allston Burrs. Burr, a loyal Harvard graduate in the Class of 1889, a member of the A.C. as well as of the A.A.C., seemed to know as much about Everest as George himself; and Mrs. Burr, 'very gentle and charming and cultivated without being highbrow,' loved the Impressionists. George would have liked to see more of the Burrs.

But away he had to go, to fill such engagements as had come through: Philadelphia again, where 1200 heard him at the University Museum; Toledo, Ohio; Buffalo (for Niagara Falls, not for a lecture); Rochester; and then, by way of Chicago to Iowa City – not far enough west for one who had dreamed of seeing the Pacific. Returning eastward, he stopped in Toronto to see his father's brother Wilfred. In the fortnight before he sailed, he visited Princeton, went up to New Hampshire for talks at Dartmouth College and St. Paul's School, and returned to Boston for a public lecture arranged by Allston Burr.

Financially, the tour was a failure, Having as yet no regular job in view, George regretfully concluded that for a while the family would have to live on less than he had hoped to provide. But there had been compensations, as he explained to Ruth a week before he boarded the *Saxonia*: 'Don't think I'm altogether disappointed by the American visit. It has been intensely interesting in all sorts of ways and has given me a real insight into their attitudes and opinions, if not a very deep one. And I have liked them on the whole very much.' He had found good friends, particularly in the A.A.C.; and as always he had enjoyed, with fellow-mountaineers and with others, times when he could breathe a little of the university atmosphere and talk not only of mountains but of books and pictures and music and world affairs.

Setting out from London for Royston one day, Hinks the geographer ran into D. H. S. Cranage, Secretary of the Board of Extra-Mural Studies at Cambridge. They shared a compartment on the train and talked about Dr. Cranage's work. For fifty years Cambridge had supported lectures at local centres for women and workingmen, and since 1909 the University had run intensive tutorial classes of the sort encouraged by the Workers' Educational Association. In the light of post-war hopes for a better world, University Extension could be expected to have an exciting and important future. Cranage spoke of a post he had to fill at Cambridge: assistant secretary and lecturer. He asked Hinks for suggestions, and Hinks recommended George Mallory.

So it came about that, on reaching home in April, Mallory was swept into the business of being a candidate. His friends mobilised in support. Arthur Benson wrote a letter, in some embarrassment, because he had already consented to back someone else; Frank Fletcher wrote, as headmaster of Charterhouse; Younghusband said that of course he would gladly do anything he could. Perhaps the most helpful of all the friends was F. E. Hutchinson, who had been present at the Charles Lamb Dinner in 1909. He was now Cranage's opposite number, Secretary of the University Extension Delegacy at Oxford; and he happened to lunch, at precisely the right moments, with Cranage himself and with W. H. Draper, Master of the Temple, whom Cranage had asked for advice. Hutchinson wrote to Mallory: 'I should, if I were in Cranage's position, catch at having you for a colleague and possible successor.'

All went well: Cranage 'caught', and in mid-May the news of George's appointment spread among his friends. Those who were in Cambridge – Benson, the Claude Elliotts, David Pye, Jim Butler – rejoiced that George and Ruth would soon be living in their midst. 'It's an excellent thing for our sober and quiescent atmosphere,' said Benson, 'to be aerated by something brisk and adventurous, and I shall look forwards confidently to your introducing quite a new spirit into our sedate academical concerns.'

Geoffrey Winthrop Young to G.M.   *18 May 1923*
Few things could have given greater delight! May I claim a little

selfish share in it? For – as you will probably *not* remember – when we were discussing Everest first, I said to Ruth, 'What George wants is a label, and this will give it.' And t'other day, when G.M.T. was talking of your chances, he used the very phrase: 'You see, he's known about now – he's ticketed!' And I chuckled!

The future now looked settled: George and Ruth and the children living in Cambridge, and George working at a job that suited him. He began at once; he took lodgings in Cambridge, leaving the family at the Holt until he could find a house for them. His enthusiasm contributed a great deal, Cranage said, to the Jubilee of Cambridge Local Lectures in July and to the various summer schools held at Cambridge in the Long Vacation. Regular lectures at Hunstanton, and classes at Halstead and Raunds, began in the autumn; the arrangement at Raunds was for a three-year University Tutorial Class. For each class Mallory had to start about four o'clock in the afternoon, with thirty miles to drive; and he could not get back to Cambridge much before midnight. The students, however, impressed him as alert and pleasant to work with – 'mostly young men and maidens in various walks of life between teachers and boot-making hands'.

Herschel House fell vacant, and the last impediment to happiness seemed to have been cleared away. The Mallorys prepared to move in at the end of October. George was to live there for just four months. The matter of Everest came up once more.

General Bruce, who had succeeded to the Presidency of the Alpine Club and to the Chairmanship of the Mount Everest Committee, was already making plans for a third expedition. No one questioned who should lead the party in 1924 – the General himself again, of course. The questions had to do rather with selection of the climbers.

On 10 April 1923 Bruce announced the appointment of a selection committee which included George Mallory. After the meeting on May 1st it seemed clear, Mallory noted, that Norton and Somervell would go out again, and that the likeliest new candidates were Bentley Beetham and Noel Odell. Beetham had been Somervell's partner in strenuous Alpine campaigns; Odell, a Cambridge geologist, had made an admirable record in the mountains and in the Arctic. Other names appear in Mallory's notes; one or two were crossed out during the meeting. The most interesting line reads simply 'Self?'

For six months this question remained unsettled. At this stage,

Mallory probably figured not at all as a potential leader of the climbing party. He was the only available man with experience of the first two expeditions; he had distinguished himself on the reconnaissance and again shown his skill, durability, and alertness on the first high climb in 1922. But he had been involved in the accident below the North Col, and he could hardly be counted an enthusiastic proponent of oxygen, and he showed little taste for anything remotely resembling a quasi-military regimen. 'He is a great dear,' General Bruce had written, 'but forgets his boots on all occasions'; and Longstaff had described him as 'a very good stout-hearted baby, but quite unfit to be placed in charge of anything, including himself'.[1] By mid-October Norton had been designated leader at Camp III and above, and Geoffrey Bruce had been appointed adjutant. The selection committee, at its meeting on October 16th, had still to choose six members of the climbing party from a short list of seven: Mallory, Somervell, Beetham, Odell, A. C. Irvine, R. B. Graham, and J. de V. Hazard.

Mallory thought of himself as an unlikely candidate; he had a new job and a new home, and he felt sure that the question would be settled for him by Cambridge reluctance or refusal to grant a leave of absence. The Mount Everest Committee thought otherwise and began to press for inclusion of Mallory in the party. Hinks remembered quite well that he had recommended Mallory for the Cambridge job:

A. R. Hinks to D. H. S. Cranage   *18 October 1923*

The Mount Everest Committee are very anxious that Mallory should be a member of the expedition next year, and that everything possible should be done by them to assist him in obtaining leave from the University. . . . I can only ask you to convey to the proper quarters the assurance that Mallory's cooperation next year is of high importance in the opinion of the Mount Everest Committee to the success of their enterprise.

Hinks sent a copy of the letter to Mallory, who was taken by surprise. Was the General really as keen as all that to have him go again? Hinks answered promptly: 'I think I can say that not only Bruce but all the members of the Committee are anxious that you should go. I have never heard any expression except of fear that

[1] C. G. Bruce to A. R. Hinks, 4 July 1922 (now in the files of the Mount Everest Foundation); T. G. Longstaff to A. F. R. Wollaston, 19 August 1922 (now in the possession of Nicholas Wollaston).

214

the University might not be able to spare you.' The Lecture Committee at Cambridge unanimously agreed on October 24th that a request of this kind could not be resisted; it recommended that Mallory be granted a six-month leave at half-pay, subject to final approval by the Syndicate which had appointed him. Both Hinks's request and Cranage's response had shown more concern than Mallory had dreamed of expecting, and now it seemed improbable that the Syndicate would reject the Lecture Committee's recommendation.

Busy in the new work at Cambridge, away from Ruth, longing for October 28th, the day when the family would move to Herschel House, Mallory faced alone the resolution of the question: 'Self?'

For Mallory this was a matter of trying to ascertain what would be right. Climbing had come to be far more than a pastime in his life; it enabled him to express himself in a way peculiarly his own; it was his art. He had made a reputation in it, and he alone had been to Everest twice before. On the other hand, he had a wife and three children, and a new job that suited him. In his family and in his work he had immediate and urgent reasons for aspiration and strenuous effort. Would it not be best, from now on, to climb with chosen companions on familiar hills not far from home, or simply to walk in good country? Was it necessary to risk everything again on Everest?

Nothing Mallory ever wrote or said has been so widely quoted as the brief answer he gave, after one of his American lectures, to the question repeatedly asked, 'Why do you want to climb Mount Everest?' Mallory replied, 'Because it is there.' The words have been explicated in sermons, used in advertisements, alluded to in countless articles and essays (usually, but not invariably, about mountaineering), adopted as the title of a later Everester's book about the crossing of Antarctica, and quoted by Prince Philip and by President Kennedy in explanation of man's efforts to travel through space and reach other planets. One writer calls the line 'a polite evasion'; another detects 'a romantic ring'; a third says that Mallory used in an ontological statement 'the language of theology'. Some adepts quote it as they quote bits from difficult poems, with knowing half-smiles, as if to say, 'You and I can grasp the sense without asking more.' Those who knew Mallory best have treated 'Because it is there' less seriously – the utterance of a tired man, not naturally patient, on hearing for the *n*th time a question that could be answered illuminatingly only if at very considerable length.[1]

'Because it is there' would serve well enough as text for a discourse on the question Mallory faced in October 1923; but there is a more substantial basis for understanding, a better starting-point, in this passage from a manuscript prepared for a lecture:[2]

Does the Mount Everest expedition serve useful ends? It may. The geologists want a stone from the top. The physiologists will be interested to know more about the limits of human endurance in a rarefied atmosphere. But I confess it is not as a potential victim of physiological experiment that I regard my own part in the expedition. And cutting out all scientific objects, do we still want Mount Everest to be climbed? Well, if I were to tell you anything else, I hope you would howl me down at once. . . .

The classic defence of the expedition made by Sir Francis Younghusband is simply this: he says by climbing Mount Everest you will stimulate the spirit of adventure throughout the English-speaking peoples of the world. Well, I can do no better than that. I hope what he says is true, and I must say I believe it is true.

But though Younghusband's words are a justification, they do not supply a motive. No one, I expect, would claim that he went to Mount Everest in order to stimulate the world; and the world, if he did, would have an unkind word for him. On the other hand, I believe I have not been on these two expeditions to witness the spectacle of myself breaking a record. As a true-hearted Englishman, I love a record deeply, with unreasoning devotion. . . . Fifty years a queen, and I clapped my hands in the cradle. A second knocked off the world's record for the mile – if I saw it announced in the morning paper, I should forget my breakfast. And I'm a positive slave to Hobbs's centuries. But were I asked to sacrifice anything of real importance merely to break a record – well, I should not repeat the question to myself. In the whole scale of values, clearly, I think, records of this sort can't weigh in the balance against the serious work of everyday life.

No. I suppose we go to Mount Everest, granted the opportunity, because – in a word – we can't help it. Or, to state the matter rather differently, because we are mountaineers.

Our case is not unlike that of one who has, for instance, a gift for

[1] A. C. Benson may have been ultimately responsible for the wording. In 1911 he urged Mallory to read Carlyle's *Life of John Sterling*: the book achieved high quality 'by being *there*'. In 1916 (see p. 116, above) Mallory thought of soldiers digging as like Millet's figures, but 'more *there*'.

[2] The first two paragraphs are very close to what James Friskin remembered from Mallory's lecture at the Broadhurst Theatre in New York.

music. There may be inconvenience, and even damage, to be sustained
in devoting time to music; but the greatest danger is in not devoting
enough, for music is this man's adventure. . . . To refuse the adventure
is to run the risk of drying up like a pea in its shell. Mountaineers, then,
take opportunities to climb mountains because they offer adventure
necessary to them.

Mallory had been adventurous, as we have seen, since boyhood.
He had loved to take chances – standing on a rock while the tide
came in, climbing about on a roof or in a quarry, swerving the
bike so as to make it just miss the post. As a mountaineer, he
acknowledged that confrontation of risk afforded him a certain
grave pleasure. No serious climber, he believed, could ever be
quite satisfied by an ascent altogether without difficulty and danger.
In an unpublished essay entitled 'Men and Mountains: The
Gambler', he said that 'mountaineering would lose its zest if there
were no dangers for the daring and skilful'. But in developing
his comparison of the mountaineer and the gamester, he took care
to point out the differences. The proper mountaineer, no fool,
recognises the dangers and either avoids them or overcomes them
by his skill; he plays the game 'only within the limits of some
strict principles':

It is clear that the stake he risks to lose is a great one with him: it is a
matter of life or death. . . . To win the game he has first to reach the
mountain's summit – but, further, he has to descend in safety. The
more difficult the way and the more numerous the dangers, the greater
is his victory. . . . He must be compared not to the foolish gambler who
takes whatever chance may come, but rather to the prudent man who
chooses carefully the risks he shall take. . . .

Great climbers have been caught – I admit it. But it has always been
for one of two reasons: either, as in the early days of the mountains,
they were ignorant, or else they were foolish in their gambling. There
have been great climbers who have grown so confident that they have
run the gauntlet of natural perils and paid for it at a great price; there
have been some who, not satisfied merely with difficulties of the ordinary
kind upon snow or ice or rock, have undertaken for their pleasure the
climbing of places which no human being could climb with safety, and
added so a fresh element of risk by pushing our sport beyond its natural
limits. Condemn them if you like, but not us who don't do these things
and don't get killed. . . .

Provided that a party has a large enough preponderance of competence over its opposite and takes the ordinary precautions, it is as
safe as people driving in motors or travelling in trains. A slight chance

of disaster there will always be in each of these cases, so long as humanity is imperfect. But when I say that our sport is a hazardous one, I do not mean that when we climb mountains there is a large chance that we shall be killed, but that we are surrounded by dangers which will kill us if we let them.

Of climbers who had met with an accident on an ascent entirely beyond their powers, Mallory once said scathingly, 'They had no *business* to be there!' To go adventuring without experience and sane judgment merited no praise.

Desire for praise: this, too, had to be weighed as a motive. As a boy, Mallory had delighted in the triumph of the Winchester VIII at Bisley; as a Cambridge undergraduate, he had enjoyed the success of the Magdalene boat under his captaincy. In the school of the future the most telling justification for games, he believed, would be that they provided opportunities for 'pure heroics'. But serious mountaineering was more than a game. No doubt the young Wykehamist had found pleasure in being known as a member of the Ice Club; but he soon learned a decent reserve in talking of his exploits, especially with strangers, and impressed most people as notably modest. He would not seek praise; in fact, he never had to. And yet, in another unpublished fragment, he wrote candidly that 'mountaineering, like the greater part of man's activities, is not as a rule wholly independent of praise':

The desire to climb mountains is commonly held among laymen to be an incomprehensible psychological freak. One explanation, nevertheless, is commonly given – that we climb to win admiration. No mountaineer will accept that. And yet, when he remembers that this explantion is freely offered, he may forget that the admiration is not completely withheld. Or, in mere indignation at its inadequacy, he may neglect the suggestion altogether. It is incomplete, of course; but it is probably true to say of most mountaineers, as one among several reasons, that they climb to win admiration:

> Fame is the spur that the clear spirit doth raise
> To scorn delights and live laborious days. . . .

'Fame' we call it for those with whose motives we are apt to sympathise; and for the others – 'Advertisement' or 'Low Competitive Spirit'. The name depends only upon the association of one quality with others. The feeling which we recognise in friends, as well as enemies, however modestly they disguise it, seems to be so deeply seated in the human breast than we can neither pass it by nor condemn it. There can be very few men capable of performing heroic deeds without some desire of being proclaimed a hero.

In Mallory's own mind, however, the desire to win fame seems clearly to have mattered less than the desire to satisfy the sense of beauty. 'A day well spent in the Alps,' he had said, 'is like some great symphony.' Or like a dance, for the climber responds to the mountains as a dancer responds to music. In jottings on 'The Art of Climbing', Mallory pointed to the interdependence of soul, mind, and body, and praised those few arts which call the body into play – 'the poise of a man's head, the manner in which the legs support his weight, and the motion of an uplifted arm or of a hand stretched out'. Dancing was one such art, and climbing was another. Elsewhere Mallory wrote that 'the same need can be satisfied by climbing a hill and writing a poem'. Like a poem, a climb had a beginning, a middle, and an end; and it could well express an inward vision. If you were Matthew Arnold, you wrote the verses about sunrise on 'the domed Vélan with his snows':

> And glorious there, without a sound,
> Across the glimmering lake,
> High in the Valais depth profound,
> I saw the morning break.

If you were George Mallory, you went on climbing; you saw again the beauty of the hills, and felt again the joy of moving skilfully and gracefully in high places as one of a party all splendidly fit and climbing in perfect harmony.

And what memories! Of that first Alpine dawn from the Vélan, and the first big climb on the Combin; of the Droites and the Verte from the Chardonnet, and the south side of Mont Blanc from the Herbetet, and the Oberland peaks from Mont Pleureur; of the Brocken spectre above the Val Sesia, and sunset on the Bosses du Dromadaire. Of the Grivola with Graham and Harry, the Nesthorn ridge with Geoffrey and Donald, the Dent Blanche with Harold Porter and Hugh Pope, the Charmoz with Harold. Of Wales also – the mountains around Pen-y-Pass, the good rock, and the congenial spirits who knew the drift of 'The Mountaineer as Artist'.

But how much of all this bore on the question of Everest?

The Mountaineer as Gambler, if he thought of his wife and children, and if he really believed in prudence, could hardly accept the odds. It was one thing to invent the Garter Traverse on Lliwedd or the new route on the Aiguille du Midi, to risk a wetting in Wales or a night out in the Alps; it was quite another thing to struggle against Everest. Mallory had felt the devilish wind, fought for his breath, and had his fingers nipped by frost. Already it had fallen to him to arrest the slip of three men and to go down himself in the avalanche that killed seven others. Bullock in 1921 had put the odds against a given party on Everest as fifty to one, and Mallory had agreed. Neither the love of adventure nor a vestigial desire for praise – 'That last infirmity of Noble mind' – could have made him forget that estimate; neither, alone, could have induced him to go out and face the blind Fury again.

Nor did the Mountaineer as Artist have any need to make a third journey. Already he had seen the Kama valley and looked up at the incredible precipices and ridges of Everest – a sight for a lifetime. Could another trip be worth the time and strength expended? Once above the North Col, the Mountaineer felt little call to play the Artist. Instead of admiring the beauties of the scene, he had to concentrate entirely on his next upward step; instead of participating in a rhythmic action suggestive of a dance, he had to struggle, with reserves of strength diminished, against a gigantic and inhuman adversary with untold reserves. A day spent on Mount Everest was all too likely to turn into a great cacophony – or a dead silence.

As for companions, a man's own choice seemed preferable to a committee's. To think who might have gone out if the year had been 1912: Young, Herford, Pope! But after all the Mount Everest Committee had picked such stalwarts as Bullock, Morshead, Norton, and Somervell. Given comrades like these, deserving of the fullest loyalty, a man could endure a certain amount of friction with others.

'Self?' The decision rested at last, I am sure, with the Mountaineer as Moralist. A professed believer in aspiration and endeavour as life-giving could not well turn away and leave unfinished a work, however difficult or unpleasant, for which he had been found extraordinarily well qualified. The highest mountain on earth now had symbolic value in many minds as a goal of aspiration; Mallory was supposed to be one of the ablest mountaineers in the country and therefore must get on with the endeavour. It was expected of him that he should try again. Moreover, the climber with knowledge of the first two expeditions could help the third with his counsel and contribute to its safety. Compelled by the sense of duty, Mallory decided to go.

George to his father   *25 October 1923*

You'll see that most likely I shall be free to go, and it will therefore rest with me to make the choice. You may imagine it isn't easy, and I look for guidance as to what is right. . . . I had largely assumed that opinion here would go the other way; and so it is an awful tug to contemplate going away from here instead of settling down to make a new life here with Ruth. We have both thought that it would look rather grim to see others, without me, engaged in conquering the summit; and now that the prospect revives, I want to have a part in the finish. Apart from that, for any fun I may get out of the expedition, or *réclame*, I wouldn't look at it for a moment; my preference is all the other way. But I don't think it can really be decided on those sort of grounds at all.

Ruth comes in, of course. She has written that she is willing I should go, and we shall discuss it this week end. Taking that for granted, my present feeling is that I have to look at it from the point of view of loyalty to the expedition and of carrying through a task begun.

George to his father   *7 November 1923*

It's all settled, and I'm to go again. I only hope this is a right decision. It has been a fearful tug. I've had to think precisely what I was wanted for. They think I can help to keep it all safe; and I think that too, a bit. And then I was guided a bit by the attitude of the Lecture Committee and the Syndicate – both unanimous to give me leave and favourably disposed to my going. They've granted me half-pay for the six months.

I saw the doctors yesterday. They say I'm absolutely A1, heart and all perfect. I hate leaving anxieties behind, but it means a lot that we now know pretty well all about the risks and how to manage for the best.

H.L.M. to George   *12 November 1923*

Though of course your decision about Mount Everest must bring us an anxious time, still I feel you are right and congratulate you on having so decided. . . . Our thoughts and prayers will be with you all the time, and (needless to say) our very heartiest wishes for your success. It is most gratifying that the Everest Committee appreciate all you have done so greatly and that the Cambridge committee have risen so nobly to the occasion. . . . Ruth, too, is very good to give you up again. . . . We are wondering much if you will be able to come and see us before you go. . . . Very much love, dear old man.

Once the decision had been made, George felt liberated. 'Life is full of interest,' he wrote on November 18th, 'and we're all very happy.' It was a busy time: lecturing and secretarial chores, and all the enjoyable settling-in at Herschel House. George and Ruth liked the study and the nursery from the start. For the dining room, which had a vast area of brown varnished woodwork, they found a brown-cream paper with Morris's dark daisy and curtains with a brown-orange ground. Even the difficulties seemed quite bearable. The first coat of green in the drawing room turned out badly, and the boundary hedge had to be replaced, and the tennis court needed a wire fence.

Norton sent the rough draft of a memorandum on Everest equipment, with a request that Mallory vet it. Evidently he meant to keep in close touch throughout the planning stage – characteristic of him, and heartening. But in mid-December, through no fault of Norton's, a contretemps developed. On November 6th General Bruce had announced that the climbing party would include Mallory, Somervell, Beetham, Odell, Irvine, and Graham. R. B. Graham, a schoolmaster at Reading, was well known to Graham Irving as a mountaineer of great staying power and charming modesty. Being a Quaker, he had firmly taken the stand of a conscientious objector during the war. For that reason, his inclusion in the party was now being protested. To Mallory's dismay and regret, Graham felt bound to resign. J. de V. Hazard filled his place.

Christmas was coming. George and Ruth took the children down to Westbrook for 'a very nice party with splendid dancing – Sir Roger for the first time in the children's lives.' Then, with George Trevelyan and Jim Butler, George and Ruth joined a small party in Derbyshire. This was country George has known as a boy, and he wrote nostalgically to the sister who had gone with her husband to Ceylon:

George to his sister Mary   *Castleton, 2 January 1924*

Do you remember coming to this place? It must have been centuries ago; I believe Gra was with us. Peveril Castle, the Peak Cavern, and the Speedwell Mine, and a hill called Mam Tor – those were the great things. We've had a small party up here walking for a week. . . . We've had some very good walks on the Peak and quite a little climbing, but murky, murky weather and mostly wet. . . .

Talking of Everest with Jim Butler, George said that he did not expect to *enjoy* the next expedition; he hated the all-day-long Tibetan wind.

Local lectures began again on January 7th. Avie came to stay, and Trafford and Doris at the same time. 'T. looks forward without a doubt to success and promotion in the future,' George wrote to Mary at Colombo, 'and is quite sure he is at the heart of Imperial Defence at present; I daresay he does his job very well.'[1] January stayed comparatively mild, but February turned very cold. It was an expense to burn the stove that heated the lower rooms and the greenhouse. Ruth had a little trouble with her back, and the children developed a mild flu, and the winter flowers suffered once or twice from frost.

On February 13th Mallory signed an agreement with the Mount Everest Committee. One paragraph read:

> I agree that I shall join the Expedition at my own risk as to the consequences and the Committee shall not be responsible for any damage, personal or otherwise, which I, or any dependent, may suffer during the continuance of the Expedition or on my journey to, or back from, Darjeeling.

There was no escaping the 'risk as to the consequences'. George went down to Taunton to stay with the Morgans and deliver a lecture. After his talk, a man in the audience exclaimed, 'How thrilled you must must be to be going out again!' Almost reproachfully, George answered, 'You know, I am leaving my wife and young children behind me.' As the time for departure came even nearer, he said to Geoffrey Keynes, 'This is going to be more like war than mountaineering. I don't expect to come back.'

Mallory, Irvine, Beetham, and Hazard were to sail on the *California* from Liverpool. George and Ruth went up and stayed with his parents at Birkenhead. Andrew Irvine's family lived near by. Sandy, who had rowed twice against Cambridge and probably would have been elected the Oxford president in 1924 if he had not been chosen for the Everest party, had taken two terms' special leave from Merton. The year before, with Odell on the Merton College expedition to Spitsbergen, he had proved himself a strong sledger and a great hand at tinkering with mechanical things. Though his experience of the mountains was limited, his natural aptitudes inspired confidence. Odell had watched him lead the Chimney Pitch in the Great Gully of Craig yr Ysfa, 'a brilliant first lead for a novice'; and Arnold Lunn, after seeing him ski in the Oberland at Christmas, said that he had never met a more

---

[1] Air Chief Marshal Sir Trafford Leigh-Mallory, K.C.B., served as Commander-in-Chief of the Allied Expeditionary Air Force in 1944. He and his wife died in November of that year when his aircraft hit a mountain near Grenoble; he was on his way to a new post as Air Commander-in-Chief in Southeast Asia.

remarkable beginner. Sandy, still an undergraduate, was twenty-one when he was picked for Everest.

On February 28th the Liverpool Wayfarers' Club gave a dinner in honour of the four climbers who were setting out. Among the guests were all the local members of the A.C. and the fathers of two of the climbers – Mallory and Irvine. On the 29th a strong wind hampered the tugboats and delayed the *California*. At last, having waved good-bye, Ruth returned to the children. George reminded Ruth that he hoped to see the Finches at Herschel House on his first week end at home.

CHAPTER 10

Everest 1924

The *California* was new and comfortable but overcrowded with tourists, some of whom, having heard Mallory lecture, came up to him with questions about the expedition or asked leave to take pictures. The three fellow-climbers seemed to be excellent folk: Beetham 'good-humoured and unselfish', Hazard 'nice and reasonable', Irvine 'sensible and not highly strung'. Mallory shared a cabin with Hazard and a table in the dining saloon with Irvine, who struck him as 'one to depend on for everything perhaps except conversation'.

Determined to be fit, Mallory took exercise in the gymnasium and threw a medicine ball with Beetham and Irvine; occasionally he ran ten times round the deck. Irvine persuaded him to enter one deck competition, a potato race, 'in which I had a brilliant success and was only knocked out in the final, where one potato was really impossible.' On the whole, the voyage spun out quite uneventfully, except for a memorable approach to Gibraltar:

George to Ruth   *8 March 1924*

I was fortunate enough to wake before sunrise and went on deck. We were steaming due east, and straight ahead was the orange glow spreading over the sky. Towards the centre of it, the long dim lines of land on either side converged and left a gap . . . twenty miles away or more. We were aiming straight for this little hole in the skyline where the light was brightest, and I had the most irresistible feeling of a romantic world: we had only to pop through the hole, like Alice through the garden door, to reach a new scene and a whole kingdom of adventures. . . .

I have finished reading Maurois' *Ariel* . . . an interesting story because, in so far as Shelley's relations with Mary were impaired, it was simply by the friction of everyday life. He was the most unselfish of men, but the glamour of Mary wore off a bit when he saw her as a housewife. She certainly had little enough of his society when he was making poems, but I'm inclined to think that she had Shelley all the time. . . .

George Mallory

I fear I don't make you very happy. Life has too often been a burden to you lately, and it is horrid when we don't get more time and talk together. Of course we have both had too much to do; and I have hated thinking that it must fall upon you to do the car, for instance, which has often been an unpleasant grind, when you might otherwise have been painting china, or one thing or another more profitable to your soul. Somehow or another, we must contrive to manage differently – to have some first charge upon available time for our life together.

George to Ruth [*17 March 1924*]

It is curious that now I am in warm sunshine I must think of you in a summer frock. March 17 – perhaps it is snowing in Cambridge. England does look a little grim from the tropics at this time of year. But you'll have an English spring. . . .

How I wish I had you with me! With so much leisure we should have enjoyed the time together. . . . Dear girl, we give up and miss a terrible lot by trying to do what is right. . . . Great love to you, dearest one. . . .

Mallory spent some of the time on board studying Hindustani, going through lists of stores, thinking about the organisation of high camps, and examining the oxygen apparatus:

George to his sister Mary *17 March 1924*

Irvine is a great dab at things mechanical and has some criticisms to make; and there are certainly a good many chances that it will go wrong or break if we use it. We broke one of the high-pressure tubes that are supposed to stand any amount of bending, putting it away into its box today. However, I rather expect we shall use it, as we can carry 50% more oxygen than last year with the same weight. Norton was keen to go up without oxygen from 26,000, but we've got to camp higher than that to have a chance. Anyway, we've got to get up this time; and, if we wait for it and make full preparations, instead of dashing up at the first moment, some of us will reach the summit, I believe. . . . I wish Irvine had had a season in the Alps.

G.M. to T. G. Longstaff *18 March 1924*

It's going to be a good party. What we shall do first God knows, and everything will depend on that. I'm dead against trying without oxygen from 26,000 – we should simply knock out three or four of the best and be jolly lucky if they had the sense to turn back in time. . . . And I'm dead against making ill-prepared dashes. It's got to be all or nothing this time. We don't want to break any more records for height unless we reach the summit; and the only way is to start as high as possible according to what the organisation will stand and wait until the whole train is laid, risking the weather. We shall be very unlucky if after all's ready we can't get a good enough day. . . .

At present, I'm inclined to think that the first job will be a strong reconnaissance with oxygen from IV to choose the best camp site and *build*. . . . There is a great danger in going higher than 26,000 feet for Camp V; there must be a limit to what porters can do, marvellous as they were, and to put the camp too near the limit is to ask for trouble. . . .

Mallory and his companions landed at Bombay and endured three days of 100° heat on the way to Darjeeling, where they joined the other members of the expedition on March 21st. The General, Norton, Geoffrey Bruce, and E. O. Shebbeare, of the Indian Forest Service, who was to have charge of transport, had been there since March 1st. Somervell had come from his medical mission in Travancore; R. W. Hingston, the medical officer and naturalist, from the R.A.F. hospital at Bagdad; Odell, from the Persian oil fields. Noel, the cinematographer, had already gone on to Kalimpong. The four from England, last to arrive, had only a brief stay at Darjeeling – five very busy days of planning and packing. After conferring with Norton, Mallory wrote again to his sister Mary at Colombo, asking for regular weather reports by post card and a telegram announcing the first unmistakable sign of the monsoon. Everything seemed to be in admirable order.

George to Ruth   *Darjeeling, 25 March 1924*

Norton has got the whole organisation under his hand, and we shall economise much time and money by dumping some of our boxes en route. All the stores for the high camps have practically been settled already. He is going to be an ideal second to Bruce.

The party looks very fit altogether. . . . The only doubts I have are whether the old ankle one way or another will cause me trouble. . . . It was very nice to see S. again, and Odell is one of the best. Really it is an amazingly nice party. . . .

On March 26th, all together, the members of the expedition left Darjeeling for Kalimpong. There they separated in two parties for the journey through Sikkim into Tibet. Mallory travelled in the second, with Norton, Odell, Hingston, Irvine, and Shebbeare. They reached Pedong on the 28th and Rongli Chu on the 29th. The country was very dry, and the sky hazy from the smoke of fires set to burn dead leaves and undergrowth. It was reported that exceptionally little snow had fallen in Tibet.

At Sedongchen George had the first letter from Ruth. Snow had indeed fallen in Cambridge, and the children had made snow men in the garden.

Ruth to George   *Herschel House, 5 March 1924*

Dearest one, I do hope you are happy and having a good voyage. I am keeping quite cheerful and happy, but I do miss you a lot. I think I want your companionship even more than I used to. I know I have rather often been cross and not nice, and I am very sorry, but the bottom reason has nearly always been because I was unhappy at getting so little of you.

George to Ruth   *Sedongchen, 30 March 1924*

Dearest one, you needn't worry that you haven't been an angel every day of your life. We went through a difficult time together in the autumn; but, though we were both conscious that we saw too little of one another last term, it seemed to me we were very happy; and I often thought how cheerful and pleasant you were when life was not being very agreeable. I'm quite sure we shall settle down to enjoy our home in Cambridge. . . .

On the 'great rhododendron march' from Sedongchen to Gnatong, everyone enjoyed the bright sun and a glorious view of Kangchenjunga in the distance. Walking up to the Jelep La with Norton, Mallory had a sense of physical well-being impaired only very slightly by consciousness of the old ankle. 'I must tell you, dearest one,' he wrote to Ruth, 'how wonderfully fit I have been these last days, much better at this stage, I'm sure, than either in '21 or '22. I feel full of energy and strength, and walk uphill here already almost as in the Alps.' This was a remarkably pleasant journey, in happy and quite sufficiently amusing company. To await the second party's arrival at the little rest house beyond the Jelep La on April 1st, the first party had left there a whisky bottle filled with cold tea.

The two parties met again at Yatung on April 2nd. The General seemed not quite himself; he sent a reconstituted first party on in Norton's charge and stayed at Yatung for a day of rest with the newcomers. Mallory went off for a long ramble with Irvine and then wrote letters. 'One way or another,' he assured Cranage in Cambridge, 'I will get back before the end of August.' A few days later, having moved on to Phari, he seized the chance for another side-trip and walked with Somervell and Odell 'up into the recesses of Chomolhari'.[1] One march beyond Phari, on the way to Kampa Dzong, he resumed his letter-writing:

George to Ruth   *7 April 1924*

It isn't easy to write, because the site of my tent dips slightly towards

[1] Somervell, *After Everest* (2nd ed., 1938), p. 111.

the head of my bed, and no amount of propping seems quite to over-
come the difficulty. If I had my bed the other way round, my head
would be at the mouth of the tent, and this would create a difficulty
about light. Besides, it is snowing slightly and may snow more; and,
though I don't mind having my feet snowed upon for the sake of fresh
air, I am unwilling to have my head snowed upon during the night. . . .

The General's trouble has been an irregular pulse, and he and
Hingston are both nervous about the effects of these altitudes on his
heart. Consequently, he is not coming with us to Kampa Dzong (last
year's route, but in six days instead of four), but by another way which
will allow him to camp lower. . . . I think it is ten to one he will be all
right.

I can't write much more in this position, and my arms are getting
cold.

The difficulties mounted. By the 9th Beetham was suffering from
dysentery, and Mallory (as he hopefully said) from 'a slight colitis
or something of the kind'. Thinking appendicitis possible, Somervell made plans for an emergency operation. Mallory felt very
feeble and made the next two marches on a diet of little more than
biscuits and jam, but began to recover soon after reaching Kampa
Dzong on the 11th. The General's condition still gave rise to
anxiety.

George to Ruth   *Kampa Dzong, 12 April 1924*

The wind and sun between them have fairly caught us all these last
three days. Norton says that he was accused by his people after the
last expedition of having acquired a permanent dint in his nose, and
he is determined to prevent the same thing happening again – but how
to do it? Personally, I limit my desire in that direction to keeping my
nose the same size as usual; I don't like to feel it swollen with sunburn.
Somervell, who started with a complexion tanned by Indian suns, is
now exactly the colour of a chestnut and, as he greases freely, no less
shiny. Beetham so far has the best beard; but then he had a start, as he
didn't shave after Kalimpong. I'm inclined to back Geoffrey Bruce
against him in the long run, as his will be blacker. The face with the
greatest number of flaky excrescences and crevasses is undoubtedly
that of Hazard, and the underlying colour in his case is vermilion. . . .

14 April 1924

Yesterday we had the news that the General is not coming on. The
possibility had been in the back of our minds since Yatung. We are all
very sorry for him, naturally. It is difficult to size up in a moment how
much difference his absence will make. I don't think the difficulties of
travelling through Tibet will be considerably increased. The General's

influence with the porters must go for something; but Norton thinks
that Geoffrey Bruce, with his more direct contact with and personal
knowledge of them, counts for more. I expect myself the porters will
work as well this year as in 1922. Still, we've lost a force, and we shall
miss him in the mess. . . .

Meanwhile, Norton takes command; and we couldn't have a better
commander. He will do it much better than I could have done had I
been in his place, if only because he can talk the lingoes freely. He has
appointed me second-in-command in his place, and also leader of the
climbers altogether. I'm bound to say I feel some little satisfaction in
the latter position. . . .

The worst news is about Beetham, who has not yet properly recovered
from dysentery and is a very weak man. It is not yet decided whether
we shall send him down to Laachen tomorrow. If he comes on and gets
bad, and Somervell (in the absence of Hingston with Bruce) has to take
him back, we shall have lost two of the best and be left without a
medical officer – a very serious position. . . .

Now about myself: I was able to feel definitely this morning that my
trouble has passed. The tenderness in my gut is no longer sensitive –
like an old bruise, rather. And I feel strong and full of energy, and
myself; and I haven't the least doubt I shall remain fit. I shall take every
care to do so. . . . I wanted you very much to comfort me when I wasn't
well, and I want you very much now to be happy with. . . .

From this time on, Mallory and Norton worked actively and
harmoniously together over the various proposals for the
campaign. It was understood that attempts would be made with
oxygen and without, that every high-climbing party must have
strong support, that eight fit climbers would be none too many,
and that assignment of porters to carry and dump loads for the
high camps would require painstaking calculations, particularly
on behalf of the climbers using oxygen. Mallory questioned
Norton's first plan, otherwise valuable, on the ground that it
called upon two climbers without oxygen to try for the summit
from Camp V at 26,500 feet; he believed that a gasless party's
chances of success depended upon the establishment of a second
camp above the North Col.

George to Ruth   *Tinki Dzong, 17 April 1924*

My tummy is in perfect order again, and I feel as fit as possible. It
was a funny go altogether and quite inexplicable. . . . Beetham came on
with us. It was Somervell's decision on the very morning of leaving
Kampa Dzong. That is to say, S. had to decide that B. would get better;
and no doubt he is right. . . . At present B. looks years older, in much

the same way as Raeburn did in '21, only at a younger stage, and has quite lost all kick; and there was no one more energetic earlier. . . .

I've had a brain-wave – no other word will describe the process by which I arrived at another plan for climbing the mountain:

(*a*) A and B, with fifteen porters (about), starting from IV (North Col), establish V, building emplacements for four tents at about 25,500, and descend.

(*b*) C and D, gasless party, go to V with another fifteen porters, of whom seven carry loads and descend; the other eight go up without loads, practically speaking, and sleep.

(*c*) C and D proceed to establish a Camp VII at 27,300 (about), with the eight porters carrying up six loads.

(*d*) E and F, gas party, on the same day as (*c*), start with ten porters (about) from IV, go without loads to V; and from that point, E and F using oxygen, they take on the stores and gas previously dumped at V about 1000 feet higher to VI at 26,500.

(*e*) Then the two parties start next morning and presumably meet on the summit

You will readily perceive the chief merits of this plan: the mutual support which the two parties can give each other; the establishment of camps without waste of reserve climbers (A and B will not have done so much that they couldn't recover); the much better chance this way of establishing VI without collapse of porters. And then, if this fails, we shall be in the best possible position to decide how the next attempt should be made: four climbers, we hope, will be available; and the camps either way will be all ready.

This plan has such great advantages over all others that Norton has taken it up at once, and this evening we had another powwow, and everyone has cordially approved. I'm much pleased about this, as you may imagine. If only for this, it seems worth while to have come. . . . It is impossible yet to say who the parties will be. N. and I have talked about it; he thinks Somervell and I should lead each one of these two parties; he puts himself in my hands as to whether he should be one of them. . . .

G.M. to a Member of the Mount Everest Committee[1]   *19 April 1924*

I must tell you, what Norton can't say in a dispatch, that we have a splendid leader in him. He knows the whole bandobast from A to Z, and his eyes are everywhere; is personally acceptable to everyone and makes us all feel happy, is always full of interest, easy and yet dignified, or rather never losing dignity, and a tremendous adventurer – he's dead keen to have a dash with the non-oxygen party. He tells me (and I tell you confidentially, as I'm sure he wouldn't have it broadcasted) that

[1] Sir Francis Younghusband, *The Epic of Mount Everest* (1926), pp. 191–192.

when the time comes he must leave it to me in consultation with Somervell to decide whether he'll be the right man for the job. Isn't that the right spirit to bring to Mount Everest?

G.M. to T. G. Longstaff   *Chiblung, 19 April 1924*

Tibet since Kampa has been too mild to be healthy. The weather to the south looks more unsettled than in 1922; thick clouds gathered all round us today. Meanwhile, my sister from Colombo hands on from the meteorological people that a southwest wind has been blowing continuously for three days, with rain showers – the preliminary condition of the monsoon current, a fortnight earlier than usual. But what does it all mean? We're going to sail to the top this time, and God with us – or stamp to the top with our teeth in the wind.

After dinner on April 22nd, Norton announced that the difficult work of allotting tasks had been completed:

A and B, to establish Camp V	Geoffrey Bruce
	Odell
C and D, to climb without oxygen	Somervell
	Norton
E and F, to climb with oxygen	Mallory
	Irvine

It is of the greatest interest to read why Mallory was picked to lead the 'oxygen party' and why Irvine was picked to go with him:

George to Ruth   *Shekar Dzong, 24 April 1924*

The question as to which of the first two parties should be led by Somervell and which by me was decided on two grounds. (1) On the assumption that the oxygen party would be less exhausted and be in the position of helping the other, it seemed best that I should use oxygen and be responsible for the descent. (2) It seemed more likely on his last year's performance that Somervell would recover after a gasless attempt to be useful again later.

It was obvious that either Irvine or Odell should come with me in the first gas party. Odell is in charge of the gas, but Irvine has been the engineer at work on the apparatus. What was provided was full of leaks and faults; and he has practically invented a new instrument, using up only a few of the old parts and cutting out much that was useless and likely to cause trouble. Moreover, the remaining parties had to be considered; and it wouldn't do to make Irvine the partner of Geoffrey Bruce, as they would lack mountaineering experience. And so Irvine will come with me. He will be an extraordinarily stout companion, very capable with the gas and with cooking apparatus. The only doubt is to what extent his lack of mountaineering experience will be a handicap. I hope the ground will be sufficiently easy.

Norton, if he is fit enough, will go with Somervell – or, if he seems clearly a better goer at the moment, Hazard. Beetham is counted out, though he's getting fitter. Odell and Geoffrey Bruce will have the important task of fixing Camp V at 25,500.

The whole difficulty of fitting people in so that they take a part in the assault according to their desire or ambition is so great that I can't feel distressed about the part that falls to me. The gasless party has the better adventure; and, as it has always been my pet plan to climb the mountain gasless, with two camps above the Chang La, it is naturally a bit disappointing that I shall be with the other party. Still, the conquest of the mountain is the great thing; and the whole plan is mine, and my part will be a sufficiently interesting one and will give me perhaps the best chance of all of getting to the top. I can't see myself coming down defeated. And I have very good hopes that the gasless party will get up. I want all four of us to get there, and I believe it can be done. We shall be starting by moonlight, if the morning is calm, and should have the mountain climbed, if we're lucky, before the wind is dangerous.

This evening four of us have been testing the oxygen apparatus and comparing the new arrangements with the old. Irvine has managed to save weight, four or five pounds, besides making a much more certain as well as more convenient instrument. I was glad to find I could easily carry it up the hill even without using the gas – and better, of course, with it. On steep ground, where one has to climb, more or less, the load is a great handicap; and at this elevation a man is better without it. The weight is about thirty pounds – rather less. There is nothing in front of one's body to hinder climbing, and the general impression I have is that it is a perfectly manageable load. My plan will be to carry as little as possible, go fast, and rush the summit. . . .

Only four marches, starting tomorrow morning, to the Rongbuk monastery! We're getting very near now. On May 3rd four of us will leave the Base Camp and begin the upward trek, and on May 17th or thereabouts we should reach the summit. . . . The telegram announcing our success, if we succeed, will precede this letter, I suppose; but it will mention no names. How you will hope that I was one of the conquerors! And I don't think you'll be disappointed.

The expedition crossed the Pang La on April 26th, reached the Rongbuk monastery on the 28th, and occupied the Base Camp on the 29th.

George to Ruth   *Rongbuk Base Camp, 30 April 1924*

The Rongbuk valley greeted us with most unpleasant weather. The day before yesterday and the following night, when we were encamped outside the Rongbuk monastery, a bitterly cold wind blew, the sky was cloudy, and finally we woke up to find a snowstorm going on. Yesterday was worse, with light snow falling most of the day. However, today has been sunny after a windy night, and the conditions on Everest have gradually improved until we were saying tonight that it would have been a pleasant evening for the mountain. It is curious that, though quite a considerable amount of snow has fallen during these last few days and the lower slopes are well covered, the upper parts of Everest appear scarcely affected. This is a phenomenon we observed often enough in 1922, and notably on the day when we made the first attempt. . . .

B[eetham] has had a truly marvellous recovery; but I can't quite believe in his being really strong yet, though he makes a parade of energy and cheerfulness. . . . I'm very fit, perhaps not just so absolutely a strong goer as in '21, but good enough, I believe; and anyway I can think of no one in this crowd stronger; and we're a much more even crowd than in '22 – a really strong lot, Norton and I are agreed. It would be difficult to say of any one of the eight that he is likely to go further or less far than the rest. I'm glad the first blow lies with me.

To re-establish Camps I and II, a little army of 150 Tibetan coolies started carrying loads up the glacier on the 30th. That night, some fifty of their countrymen created a problem by deserting from the Base Camp. Norton, Shebbeare, and Geoffrey Bruce immediately went up to Camp I and found, to their relief, no sign of discontent. Meanwhile, Mallory busied himself with provisions for the high camps and with a plan for the high-climbing porters. There would be two teams of twenty porters each: 'A', to accompany the first party of climbers to Camp III and assist in putting Camp IV on the North Col; 'B', to start up a day later and work between Camp II and Camp III. A reserve team of twelve would wait at the Base Camp.

George to his sister Mary   *Rongbuk Base Camp, 2 May 1924*

The atmosphere has been just as it is during the monsoon and much warmer than in '22; we have to prepare for an early monsoon, though I daresay these conditions may only tend to delay it. At present the mountain is very windy and sprinkled with fresh snow, and looks most unpleasant for climbing. . . .

I can't tell you how full of hope I am this year. It is all so different from '22, when one was always subconsciously dissatisfied because we had no proper plan of climbing the mountain. And this year it has been a chief object with Norton and me to organise the whole show as it should be organised.

'Much warmer than in '22' – but the ink began to freeze. Finishing

the letter two days later at Camp II, George explained the make-up
of the two summit parties and concluded:

Well, then, on May 17th the four of us should join up somewhere
about the base of the final pyramid; and, whether we get up or not, it
will be my job to get the party off the mountain in safety. And I'm keen
about that part, too. No one, climber or porter, is going to get killed
if I can help it. That would spoil all.

From now on, the campaign evolved in three phases, each of
them a losing battle that necessitated changes in the schedule and
diminished the chances of success. Mallory, Irvine, Odell, and
Hazard, with the porters of team 'A', had arrived at Camp II on
May 4th, intending to re-establish Camps III and IV. Very bad
weather, and the consequent demoralisation of the porters,
worked against them. George made a journal-like report for Ruth:

May 4th. ... Camp II looked extraordinarily uninviting, although
already inhabited by an N.C.O. and two others, in charge of the stores
(150 loads or so) which had already been carried up by Tibetans. A low
irregular wall surrounded a rough compound, which I was informed
was the place for the sahibs' tents; and another, already covered by the
fly of a Whymper tent, was the home of the N.C.O. The sahibs' compound was soon put sufficiently in order; two Whymper tents were
pitched there for the four of us. ...

No tents were provided here for porters. The intention was to build
comfortable huts (or 'sangars', as we call them), using the Whymper flies
for roof; but no sangars had yet been built, and accommodation for
twenty-three men is not so easily provided in this way. However, I soon
saw that the ground would allow us to economise walls; and Irvine
and I, with three or four men, began building [an] oblong sangar, the
breadth only about seven feet. Other men joined in after resting. It is
an extraordinary thing to watch the conversion of men from listlessness
to some spirit of enterprise. A very little thing will turn the scale. On
this occasion, the moving of a huge stone to form one corner started
the men's interest, and later we sang! And so these rather tired children
were persuaded to do something for their comfort. Without persuasion,
they would have done nothing to make life tolerable.

Towards 3:00 p.m. Odell and I (Irvine seemed tired after prodigious
building efforts) went on to reconnoitre next day's march over the
glacier. ... In an hour and a half the first and most difficult part of the
way from II to III had been established.

4th to 5th. An appalling night: very cold, considerable snow fall, and
a violent wind.

5th. Result: signs of life in camp (the first audible ones in camps up to and including II are the blowing of a yak-dung fire with Tibetan bellows) . . . were very late. The men, too, were an extraordinarily long time getting their food this morning. The N.C.O. seemed unable to get a move on; and, generally speaking, an Oriental inertia was in the air. It was with difficulty, in fact, that the men could be got out of their tents; and then we had further difficulty about loads. One man, a regular old soldier, having possessed himself of a conveniently light load, refused to take a heavier one which I wanted taken instead. I had to make a great show of threatening him with my fist in his face before he would comply. And so, with much argument about it and about, as to what should be left behind, as to coolie rations and blankets and cooking pots and the degree of illness of three reporting sick, we didn't get fairly under way until 11:00 a.m. . . .

Snow had fallen in the night. The glacier which had looked innocent enough the evening before was far from innocent now. The wind had blown the higher surfaces clear; the days, I suppose, had been too cold for melting; and these surfaces were hard, smooth, rounded ice, almost as hard as glass and with never a trace of roughness; and between the projecting humps lay the new powdery snow. The result of these conditions was much expenditure of labour either in making steps in the snow or cutting them in the ice; and we reached a place known as the Trough – a broad, broken trough in the ice, fifty feet deep, about a third of the way up – knowing we should have all we could do to reach Camp III.

Accordingly, we roped up all the men in three parties. This, of course, was a mere device to get the men along, as there isn't a crevasse in the glacier until rounding the corner to III. We followed along in the Trough for some way, a lovely warm place, and then came out of it onto the open glacier, where the wind was blowing up the snow maliciously. The wind luckily was at our backs until we rounded the corner of the North Peak – and then we caught it, blowing straight at us from the North Col. As the porters were now nearly exhausted and feeling the altitude badly, our progress was a bitter experience.

I was acting as lone horse, finding the best way, and consequently arrived first in camp. It was a queer sensation reviving memories of that scene, with the dud oxygen cylinders piled against the cairn which was built to commemorate the seven porters killed two years ago. The whole place had changed less than I could have believed possible, seeing that the glacier is everywhere beneath the stones. My boots were frozen hard on my feet, and I knew we could do nothing now to make a comfortable camp. I showed the porters where to pitch their tents at 6:00 p.m., got hold of a rucksack containing four Unna cookers, dished out three and Meta for their cooking to the porters, and one to our own cook. Then we pitched our own two Meade tents with doors facing about a yard apart for sociability.

The porters seemed to me very much done up; and, considering how cold it was even at 6:00 p.m., I was a good deal depressed by the situation. Personally, I got warm easily enough; our wonderful Kami produced some sort of a hot meal, and I lay comfortably in my sleeping bag. The one thing I could think of for the porters was the high-altitude sleeping sacks (intended for IV and upwards) now at II, which I had not ordered to come on next day with the second party of porters. ... The only plan was to make an early start next morning and get to II in time to forestall the departure of 'B' party. I remember making this resolve in the middle of the night and getting up to pull my boots inside the tent from under the door. I put them inside the outer covering of my flea bag and near the middle of my body, but of course they remained frozen hard, and I had a tussle to get them on in the morning.

Mallory started from Camp III at 7:00 a.m. on May 6th, leaving directions that as many 'A' porters as possible should come a quarter of the way down and help to carry 'B' party's loads. He was too late to catch 'B' party at Camp II; he met them about 9:00 a.m. below the Trough. Some of them, disinclined to go from II to III and back in one day, had increased their loads with blankets, intending to sleep at III.

This was the last thing I wanted. My chief idea at the moment was to get useful work out of 'B' party without risking their morale or condition as I saw we were risking that of 'A'. So, after despatching a note to Noel at II, I conducted 'B' party slowly up the glacier. After making a convenient dump and sending down 'B' party, I got back to Camp III [in the] early afternoon, somewhat done and going very slowly at the last from want of food.

In camp, nothing doing. All porters said to be sick, and no one fit to carry a load. Irvine and Odell volunteered to go down to the dump and get up one or two things specially wanted. ... The sun had left the camp some time before they returned. A very little wall-building was done this day, notably round the N.C.O.'s tent; otherwise nothing to improve matters. The temperature at 5:00 p.m. (we hadn't thermometers the previous night) was observed to be 2° F. – 30° of frost an hour before sunset. ... I gathered that sahibs as well as porters were suffering from altitude lassitude.

May 7th. The night had been very cold: $-21\frac{1}{2}°$; i.e., 53° of frost. Personally, I had slept beautifully warmly and yet was not well in the morning. Odell and Irvine also seemed distinctly unfit. I decided to send Hazard down with some of 'A' party to meet at the dump and bring up ten of 'B'. (It had been arranged that this party were to come up again.) Investigations again showed that no porters were fit to carry loads. Several were too unwell to be kept up at III; not one had a spark of energy or seemed inclined to do a hand's turn to help himself. The only live man in camp was our admirable Kami. I decided to send down the whole lot and to send up 'B' next day to establish the camp and prove it habitable.

While Hazard went off to meet 'B', I collected the men at III. They had to be more or less pulled from their tents. An hour and a half must have been taken up in their getting a meal of tea and tsampa, which they must clearly have before going down; and much time, too, in digging out the sicker men who tried to hide away in their tents. One of them, who was absolutely without a spark of life to help himself, had swollen feet; and we had to pull on his boots without socks. He was almost incapable of walking; I supported him with my arm for some distance and then told off a porter to do that. Eventually, roped in three parties in charge of the N.C.O., I sent them off by themselves from the dump, where shortly afterwards I met Hazard. Four men of 'B' had gone on to III, but not to sleep. Three others, whom we now proceeded to rope up and help with their loads, alone consented to stay there.

A second day therefore passed with only seven more loads got to III and nothing done to establish the camp in a more comfortable manner, unless it may be counted that this third night the six men would each have a high-altitude sleeping bag. And meanwhile the morale of 'A' had gone to blazes. It was clear to me that the morale of porters altogether must be restored if possible at once by bring[ing] 'B' party up and giving them a day's rest to make camp.

Mallory made another early start from Camp III on May 8th and reached Camp II at 9:00 a.m. Norton and Somervell had come there on the 7th, and Geoffrey Bruce arrived during the day.

N. agreed with my ideas; and we despatched all remaining 'B' party to III with Somervell, to pick up their loads at the dump and carry them on. 'A' had been filled up the previous night with hot food and were now lying in the sun, looking more like men.

The only question was whether in future to re-establish the correct standard and make them carry all the way to III and back, as was always done in 1922. I was strongly opposed to this idea. The best way of re-establishing their morale, I thought, would be to give them a job well within their powers; and, if they improved as I hoped, they might well carry loads the three-quarters journey to the dump on three successive days, while 'B' could ferry the last quarter once and twice on the two of the days when they would not be engaged in making camp. This was agreed to, more particularly by Geoffrey Bruce, who really runs the porters altogether. . . .

A day of great relief, this, with the responsibility shared or handed over, and much lying in the sun, and untroubled sleep at II.

On May 9th Mallory, Norton, and Geoffrey Bruce shepherded 'A' party as far as the dump and seven 'fresh heroes from the Base' all the way to Camp III. The men needed a good deal of driving. Snow fell, and beyond the Trough a violent wind was blowing. At moments all but the nearest figures were completely hidden from sight.

On such a day I didn't expect III to be more congenial than it had been. However, it was something to be greeted by the cheery noise of the Roarer Cooker. The R.C. is one of the great inventions of the expeditions ... a sort of super-Primus stove. Irvine and Odell had evidently been doing some useful work. It had been a triumph getting the R.C. to Camp III. It is an extravagant load, weighing over forty pounds; and it now proved to be even more extravagant of fuel than had been anticipated. Moreover, its burning was somewhat intermittent; and, as the cook, even after instruction, was still both frightened and incompetent when this formidable stove was not functioning quite sweetly and well, a sahib had often to be called in to help. Nevertheless, the R.C. succeeded in cooking food for the troops; and, however costly in paraffin oil that meal may have been, it made the one great difference between Camp III as 'A' party experienced it and Camp III now.

Otherwise, on this day set apart for the edification and beautification of this camp, the single thing that had been done was the erection of one Meade tent to accommodate two more sahibs (only two more because Hazard came down this day) – and no blame to anyone. 'B' party was much as 'A' party had been – in a state of Oriental inertia. It is unfair perhaps to our porters to class them with Orientals in general, but they have this Oriental quality – that after a certain stage of physical discomfort or mental depression is reached they simply curl up. Our porters were just curled up inside their tents. And it must be admitted that the sahibs were most of the time in their tents, no other place being tolerable. ...

And so presently in my old place, with Somervell now as a companion instead of Hazard, I made myself comfortable; i.e., I took off my boots and knickers, put on my footless stockings knitted for me by my wife for [the] last expedition and covering the whole of my legs, a pair of grey flannel bags, two pairs of warm socks besides my cloth-sided shoes, and certain garments too for warming the upper parts – a comparatively simple matter. The final resort in these conditions of course is to put one's legs into a sleeping bag. Howard and I lay warmly enough, and presently I proposed a game of picquet, and we played cards for some time until Norton and Geoff came to pay us a visit and discuss the situation.

Someone a little later tied back the flaps of the two tents facing each other, so that after N. and G. had retired to their tent the other four of us were inhabiting as it were one room, and hopefully talked of the genius of Kami and the Roarer Cooker, and supposed that a hot evening meal might some time come our way. Meanwhile, I produced *The Spirit of Man* and began reading one thing and another. Howard reminded me that I was reproducing on the same spot a scene which occurred two years ago when he and I lay in a tent together. We all agreed that 'Kubla Khan' was a good sort of poem. Irvine was rather poetry-shy, but seemed to be favourably impressed by the Epitaph to Gray's 'Elegy'. Odell was much inclined to be interested and liked the last lines of 'Prometheus Unbound'. S., who knows quite a lot of English literature, had never read a poem of Emily Brontë's and was happily introduced. – And suddenly hot soup arrived.

The following night was one of the most disagreeable I remember. The wind came in tremendous gusts; and, in spite of precautions to keep it out, the fresh snow drifted in. If one's head was not under the bedclothes, one's face was cooled by the fine cold powder; and in the morning I found about two inches of snow all along my side of the tent.

May 10th. It was impossible to guess how much snow had fallen during the night when first one looked out. The only certain thing was the vile appearance of things at present. In a calm interval one could take stock of a camp now covered in snow – and then would come the violent wind, and all would be covered in the spindrift. Presently Norton and Geoff came into our tent for a powwow. . . .

On two points all were agreed: they would have to wait two or three days before making any attempt to reach the North Col, and they had to prevent further deterioration of the porters' morale. Speaking from the porters' point of view, Geoffrey Bruce favoured a retreat. Mallory countered with arguments which Norton accepted: the weather could now be expected to improve; if it did not, the decision to retreat could be made on the following day; morale would suffer more from an immediate retreat than from a holding-on at Camp III. But to keep all six climbers there would require inordinate consumption of fuel. It was decided that Norton, Somervell, and Odell should stay, to make the first attempt on the North Col if they could, and that Mallory and Irvine should go down to Camp II and then return to 'finish the good work'.

On May 11th, after a restful night at Camp II with Beetham and Noel, Mallory received a half-expected message from Norton, saying 'that he had decided to evacuate III for the present and retire all ranks to the Base Camp'.

George to Ruth   *Camp II, 11 May 1924*

It has been a very trying time with everything against us. The porters have seemed from the start short of acclimatisation and up against it. . . . I'm convinced Norton has been perfectly right. We pushed things far enough. Everything depends on the porters, and we must contrive to bring them to the starting point (i.e., No. III) at the top of their form. I expect we were working all the time in '22 with a smaller margin than we knew; it certainly amazed me that the whole bandobast, so far as the porters were concerned, worked so smoothly. Anyway, this time the conditions at III were much more severe; not only were the temperatures lower, but wind was more continuous and more violent. . . . Personally, I felt as though I were going through a real hard time in a way I never did in '22.

The respite at the Base Camp lasted six nights. On the 15th Norton took the expedition down to the Rongbuk monastery, to receive the lama's blessing. According to Noel, who consulted an interpreter, the lama said, 'Your turning back brings pleasure to the demons. They have forced you back, and will force you back again.'[1] The toll had indeed been heavy. One of the Gurkha N.C.O.'s died of a cerebral haemorrhage; one porter was down with badly frostbitten feet, and another with a broken bone in his leg; two more had severe bronchitis. Beetham had developed sciatica; Odell and Hazard seemed rather slow in acclimatising; and all the climbers who had spent time at Camp III showed signs of fatigue. Looking back to this time, Somervell wrote: 'It was largely this first week at No. 3 Camp that reduced our strength and made us – by the time when we finally climbed as far as we could, three weeks later – thin and weak and almost invalided, instead of being fit and strong as we had been during the 1922 ascent.'[2]

At Noel's invitation, Mallory shared the photographic tent at the Base Camp. 'He seemed to be ill at ease,' Noel wrote, 'always scheming and planning. It was obvious to me he felt this setback more acutely than any of us.'[3] Mallory himself insisted that he still had strength and hopes:

George to Ruth   *Base Camp, 16 May 1924*

I must tell *you* that, with immense physical pride, I look upon myself as the strongest of the lot, the most likely to get to the top, with or without gas. I may be wrong, but I'm pretty sure Norton thinks the

---

[1] John Noel, *Through Tibet to Everest* (1927), p. 231.
[2] Somervell, *After Everest* (2nd ed., 1938), p. 119.   [3] Noel, *op. cit.*, p. 233.

same. He and I were agreeing yesterday that none of the new members, with the possible exception of Irvine, can touch the veterans, and that the old gang are bearing everything on their shoulders. . . . It *is* an effort to pull oneself together and do what is required high up, but it is the power to keep the show going when you don't feel energetic that will enable us to win through if anything does.

Irvine . . . has been wonderfully hard-working and brilliantly skilful about the oxygen. Against him is his youth (though it is very much for him, some ways) – hard things seem to hit him a bit harder – and his lack of mountaineering training and practice, which must tell to some extent when it comes to climbing rocks or even to saving energy on the easiest ground. However, he'll be an ideal companion, and with as stout a heart as you could wish to find. If each of us keeps his strength as it is at present, we should go well together.

Somervell seems to me a bit below his form of two years ago; and Norton is not particularly strong, I fancy, at the moment. Still, they're sure to turn up a pretty tough pair. I hope to carry all through now with a great bound. . . . Howard and I will be making the way to Chang La again, four days hence; and eight days later – who can tell? Perhaps we shall go to the top on Ascension Day, May 29th.

George to his mother   *Base Camp, 16 May 1924*

Irvine is the star of the new members. He is a very fine fellow, has been doing excellently up to date, and should prove a splendid companion on the mountain. I should think the *Birkenhead News* – is it? – ought to have something to say if he and I reach the top together.

The second phase of the campaign opened on May 17th, when the high climbers again started up from the Base Camp. During the week that ensued, the important achievement was the fixing of Camp IV. On the 20th Mallory, Norton, and Odell, with Lhakpa Tsering, made a new route from Camp III to the North Col: avoiding the slope swept by the avalanche in 1922, they followed rather the difficult upward course of a long crevasse in the ice cliff. Near the foot of it, Mallory led 200 feet up an ice wall and a narrow chimney. 'Confronted with a formidable climbing obstacle Mallory's behaviour was always characteristic,' Norton wrote: 'you could positively see his nerves tighten up like fiddle strings. Metaphorically he girt up his loins, and his first instinct was to jump into the lead. Up the wall and chimney he led here, climbing carefully, neatly, and in that beautiful style that was all his own.'[1] The party reached the campsite at 2:30 p.m., and Mallory and Odell went on to reconnoitre the way to the Col itself. At

[1] F. F. Norton, in *The Fight for Everest* (1925), pp. 77–78.

3:45 p.m., thoroughly tired, the four started down – and, in Norton's words, 'the less said about the descent the better.' George told the whole story to Ruth:

The first visit to the North Col was a triumph of the old gang. Norton and I did the job; and the cutting, of course, was all my part. So far as one can enjoy climbing above Camp III, I enjoyed the conquest of the ice wall and crack (the crux of the route) and making the steps, too, in the steep final 200 feet. Odell did very useful work leading the way on from the camp to the Col; I was practically bust to the world and couldn't have led that half hour, though I still had enough mind to direct him.

We made a very bad business of the descent. It suddenly occurred to me that we ought to see what the old way down was like. Norton and I were ahead, unroped, and Odell behind, in charge of a porter who had carried up a light load. We got onto ground where a practised man can just get along without crampons (which we hadn't with us), chipping occasional steps in very hard snow or ice. I was all right ahead, but Norton had a nasty slip, and then the porter, whose knot didn't hold, so that he went down some way and was badly shaken.

Meanwhile, I, below, finding the best way down, had walked into an obvious crevasse. By some miscalculation I had thought I had prodded the snow with which it was choked, and where I hoped we could walk, instead of cutting steps at the side of it – all the result of mere exhaustion, no doubt. But the snow gave way, and in I went with the snow tumbling all round me, down luckily only about ten feet before I fetched up half-blind and breathless to find myself most precariously supported only by my ice-axe, somehow caught across the crevasse and still held in my right hand – and below was a very unpleasant black hole. I had some nasty moments before I got comfortably wedged and began to yell for help up through the round hole I had come through, where the blue sky showed – this because I was afraid any operations to extricate myself would bring down a lot more snow and perhaps precipitate me, into the bargain.

However, I soon got tired of shouting – they hadn't seen me from above – and, bringing the snow down a little at a time, I made a hole out towards the side (the crevasse ran down a slope) after some climbing, and so extricated myself, but was then on the wrong side of the crevasse, so that eventually I had to cut across a nasty slope of very hard ice and, further down, some mixed unpleasant snow before I was out of the wood. The others were down by a better line ten minutes before me. That cutting against time at the end, after such a day, just about brought me to my limit. . . .

My one personal trouble has been a cough. It started a day or two before leaving the Base Camp, but I thought nothing of it. In the high camp it has been the devil. Even after the day's exercise I have described, I couldn't sleep, but was distressed with bursts of coughing fit to tear one's guts – and so headache and misery altogether. Besides which, of course, it has a very bad effect on one's going on the mountain. Somervell also has a cough which started a little later than mine, and he has not been at his physical best.

On the following day, May 21st, Somervell, Irvine, and Hazard, with twelve porters, carried the first loads to Camp IV. Light snow fell at intervals. Somervell and Irvine returned to Camp III; Hazard and the twelve porters remained at Camp IV, to await the arrival on the 22nd of Odell and Geoffrey Bruce, who were to go on up with the porters and establish Camp V at 25,500 feet. But snow fell all through the night of the 21st and continued until mid-afternoon on the 22nd. Odell and Bruce could not think of starting. During the night of the 22nd, the temperature dropped to − 24° F.; and on the 23rd Hazard decided to come down. He reached Camp III at 5:00 p.m., with only eight of the twelve porters. 'It is difficult to make out how exactly it happened,' Mallory wrote; 'but evidently he didn't shepherd his party properly at all, and in the end four stayed up, and one of these badly frostbitten.'

'The situation,' Norton said, 'had suddenly taken a very serious turn.' There was only one thing to do. On May 24th the old gang – Mallory, Norton, Somervell – turned out to rescue the four stranded porters. Despite the new snow, despite the racking coughs of Mallory and Somervell, they succeeded, but at a cost; they did what was required, but they paid with yet more of their physical well-being. George wrote to Ruth:

Had the snow been a bit worse that day we went up to bring them down, things might have been very bad indeed. Poor old Norton was very hard hit altogether, hating the thought of such a bad muddle, and himself really not fit to start out next day. Nor were any of us, for that matter; and it looked ten to one against our getting up with all that snow about, let alone get[ting] a party down.

I led from the camp to a point some little distance above the flat glacier. The snow wasn't so very bad, as there had been no time for it to get sticky. Still, that part, with some small delays, took us three hours. Then S. took us up to where Geoff and Odell had dumped their loads the day before, and shortly afterwards Norton took on the lead. Luckily, we found the snow better as we proceeded. N. alone had crampons and was able to take us up to the big crevasse without step-cutting. Here we had half an hour's halt, and at 1:30 I went on again for the steep 200 feet, and so to the point where the big crevasse joins the corridor.

From here there were two doubtful stretches. N. led up the first while the two of us made good at the corner of the crevasse. He found the snow quite good. And S. led across the final slope, following Hazard's just discernible tracks, in the wrong place, but of some use now because the snow had bound better there. N. and I had an anxious time belaying; and it began to be cold, too, as the sun had left us. S. made a very good show getting the men off. . . . Time was pretty short, as it was 4:30 when they began to come back, using S.'s rope as a handrail. Naturally, the chimney took some time. It was just dark when we got back to camp.

Noel and Odell, with two or three porters, had gone out to meet them, carrying hot soup in thermos flasks. 'When we met,' Noel wrote, 'the whole lot of them sank down in the snow. They were absolutely done! The porters were like drunken men, not knowing what was happening. Norton, Somervell, and Mallory hardly spoke.'[1]

A second retreat, from III to II on May 25th and thence to I, was plainly inevitable. 'Dear Girl, this has been a bad time altogether,' George wrote to Ruth. 'I look back on tremendous efforts and exhaustion and dismal looking out of a tent door onto a world of snow and vanishing hopes. And yet, and yet, and yet there have been a good many things to set on the other side. The party has played up wonderfully.'

On May 26th, at Camp I, seven members of the expedition planned the third phase of the campaign. Setting aside the previous arrangements, they decided to send up two parties without oxygen. On the same day, at Norton's request, Mallory wrote part of the expedition's latest dispatch:[2]

The issue will shortly be decided. The third time we walk up East Rongbuk glacier will be the last, for better or worse. We have counted our wounded and know, roughly, how much to strike off the strength of our little army as we plan the next act of battle.

Noel observed that Mallory looked ill and spent much time in his sleeping bag; he believed that Mallory's strength had been sapped and that only his nerves could carry him further.

George to Ruth   *Camp I, 27 May 1924*
    N. has been quite right to bring us down for rest. It is no good sending

[1] Noel, *Through Tibet to Everest* (1927), p. 248.   [2] *A.J.*, 36:203–208 (Nov. 1924).

men up the mountain unfit. The physique of the whole party has gone down sadly. The only chance now is to get fit and go for a simpler, quicker plan. The only plumb fit man is Geoffrey Bruce. N. has made me responsible for choosing the parties of attack, himself first choosing me into the first party if I like. But I'm quite doubtful if I shall be fit enough. . . .

The candle is burning out, and I must stop.

Darling, I wish you the best I can – that your anxiety will be at an end before you get this, with the best news, which will also be the quickest. It is fifty to one against us, but we'll have a whack yet and do ourselves proud. Great love to you.

G.M. to David Pye   *Camp I, 28 May 1924*

We are on the point of moving up again, and the adventure appears more desperate than ever. . . . All sound plans are now abandoned for two consecutive dashes without gas. Geoffrey Bruce and I the first party (provided I'm fit), and Norton and Somervell in the second – old gangers first, but in fact nothing but a consideration of what is most likely to succeed has come in. If the monsoon lets us start from Camp IV, it will almost certainly catch us on one of the *three* days from there. Bright prospects!

George to his mother   *Camp I, 28 May 1924*

The train is all laid now. . . . It will be a great adventure, if we get started before the monsoon hits us, with just a bare outside chance of success and a good many chances of a very bad time indeed. I shall take every care I can, you may be sure.

Norton, Somervell, Irvine, and Geoff here with me – a good party. Oxygen is condemned in order to save porters, or Irvine and I would have been together.

Much love to you both.

George to his sister Mary   *Camp I, 28 May 1924*

I'm due to make the first dash with Geoffrey Bruce and arrive at the top seven days hence, but we may be delayed or caught by the monsoon or anything. . . . This party has been badly knocked; but we still have some guts among us, I hope.

Mallory and Bruce moved up to Camp III on May 30th and to Camp IV on the 31st. On the next day, in a blasting northwest wind, they climbed with eight porters to 25,200 feet and established Camp V. Only four porters actually reached the campsite with their loads; the others sat down, quite played out, some 300 feet from the goal. While Mallory set up two little tents, Bruce and the 'Tiger' Lobsang retrieved the loads that had been dumped. Five porters then descended to Camp IV; three stayed the night.

According to the new schedule, Mallory and Bruce were to establish Camp VI at about 27,000 feet on June 2nd and to try for the summit on June 3rd. On the morning of the 2nd, however, only one porter was able and willing to go on; the other two had had enough. Not even Geoffrey Bruce could move them. There was no choice but to withdraw to Camp IV – another frustration, but a good thing for Bruce, because the carrying of porters' loads above 25,000 feet had strained his heart.

Half-way down to Camp IV, Mallory and Bruce met Norton and Somervell, moving up in their turn, with six porters. This second assault party had better fortune and attained great heights. After a fairly comfortable night at Camp V, Norton and Somervell, with three of the porters, climbed on June 3rd to 26,800 feet and at 1:30 p.m. made Camp VI in a cleft on the north ridge. The porters descended to Camp IV. On June 4th, a brilliant day with little wind, Norton and Somervell started at 6:45 a.m. – upward again, labouring painfully for every foot of altitude they gained. They were the first to make a choice of route onward from the north ridge. Instead of taking to the crest of the northeast ridge, which is broken by two rock 'steps', they kept about 500 feet below it on the north face and climbed diagonally along a band of yellow sandstone toward the couloir which cut between them and the final pyramid.

At 28,000 feet the almost unbeatable Somervell, shaken by his very bad cough, decided to stop. Norton, though he had begun to see double, struggled on alone for an hour, across the couloir on steep slabs and treacherous snow, to an altitude reckoned as 28,126 feet; he stood at 1:00 p.m. less than a thousand feet below the summit, but knew that he must turn back. He rejoined Somervell, and slowly they made their way down. Near Camp V, a little before nightfall, Somervell barely survived a desperate bout of breathlessness by forcing from his throat an obstructive slough of mucous membrane. Lower down, Norton began trying to make himself heard at Camp IV: 'We want drink, we want drink.' Mallory and Odell met them well above the North Col; and at 9:30 p.m. the party reached Camp IV, where Irvine was brewing tea and soup. By midnight Norton had gone snow-blind.

During the day Mallory had gone down to Camp III with Irvine, ascertained that some of the porters were still fit, and then climbed back to Camp IV in the remarkably fast time of two hours and a half. He simply would not give up. He informed Norton that night, as they lay in their sleeping bags, that he wanted to make one more attempt, carrying oxygen – himself and Irvine, the oxygen party as originally planned. It is easy to argue at a distance over questions that had to be settled on the spot. Was Mallory fit to go up again? Were Irvine's sturdiness and mechanical genius enough to offset his inexperience? Had Odell, the supposedly slow acclimatiser, the only other candidate for an oxygen party, by now come into his powers? Should Norton as leader have overruled his second-in-command? In fact, though he would have picked Odell, Norton supported Mallory's plan, which, as he said, 'now represented our last chance of success.'[1]

June 5th was a day of preparation. To Odell and Hazard fell the immense responsibility for support: Hazard, after helping to escort Norton down to Camp III, would return to IV; Odell would climb to V and VI a day after the assault party. Mallory and Irvine set out from IV, with eight porters, at 8:40 a.m. on June 6th; they travelled well and spent that night at V, having sent down four of the porters. The weather looked altogether promising. On June 7th they reached Camp VI, and Mallory sent down two notes with the other four porters:

G.M. to Noel Odell[2]

We're awfully sorry to have left things in such a mess – our Unna cooker rolled down the slope at the last moment. Be sure of getting back to IV tomorrow in time to evacuate before dark as I hope to. In the tent I must have left a compass – for the Lord's sake rescue it; we are without. To here on 90 atmospheres for the two days – so we'll probably go on two cylinders – but it's a bloody load for climbing. Perfect weather for the job.

G.M. to John Noel[3]

We'll probably start early tomorrow (8th) in order to have clear weather. It won't be too early to start looking for us either crossing the rock band or going up skyline at 8:00 p.m.

'P.m.' was obviously a slip. Mallory intended to arrive at the foot of the final pyramid, some 650 feet from top, soon after 8:00 a.m. on June 8th.

On the 7th Odell had climbed to Camp V with two porters, whom he sent down at once; and on the 8th he started alone for

[1] *A.J.*, 36:265 (Nov. 1924).
[2] Reproduced, with one word altered, as the frontispiece of *A.J.*, 37 (May 1925).
[3] Reproduced by Noel in *Through Tibet to Everest* (1927).

Camp VI. The early morning was clear and not unduly cold; later, clouds began to form, and sleet and light snow fell intermittently. Odell has never wavered in his belief that, from about 26,000 feet, he caught the last glimpse of Mallory and Irvine, hours behind schedule, but 'going strong for the top':[1]

At 12:50, just after I had emerged in a state of jubilation at finding the first definite fossils on Everest, there was a sudden clearing of the atmosphere, and the entire summit ridge and final peak of Everest were unveiled. My eyes became fixed on one tiny black spot silhouetted on a small snow crest beneath a rock step in the ridge, and the black spot moved. Another black spot became apparent and moved up the snow to join the other on the crest. The first then approached the great rock step and shortly emerged at the top; the second did likewise. Then the whole fascinating vision vanished. . . .

[1] *A.J.*, 36:223 (Nov. 1924).

Epilogue

Odell, alone, climbed twice to Camp VI and searched even beyond it for traces; he gave up all hope on June 10th and descended. Norton despatched a runner to Phari Dzong with a report which was telegraphed to London on June 19th. Ruth received the news in Cambridge from a representative of the press. She went out for a long walk with old friends. The report appeared in the English papers on June 21st. Acting for the Mount Everest Committee, Sir Francis Younghusband forwarded to Ruth a message asking that the King's sincere sympathy be conveyed to the families of 'these two gallant explorers'. Younghusband added: 'What the King says is what everyone is saying, and I am sure that a more chivalrous mountaineer than your husband never existed.'

Public tributes, spoken and printed, made it clear that memories of George would stay alive. Arthur Benson, now Master of Magdalene, at a memorial service in the college chapel, emphasised Mallory's self-disregard:[1]

This was, I think, the essence of his wonderful charm, that he was so unconscious of his great personal beauty, his gifts, and his achievements, while his sympathy with those with whom he came in contact, their tastes, their preferences, their opinions, was deep and genuine.

Sir Arthur Shipley, Master of Christ's, remembered Mallory's candour: 'He was essentially honest in thought and in deed and at times outspoken – so outspoken, in fact, that a momentary irritation was sometimes produced; but that invariably passed away and was immediately forgotten.'[2] At Charterhouse Frank Fletcher said: 'With us he has left special memories of a dear friend, memories of clean strength and glorious endurance and high

---

[1] Reported in *The Times*, 30 June 1924, p. 17.   [2] *Country Life*, 5 July 1924, p. 29.

adventure, and a love of beauty and beautiful things, which is one form of the love of God.'[1]

In the *Alpine Journal* Graham Irving wrote of George as 'an ever-young and singularly lovable personality'.[2] Geoffrey Young described him as 'the magical and adventurous spirit of youth personified':[3]

Neither time nor his own disregard could age or alter the impression which the presence of his flame-like vitality produced. There are natures whose best expression is movement. Mallory could make no movement that was not in itself beautiful. Inevitably he was a mountaineer, since climbing is the supreme opportunity for perfect motion. . . .

David Pye wrote: 'To Mallory the scarcely visible black speck moving slowly, intelligently, among the vast eccentricities of nature was an epitome of the always growing story of the human spirit.'[4]

For the memorial service in St. Paul's Cathedral on October 17th, the Bishop of Chester, from whose diocese both Mallory and Irvine had come, chose as his text the Latin version of Psalm 84:5 – *Ascensiones in corde suo disposuit*.[5] That same evening, in the Albert Hall, at a joint meeting of the Alpine Club and the Royal Geographical Society, Colonel Norton said of Mallory:[6]

A fire burnt in him, and it made him one of the two most formidable antagonists Everest has ever had. He was absolutely determined to conquer the mountain, and no one knows better than I do how for several months this year he devoted his whole mind and will to this object.

At the same time those who suggest that he may have taken chances to achieve success in his last climb misrepresent him. For equally strong as his will to conquer was his sense of responsibility as leader of a party, and I know that he was prepared – nay, determined – to turn back however near the summit if it could not be reached in time to return in safety. . . .

His death leaves us the poorer by a loyal friend, a great mountaineer, and a gallant gentleman.

[1] Reported by W. F. O'Connor in a letter to *The Times*, 24 June 1924, p. 17. Lieut.-Colonel O'Connor, an Old Carthusian, had accompanied Younghusband to Lhasa in 1903–1904; he was now British Envoy in Nepal.
[2] *A.J.*, 36:385 (Nov. 1924).
[3] *The Nation and the Athenaeum*, 5 July 1924, p. 438. G.W.Y. wrote this memorial at the request of Maynard Keynes.
[4] *The Cambridge Review*, 24 Oct. 1924, p. 43.   [5] *A.J.*, 36:274–275 (Nov. 1924).
[6] *A.J.*, 36:250 (Nov. 1924).

There are memorials to George Mallory in the parish church at Mobberley, in the cathedral at Chester, and in Cloisters at Winchester. Mallory Court, a gift of Benson, was dedicated at Magdalene in 1925. David Pye's memoir, *George Leigh Mallory*, was published in 1927. By 1933, when the discovery of an ice-axe on the slabs of Everest under the crest of the northeast ridge, 250 yards short of the first 'step' (27,950 feet), stimulated fresh speculation concerning the fate of Mallory and Irvine, their story, like that of Captain Scott and his companions, had become a twentieth-century legend. A new generation of mountaineers read Pye's memoir and the big Everest books and Younghusband's *Epic of Mount Everest*; there were some who knew by heart, and would quote on occasion as they climbed, 'A day well spent in the Alps is like some great symphony' and 'Have we vanquished an enemy? None but ourselves.' Auden and Isherwood in *The Ascent of F6*, and Michael Roberts in his 'Elegy for the Fallen Climbers', alluded to Mallory and Irvine as if all the world would understand. A German book about Mallory appeared in 1931, and a French book in 1947.[1]

In the Fifties renewed attemps on Everest focussed attention on the Western Cwm, which Mallory had discovered and named. Wilfrid Noyce, a member of the successful expedition led by John Hunt in 1953, wrote that 'the Western Cwm conjured up for us the figure of Mallory, peering from the col beside Lingtren'. On 29 May 1953 Edmund Hillary and Tenzing reached the summit. Noyce was waiting for them when they returned to the South Col: 'Ed said suddenly and apropos of nothing (though he will have forgotten it), "Wouldn't Mallory be pleased if he knew about this?" '[2]

He is 'Mallory of Everest' now. A book so entitled appeared in 1967. But Mallory had been dearly loved as George before he ever set foot upon that mountain. In 1924 his friends felt utterly stricken. For years their interest and their fondness had been so warm that, if two of them started talking about him, they found it difficult to stop. They could see even now, and themselves fully believe, that his disappearance on the highest mountain in the world had been an occurrence kindling to the imagination; but they could hardly bring themselves to understand that George

---

[1] Wilhelm Ehmer, *Um den Gipfel der Welt: Die Geschichte des Bergsteigers Mallory*; and Joseph Peyré, *Mallory et son Dieu: Premier Héros de l'Everest*.

[2] *South Col* (1954), pp. 99, 237–238.

would not again be seen moving with ineffable grace on the mountains, or heard speaking in his unforgettable voice about beautiful things and right actions.

Letters written soon after his death, private utterances which complement the public tributes, throw yet more light on the reasons why friends and fellow-mountaineers have gone on talking about him as if the decades were only years.

Montague Rendall to Ruth   *25 June 1924*

I always thought him, as a boy, a real knight of chivalry, moving in a world most of us didn't know, or knew only by hearsay and hardly believed in. . . . I never forget how noble it was of you to let him go: his sacrifice is largely your sacrifice.

Geoffrey Keynes to Ruth   *21 June 1924*

I knew long ago that this was going to happen, but that doesn't make the fact any easier to bear. . . . You are the only person who could possibly know how much I loved George, and so I feel that I know something of what you have got to bear. . . . If only I could be of some real comfort to you!

George Trevelyan to Ruth   *6 July 1924*

Of course he was younger than me, and I was not a climber, and I can claim but a very small share in him. But I am deeply grateful for what I have seen of him. It has been one of the great spiritual experiences of my life. . . . And the picture of him – in form and moving how express and admirable! – is stamped on my memory as hardly any other man's.

Robert Graves to Ruth   *22 June 1924*

George was my first real friend, and he always remained so; in fact, I never said any of the spiteful things I say about my other friends about him – I couldn't. . . . My only consolation at the moment is that he once told me on Snowdon that he hoped he'd die like that, climbing, and that you are a climber and can understand what he was after; and that anyhow you'll not have lost your head. So like George to choose the highest and most dangerous mountain in the world! I did love him.

Mary O'Malley to Ruth   *21 June 1924*

He was always taking one on further, showing one new roads and a fresh point of view. You know how he did that to people, better than anyone. He was so sound, so clear; he had such an extraordinarily delicate perception for all those things that he shaped one's own views without one's knowing it. . . . He had such an appetite for beauty. And no one ever had a greater genius for appreciation.

And in ethical things I think he was even more remarkable. In any question, big or little, of right or wrong, one felt sure that he would

George Mallory

instinctively be absolutely right. I remember how he talked about that kind of thing and still more how he *did*.

*Geoffrey Winthrop Young to Ruth*30 June 1924

I was in France, and until we knew more I *could* not write. And I can't really now: it is a long numbness of pain, and yet but a shadow of yours, for indeed one cannot think of you separately. An unspeakable pride in that magnificent courage and endurance, that joyous and supreme triumph of a human spirit over all circumstances, all mortal resistance; and the loss unutterable. . . .

Ruth to Geoffrey Winthrop Young

I know George did not mean to be killed; he meant not to be so hard that I did not a bit think he would be. . . . I don't think I do feel that his death makes me the least more proud of him. It is his life that I loved and love. I know so absolutely that he could not have failed in courage or self-sacrifice. Whether he got to the top of the mountain or did not, whether he lived or died, makes no difference to my admiration for him. I think I have got the pain separate. There is so much of it, and it will go on so long, that I must do that. . . .

Oh Geoffrey, if only it hadn't happened! It so easily might not have.

It is not difficult for me to believe that George's spirit was ready for another life, and his way of going to it was very beautiful. . . . I don't think all this pain matters at all. I have had far more than my share of joy and always shall have had.

Isn't it queer how all the time what matters most is to get hold of the rightness of things? Then some sort of peace comes.

Sources and Acknowledgments

Unpublished Materials

The papers preserved by George and Ruth Mallory have been at hand throughout the preparation of this book. They include a large number of family letters, hundreds of letters that George and Ruth wrote to each other, letters from many friends, George's notebooks and manuscripts of essays and lectures, and dozens of photographs. This store has been most helpfully augmented by George's sisters. Mrs. Brooke supplied well over a hundred of George's letters to their parents; Mrs. Longridge, thirty-seven of George's letters to her. Ruth's sisters, Miss Turner and Mrs. Morgan, also added to the store.

For other letters written by George Mallory, I am indebted to Mrs. Costley-White, Sir Geoffrey Keynes, Mrs. T. G. Longstaff, the Right Reverend E. R. Morgan, Lady O'Malley, Lady Pye, Nicholas Wollaston, and Geoffrey Winthrop Young. Thanks to T. S. Blakeney, I have seen in the files of the Mount Everest Foundation letters from Mallory to General Bruce, A. R. Hinks, and Sir Francis Younghusband. The Harvard Mountaineering Club lent a postcard and a letter sent by Mallory to Allston Burr.

I have sought permission for all quotations from letters addressed to George or Ruth Mallory; and I owe thanks to the Master and Fellows of Magdalene College, Cambridge (for A. C. Benson); Wilfrid Blunt (for Sir Sydney Cockerell); the Headmaster of Charterhouse (for G. H. Rendall and for Sir Frank Fletcher); Lady Gaselee (for Sir Stephen Gaselee); Robert Graves; Sir Geoffrey Keynes (for himself and for Rupert Brooke); the Right Reverend E. R. Morgan; Lady O'Malley (for herself and for Mrs. W. A. Wills); Mrs. Mark Pryor (for Jacques Raverat); Max Rendall (for Montague Rendall); Mrs. James Strachey (for Lytton Strachey); Mrs. J. R. H. M. Moorman (for G. M. Trevelyan); Lady Wilson (for the late Sir Steuart Wilson's brother Hugh); and Geoffrey Winthrop Young.

The Mount Everest Foundation has allowed me to quote from letters of J. P. Farrar and Sir Francis Younghusband to Mallory, letters of A. R. Hinks to Mallory and to D. H. S. Cranage, a letter of General Bruce to Hinks, and the medical reports on Mallory by H. Graeme Anderson, M.D., and F. E. Larkins, M.D. Mrs. Longstaff has granted permission to quote from a letter written by her husband to A. F. R. Wollaston.

To the heirs or representatives of letter-writers whom I have been unable to trace, I should like to express both regret and hope for approval. Among the letters I have found illuminating, but not quoted, are those of Will Arnold-Forster, Alan Goodfellow, Duncan Grant, Sir Edward Marsh, Noel Odell, Sir David Pye, Raymond Rodakowski, T. Howard Somervell, and F. F. Urquhart.

Data concerning letters from which I have quoted at length will be found in the text. Some short passages I have incorporated without giving the dates or naming the recipients. For the sake of clarity, I have at times altered George's punctuation and Ruth's spelling. I have deleted the beginnings and endings of letters, but indicated with dots every omission from a quoted passage. The letters of George and Ruth, kept apart for months at a time by war and by the Everest expeditions, include many passages that have seemed, even after forty or fifty years, inviolably theirs.[1] As Will Arnold-Forster said in 1924, 'You've always been, you two, such a good unit – the Mallorys.'

Their friends have shown great interest and generosity. Graham Irving lent me the Minutes of the Ice Club for 1904 and 1905; Sir Geoffrey Keynes, the Climbing Diary he kept with George in 1907 and 1908. Harold Porter made excerpts from his scrupulously detailed Climbing Diary and later showed me the original; Geoffrey Winthrop Young paged through his Pen-y-Pass Book with me and produced a voluminous file which included his notes on transcripts of George's letters and in the margins of the published memoir, *George Leigh Mallory*. Lady O'Malley ('Ann Bridge') sent me a copy of her invaluable manuscript memoir from which I have quoted freely and gratefully.

In the Cambridge University Library, I read the manuscript diary of Charles Sayle and the letters of Hugh Wilson; and I

---

[1] I am reminded of a comment by E. L. Strutt and D. W. Freshfield, *A.J.*, 39:118 (May 1927), on an Austrian review of *The Fight for Everest: 1924* in a German translation published at Basel. Dr. G. Lammer, 'most terrible of all Alpine critics,' apparently supposed that omission of sentimental expressions from Mallory's letters to his wife in their published form showed – a lack of sentiment!

thank the Librarian for permission to quote therefrom. At the Alpine Club I found Geoffrey Winthrop Young's statement of Mallory's qualifications for membership and Mallory's last note to Odell. Nicholas Wollaston sent the manuscript of a lecture by his father, A. F. R. Wollaston. At Pen-y-Pass I read the Gorphwysfa Visitors' Book and the Climbers' Book, and at Arolla the guest-book of the Hôtel du Mont Collon.

For helpful answers to inquiries and for other assistance, I thank John Case, Miss Craies, Professor G. I. Finch, Len Frank, the late James Friskin, Basil Goodfellow, Francis Irving, Mrs. John Longland, Dr. W. W. McLean, Miss C. M. Ramsey, Dr. Grant Sanger, Miss Susan Schoenfeld, L. G. Shadbolt, Frank Solari, John Sparrow, Professor Arnold Toynbee, the late Allen O. Whipple, and the Headmasters of Charterhouse, Repton, and Winchester. Audiences at the American Alpine Club and at the Andiron Club, both in New York, listened to parts of the book and raised valuable questions.

Books

Quotations from books are footnoted.

I have long admired the late Sir David Pye's *George Leigh Mallory* (Oxford University Press, 1927), and I thank Lady Pye for her permission to quote and for her continuing interest in this new book. Other friends of George Mallory who have written at some length about the years before Everest include Robert Graves, R. L. G. Irving, the late H. E. G. Tyndale, and of course Geoffrey Winthrop Young. Their books are listed below. Mallory himself produced just one book, *Boswell the Biographer* (Smith, Elder and Co., 1912), and one pamphlet, *War Work for Boys and Girls* (George Allen and Unwin Ltd., 1916).

In Chapters I–VI, I quote with the permission of Edward Arnold (Publishers) Ltd. from J. M. A. Thomson's and A. W. Andrews's *The Climbs on Lliwedd* (1909); of Associated Book Publishers Ltd. from H. E. G. Tyndale's *Mountain Paths* (Eyre and Spottiswoode Ltd., 1948) and from Geoffrey Winthrop Young's *On High Hills* (Methuen and Co. Ltd., 1927) and *Mountains with a Difference* (Eyre and Spottiswoode Ltd., 1951); of G. Bell and Sons Ltd. from *Arthur Christopher Benson as Seen by Some Friends* (1925); of Curtis Brown Ltd. from Sir Frank Fletcher's *After Many Days* (Robert Hale Ltd., 1937) and from R. L. G. Irving's

The Romance of Mountaineering (J. M. Dent and Sons Ltd., 1935); of Hodder and Stoughton Ltd. from Lord Beveridge's *Power and Influence* (1953); of Crosby Lockwood and Son from *The Mountains of Snowdonia*, edited by H. R. C. Carr and G. A. Lister (2nd ed., 1948); of the Master and Fellows of Magdalene College, Cambridge, from A. C. Benson's *From a College Window* (Smith, Elder and Co., 1906) and his *Diary*, edited by Percy Lubbock (Hutchinson and Co. Ltd., n.d.), and from *The Magdalene Boat Club, 1828–1928* (Cambridge University Press, 1930); of A. P. Watt and Son from E. F. Benson's *Final Edition* (Longmans, Green and Co., 1940) and from Robert Graves's *Good-bye to All That* (Jonathan Cape, 1929); and of Lady Wilson from *Letters of Hugh Stanley Wilson to His Family and Friends* (Cambridge University Press, 1919).

Among other books helpful in the preparation of Chapters I–VI were these: A. P. Abraham, *Rock-Climbing in Skye* (Longmans, Green and Co., 1908); G. D. Abraham, *Swiss Mountain Climbs* (Mills and Boon, 1911); George and Ashley Abraham, *Rock-Climbing in North Wales* (Keswick: G. P. Abraham and Sons, 1906); A. C. Benson, *Magdalene College, Cambridge* (Cambridge: Bowes and Bowes, 1923); T. Graham Brown, *Brenva* (J. M. Dent and Sons, 1944); J. D'E. Firth, *Rendall of Winchester* (Oxford University Press, 1954); Christopher Hassall, *Edward Marsh* (Longmans, Green and Co., 1959) and *Rupert Brooke* (Faber and Faber, 1964); Michael Holroyd, *Lytton Strachey* (William Heinemann Ltd., 1967–68); R. L. G. Irving, *Ten Great Mountains* (J. M. Dent and Sons, 1940) and *A History of British Mountaineering* (B. T. Batsford, 1955); O. G. Jones, *Rock-Climbing in the English Lake District* (Keswick: G. P. Abraham and Sons, 1900); Sir Arnold Lunn, *The Mountains of Youth* (new ed., Eyre and Spottiswoode, 1949) and *A Century of Mountaineering, 1857–1957* (George Allen and Unwin Ltd., 1957); Sir Edward Marsh, *A Number of People* (William Heinemann and Hamish Hamilton, 1939); *A History of Mobberley Village*, by Members of the Women's Institute (Altrincham: John Sherratt and Son, 1952); *Oxford Mountaineering Essays*, edited by Arnold Lunn (Edward Arnold, 1912); C. R. Sanders, *Lytton Strachey: His Mind and Art* (New Haven, Conn.: Yale University Press, 1957); E. W. Steeple, G. Barlow, and H. MacRobert, *Island of Skye* (Edinburgh: Scottish Mountaineering Club, 1931); Arthur Stringer, *Red Wine of Youth: A Life of Rupert Brooke* (Indianapolis and New York: Bobbs-Merrill Co., 1948); Geoffrey Winthrop Young, *Mountain*

Craft (Methuen and Co., 1920) and *The Grace of Forgetting* (Country Life, 1953); and Geoffrey Winthrop Young, Geoffrey Sutton, and Wilfrid Noyce, *Snowdon Biography* (J. M. Dent and Sons, 1957). In tracing 40th S.B.'s movements in Picardy, I depended mainly on the Official History of the War.

Mallory's contribution to the Everest books of the Twenties were as follows: 'The Reconnaissance of the Mountain', Chapters XII–XVII in Lieutenant-Colonel C. K. Howard-Bury's *Mount Everest: The Reconnaissance, 1921* (1922), pp. 183–279; and 'The First Attempt' and 'The Third Attempt', Chapters IV–VI and X–XI in Brigadier-General the Hon. C. G. Bruce's *The Assault on Mount Everest, 1922* (1923), pp. 121–224 and 173–295. 'Mallory's Letters' constitute Part II of Lieutenant-Colonel E. F. Norton's *The Fight for Everest: 1924* (1925), pp. 207–239. For permission to quote from these books, I am indebted to Edward Arnold (Publishers) Ltd. All passages from Mallory's letters, however, have been re-edited from the manuscripts.

For permission to quote in Chapter VII–X, I am further indebted to Edward Arnold (Publishers) Ltd. for J. B. L. Noel's *Through Tibet to Everest* (1927) and Sir Francis Younghusband's *The Epic of Mount Everest* (1926); to Sir Rupert Hart-Davis for John Morris's *Hired to Kill* (1960); to W. H. Murray for his *The Story of Everest* (J. M. Dent and Sons, 1953); to William Heinemann Ltd. for Wilfrid Noyce's *South Col* (1954); and to Hodder and Stoughton Ltd. for T. Howard Somervell's *After Everest* (2nd ed., 1938).

Among other books helpful in the preparation of Chapters VII–X were these: René Dittert, Gabriel Chevalley, and Raymond Lambert, *Forerunners to Everest*, translated by Malcolm Barnes (George Allen and Unwin Ltd., 1954); G. I. Finch, *The Making of a Mountaineer* (Arrowsmith, 1924); Brigadier Sir John Hunt, *The Ascent of Everest* (Hodder and Stoughton, 1953) and *Our Everest Adventure* (Leicester: Brockhampton Press, 1954); T. G. Longstaff, *This My Voyage* (John Murray, 1950); Kenneth Mason, *Abode of Snow* (Rupert Hart-Davis, 1955); Hugh Ruttledge, *Everest 1933* (Hodder and Stoughton, 1934) and *Everest: The Unfinished Adventure* (Hodder and Stoughton, 1937); George Seaver, *Sir Francis Younghusband* (John Murray, 1952); Eric Shipton, *The Mount Everest Reconnaissance Expedition* (Hodder and Stoughton, 1952); F. S. Smythe, *Camp Six* (new ed., A. and C. Black Ltd., 1956); H. W. Tilman, *Mount Everest 1938* (Cambridge

University Press, 1948); J. R. Ullman, *Americans on Everest* (Michael Joseph, 1965); and A. F. R. Wollaston, *Letters and Diaries*, edited by Mary Wollaston (Cambridge University Press, 1933).

Journals

Quotations from journals are footnoted.

Without my files of the *Alpine Journal* (1863–1968), the *Climbers' Club Journal* (for 1898–1923) and *Climbers' Club Bulletin* (for 1911–1926), and the *Geographical Journal* (for 1922–1924), I should have felt quite lost. For permission to quote, I give my thanks to the Editors and to the Alpine Club, the Climbers' Club, and the Royal Geographical Society.

Before 1921 Mallory's own principal contributions to journals were 'The Mountaineer as Artist', *C.C.J.*, 13:28–40 (March 1914); 'Mont Blanc from the Col du Géant by the Eastern Buttress of Mont Maudit', *A.J.*, 32:148–162 (Sept. 1918); 'Our 1919 Journey', *A.J.*, 33:166–185 (Nov. 1920), read before the A.C. on 4 May 1920; and 'Geoffrey Winthrop Young on Mountain Craft', *C.C.J.*, 14:106–119 (Dec. 1920).

Concerning the years before Everest, the following articles have been particularly informative: an unsigned review, probably by R. L. G. Irving, of D. R. Pye's *George Leigh Mallory* (*Wykehamist*, 25 July 1927); A. C. Benson's memorial to Charles Sayle (*Library*, Dec. 1924); Karl Blodig's 'Ostertage in North Wales' (*C.C.J.*, Feb. 1912); Sir Claude Elliott's memorials in the *A.J.* to Geoffrey Winthrop Young (May 1959) and to Sir David Pye (Nov. 1960); A. S. F. Gow's memorial to Sir Stephen Gaselee (*Proceedings of the British Academy*, 1943); R. L. G. Irving's 'Five Years with Recruits' (*A.J.*, Feb. 1909), 'Mont Blanc by the S.E. Ridge of Mont Maudit' (*A.J.*, Nov. 1911), 'When We Were Very Young' (*A.J.*, May 1944), 'A Great Mountaineer' (*Listener*, 3 Jan. 1946), 'Unclouded Days, 1901–14' (*A.J.*, Nov. 1957), and memorials in the *A.J.* to H. O. S. Gibson (Feb. 1918), H. E. G. Tyndale (Nov. 1948), and G. H. Bullock (Nov. 1956); Sir Geoffrey Keynes's 'Henry James in Cambridge' (*London Magazine*, March 1959); W. W. McLean's 'First Impressions of the Alps' (*C.C.J.*, Dec. 1920); H. E. L. Porter's 'A New Climb on the Dent Blanche' (*C.C.J.*, Feb. 1913) and 'Garter Traverse – Lliwedd' (*A.J.*, Nov. 1926); D. R. Pye's 'A Fortnight in Skye' (*Scottish Mountaineering Club Journal*, April 1919); C. D. Robertson's 'Alpine Humour'

(*A.J.*, May 1910); H. E. G. Tyndale's 'First Affections' (*A.J.*, Nov. 1942); and Geoffrey Winthrop Young's 'The Nesthorn: A First Ascent' (*C.C.J.*, Dec. 1920), 'As It Was in the Beginning' (*Out of Doors*, Christmas 1946), and memorials in the *A.J.* to C. D. Robertson (May 1910), H. R. Pope (Nov. 1912), H. O. Jones (Feb. 1913), and J. P. Farrar (May 1929). From some of these articles I have drawn brief quotations, with the consent of the Editors concerned or of the writers.

In the Everest years, Mallory contributed twice to journals: 'Mount Everest: The Reconnaissance', *G.J.*, 59:100–109 (Feb. 1922), and *A.J.*, 34:215–225 (May 1922), read at the joint meeting of the R.G.S. and the A.C. on 20 December 1921; and 'The Second Mount Everest Expedition'/'The First High Climb', *A.J.*, 34:425–439 (Nov. 1922), and *G.J.*, 60:400–412 (Dec. 1922), read at the joint meeting of the R.G.S. and the A.C. on 16 October 1922. To this list must be added the dispatches Mallory helped to write for *The Times*, particularly the account of the first high climb in 1922 (*Times*, 16 June 1922) and a portion of Dispatch No. 7, 26 May 1924 (*Times*, 16 June 1924; *A.J.*, Nov. 1924), both of which I quote with the consent of the Editors.

Among the most interesting articles about Everest by other hands were these: G. H. Bullock's Diary of the 1921 Expedition (*A.J.*, May and Nov. 1962); J. P. Farrar's 'The Everest Expeditions: Conclusions' (*A.J.*, Nov. 1922); G. I. Finch's 'The Second Attempt on Mount Everest' (*A.J.*, Nov. 1922); R. W. G. Hingston's 'Physiological Difficulties in the Ascent of Mount Everest' (*A.J.*, May 1925); A. R. Hinks's 'The Mount Everest Maps and Photographs' (*A.J.*, May 1922); C. K. Howard-Bury's 'Some Observations on the Approaches to Mount Everest' (*G.J.*, Feb. 1921) and 'The 1921 Mount Everest Expedition' (*G.J.*, Feb. 1922; *A.J.*, May 1922); J. B. L. Noel's 'A Journey to Tashirak in Southern Tibet, and the Eastern Approaches to Mount Everest' (*G.J.*, May 1919); E. F. Norton's 'The Personnel of the Expedition' and 'The Climb with Mr. Somervell to 28,000 Feet' (*A.J.*, Nov. 1924), and 'The Problem of Mount Everest' (*A.J.*, May 1925); N. E. Odell's portion of Dispatch No. 9, 14 June 1924 (*Times*, 5 July 1924; *A.J.*, Nov. 1924), and his 'The Last Climb' and memorial to A. C. Irvine (*A.J.*, Nov. 1924); and P. J. H. Unna's 'The Oxygen Equipment of the 1922 Everest Expedition' (*A.J.*, May 1922) and 'Everest Expedition, 1922: Notes on Illustrations' (*A.J.*, Nov. 1922).

George Mallory

I have quoted with permission from memorials to George Mallory by R. L. G. Irving (*A.J.*, Nov. 1924); David Pye (*Cambridge Review*, 24 Oct. 1924; reprinted in *Oxford and Cambridge Mountaineering 1924*); Sir Arthur Shipley (*Country Life*, 5 July 1924); T. Howard Somervell (*Journal of the Fell and Rock Climbing Club*, 1924); Geoffrey Winthrop Young (*The Nation and the Athenaeum*, 5 July 1924); and an unidentified writer, probably Montague Rendall, in *The Wykehamist* (19 July 1924). Addresses by Frank Fletcher at Charterhouse on June 22nd and by A. C. Benson at Magdalene on June 24th were reported in *The Times* (24 and 30 June 1924). The *A.J.* (Nov. 1924) published an account of the memorial service on October 17th in St. Paul's.

Illustrations

Prints of almost all the photographs here reproduced were among the many preserved by the Mallorys. Mrs. Brooke and Miss Turner, Lady Pye, Sir Geoffrey Keynes, Harold Porter, and Jocelin Winthrop Young sent additional prints and several negatives, for all of which I have been most grateful. G.W.Y. expressed particular pride in the photograph he made as he followed Mallory and Knubel down the Moine ridge of the Aiguille Verte on 13 August 1909; he considered it the best ever taken of Mallory climbing. 'In poise, and in the atmosphere of mountain "reverence" that pervades it, it is the best I know.' Of the pictures here reproduced, he was responsible for those of Mallory at Zermatt in 1910 and of Mallory and Herford at Pen-y-Pass in 1913.

The view of Mont Blanc and Mont Maudit appears to have been George Mallory's own, for the negative remained in his collection.

Messrs. G. P. Abraham Ltd. (Photographers), Keswick, granted permission to reproduce the photograph of Craig yr Ysfa. For the pictures of the Mont Collon and the Charmoz, I am indebted to the Alpine Club, to which the late Sydney Spencer left his negatives. The picture of the Nesthorn was taken by Ernest Edwards; it appeared in *The Oberland and its Glaciers* (Alfred W. Bennett, 1866), by the Rev. H. B. George, Editor of the *Alpine Journal*. I wish that I had some way of thanking the late Marcus Heywood for his pictures of Pen-y-Pass in 1909; the unidentified photographer who had his camera at Pythagoras House in July of that year; and Adrian Harding for his portraits of George and Ruth.

Sources and Acknowledgments

All the Everest photographs have been made available by the Mount Everest Foundation. The first two, of the northern approach to the mountain, were made by George Mallory in 1921. The routes not taken in 1921 were photographed by a later expedition. The picture of the Northeast Ridge from the Lhakpa La was made in 1921 by C. K. Howard-Bury, and the telephoto of the North Face in 1922 by J. B. L. Noel. The two pictures of the climb to 26,800 feet in 1922 were taken by T. H. Somervell.

The three maps on pages 264–266 were drawn by Neil Hyslop.

Alps from Mont Blanc to the Grand Combin
and Gran Paradiso

264

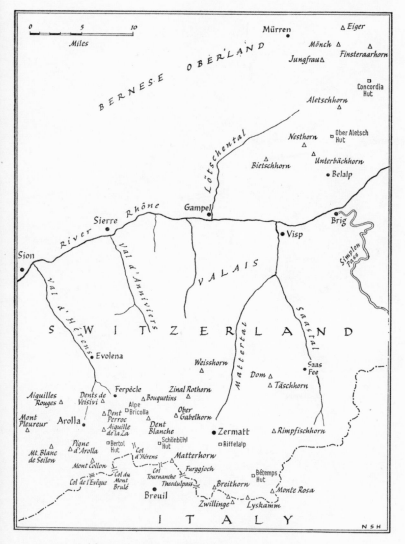

Alps from Mont Pleureur to Monte Rosa
and the Finsteraarhorn

265

MOUNT EVEREST
From a sketch-map based on Major Wheeler's
surveys in 1921, showing the camps
established in 1924

Index of Persons and Groups

Abominable Snowman, 174
Abraham brothers, of Keswick,
41, 42, 64, 181, 258, 262
Allen, Lancelot, at Charterhouse,
64, 65
Alpine Club, 21, 25, 46, 47, 48,
67, 71–72, 78, 134, 147–148,
177–178, 179, 182, 205, 207,
224, 251, 257, 262; *Alpine
Journal*, 22, 48, 55, 58–59,
64, 74–76, 83–84, 120–121,
131, 134–142, 251, 260–262
American Alpine Club, 209, 211,
257
Andrews, A. W., 44 n 1, 48, 69,
88, 257
Arnold-Forster, W. E., 91, 93,
94, 102, 103, 118, 256

Bankes-Price, John, the 'bear' in
the Alps (1910), 63–64
Bartholomew, A. T., 47, 51
Beetham, Bentley, member of
1924 Everest expedition,
213, 214, 222, 223, 225, 229,
230–231, 233, 234, 241
Bell, Sir Charles, 147
Bell, Clive, 49, 50; Mrs. Bell
(Vanessa Stephen), 49, 50
Bell, Lieut., 107, 112, 115
Benson, A. C., in G.M.'s
Cambridge years, 34–35, 40,
45, 49, 52, 53; thereafter,
69, 92, 212, 216 n 1, 250,
252, 255, 257, 258, 260, 262;

letters from G.M., 38, 73,
78, 101, 103 and n 1; letters
to G.M., 34–35, 35, 53, 63,
65, 66
Benson, E. F., 45, 86 n, 258
Benson, R. H., 35, 40
Beveridge, W. H. (Lord
Beveridge), 64, 69, 94, 258
Blodig, Karl, in Wales (1911),
69–70, 74, 260
'Bridge, Ann.' *See* O'Malley
Brock, A. Clutton, 97, 105, 108,
210; Mrs. Brock, 105
Bron, Othon, in the Alps (1920),
144–145
Brooke, Justin, at Cambridge,
38, 39
Brooke, Ralph, 96, 97, 98, 105,
106, 121; Mrs. Brooke
(Mary Henrietta Leigh-
Mallory, G.M.'s elder
sister), 9, 16, 20, 43, 60, 85,
96, 97, 98, 255, 262; letters
from G.M., 222–223, 226,
227, 234, 246
Brooke, Rupert, at Cambridge,
36, 39, 40–41, 43, 44, 45, 47,
51, 53–54; thereafter, 80,
85, 103 and n 1; 255, 258
Bruce, Brig.-Gen. the Hon.
C. G., 147, 148; leader of
1922 Everest expedition,
179–180, 183, 184, 187–188,
198, 203, 204, 214; leader of
1924 Everest expedition,

267

Index of Place-Names